Sepphoris in Galilee

Sepphoris in Galilee

Crosscurrents of Culture

Edited by Rebecca Martin Nagy

Carol L. Meyers

Eric M. Meyers

Zeev Weiss

North Carolina Museum of Art 1996

Distributed by Eisenbrauns, Winona Lake, Indiana

Published on the occasion of the exhibition "Sepphoris in Galilee: Crosscurrents of Culture," organized by the North Carolina Museum of Art.

This exhibition is made possible through the generosity of the State of North Carolina, Department of Cultural Resources, and the State of Israel, Ministry of Foreign Affairs.

EXHIBITION ITINERARY

North Carolina Museum of Art
Raleigh, North Carolina
17 November 1996–6 July 1997

Kelsey Museum of Archaeology
and the University of Michigan Museum of Art
Ann Arbor, Michigan
7 September 1997–14 December 1997

Michael C. Carlos Museum
Emory University, Atlanta, Georgia
24 January 1998–12 April 1998

Library of Congress Catalogue Number 96-069214
ISBN 0-88259-971-2
Copyright 1996 North Carolina Museum of Art

The North Carolina Museum of Art, Lawrence J. Wheeler, Director, is an agency of the State of North Carolina, James B. Hunt, Jr., Governor, and the Department of Cultural Resources, Betty Ray McCain, Secretary.

Front Cover: **Hunter Mosaic from the Nile festival building (detail)**
Sepphoris; Hebrew University Expedition
Byzantine period, c. 5th century C.E.
Israel Antiquities Authority 93-2887
Photo: Gabi Laron
Frontispiece: **Nilotic Mosaic from the Nile festival building (detail)**
Sepphoris; Hebrew University Expedition
Byzantine period, c. 5th century C.E.
Photo: Gabi Laron

Editor: Leslie Watkins
Design of catalogue: Jennie Malcolm and Nancy Sears
Design of exhibition: Stephanie Miller, Jim Deskevich, and the North Carolina Museum of Art Design Department
Printer: Editoriale Bortolazzi Stei, Verona, Italy

Lenders to the Exhibition

The Burke Library,
Union Theological Seminary, New York

Department of Religion,
Duke University, Durham, North Carolina

Franciscan Custody of the Holy Land

Institute of Archaeology,
The Hebrew University of Jerusalem

Israel Antiquities Authority

The Israel Museum, Jerusalem

Kelsey Museum of Archaeology,
University of Michigan, Ann Arbor

The Library of The Jewish Theological
Seminary of America, New York

North Carolina Museum of Art, Raleigh

Private Collection, Durham, North Carolina

Rare Book Collection, Wilson Library,
University of North Carolina at Chapel Hill

Semitic Museum,
Harvard University, Cambridge, Massachusetts

Special Collections Library,
Duke University, Durham, North Carolina

W. F. Albright Institute of Archaeological Research,
Jerusalem

Major Contributors

to the Israel/North Carolina Cultural Exchange

State of North Carolina,
    Department of Cultural Resources
State of Israel, Ministry of Foreign Affairs

The Mary Duke Biddle Foundation
BB&T
The Blumenthal Foundation
Joseph M. Bryan, Jr.
Carolina Power & Light Company
Charlotte Jewish Federation
City of Raleigh Arts Commission
Nathan Cummings Foundation, secured by Beatrice
    Cummings Mayer
EL AL
First Citizens Bank
A.J. Fletcher Foundation
Glaxo Wellcome
John Wesley and Anna Hodgin Hanes
The Kaplan Family Foundation
Sara Lee Corporation
Miller Brewing Company
NationsBank
Tannenbaum-Sternberger Foundation
Time Warner Cable
The Wachovia Bank of North Carolina
Wake County Jewish Federation
Winston/Salem Jewish Community Council

Mr. and Mrs. Arthur Bluethenthal
Anna Lou Cassell
Mr. and Mrs. Benjamin Cone Jr.
Mr. Bernard Gutterman
Randall Kaplan and Kathy Manning
Mr. and Mrs. Sidney H. Siegel

The Adelman Family Fund
Richard D. Adelman
Herbert and Ann Brenner Fund
Mr. and Mrs. Norman R. Cohen
Mr. and Mrs. Robert C. Cone
Barbara and Harvey Colchamiro
Richard S. Deckelbaum
Lynn and Barry Eisenberg
Jean B. Falk
Sara Frooman
Global Software
Ronald and Susan Green
Greensboro Jewish Federation
Arthur Gordon
Mary Gut
Mr. and Mrs. R. Philip Hanes, Jr.
Horn and Stronach
    Marketing Advertising & Public Relations
Robert S. Kadis
Ms. Linda Kornberg
Mr. and Mrs. Arthur H. Kurtz
Mr. and Mrs. Robert J. Lee
Dr. and Mrs. I. Joel Leeb
Mr. and Mrs. Henry Levinson
Dr. and Mrs. Myron B. Liptzin
Mazel Tov Gifts
Mr. and Mrs. Paul J. Michaels
Kay and Dave Phillips Foundation
Mr. and Mrs. Marshall Rauch
Stanley Robboy
Susan Rosenthal
Mr. and Mrs. Norman G. Samet
Dr. and Mrs. Paul Sarazen
Mr. and Mrs. Daniel Satisky
Gordon Smith, III
Ann and Wade Smith

Contributors to the Catalogue

Essays

Jaroslav Folda
University of North Carolina at Chapel Hill

Sean Freyne
Trinity College, University of Dublin, Ireland

Isaiah Gafni
The Hebrew University of Jerusalem

Kenneth G. Hoglund
Wake Forest University, Winston-Salem, North Carolina

Carol L. Meyers
Duke University, Durham, North Carolina

Eric M. Meyers
Duke University, Durham, North Carolina

Stuart S. Miller
University of Connecticut at Storrs

Ehud Netzer
The Hebrew University of Jerusalem

Lucille A. Roussin
New York, New York

E. P. Sanders
Duke University, Durham, North Carolina

Binyamin Shalev
The Zippori Project

James F. Strange
University of South Florida at Tampa

Tsvika Tsuk
Israel National Parks Authority

Seth Ward
University of Denver, Denver, Colorado

Zeev Weiss
The Hebrew University of Jerusalem

Catalogue Entries

Marva Balouka
Israel Antiquities Authority, Jerusalem

Sarah H. Cormack
Duke University, Durham, North Carolina

Michal Dayagi-Mendels
The Israel Museum, Jerusalem

Alysia Fischer
Fellow, W.F. Albright Institute of Archaeological Research, Jerusalem

Rafael Frankel
Haifa University, Israel

Elise A. Friedland
Kelsey Museum of Archaeology, University of Michigan, Ann Arbor

Beth Glazier-McDonald
Centre College, Danville, Kentucky

Stephen Goranson
University of North Carolina at Wilmington

Dennis E. Groh
Illinois Wesleyan University, Bloomington

John S. Jorgensen
Duke University, Durham, North Carolina

Eric C. Lapp
Fellow, American School of Classical Studies,
Athens, and W. F. Albright Institute of
Archaeological Research, Jerusalem

Thomas R. W. Longstaff
Colby College, Waterville, Maine

C. Thomas McCollough
Centre College, Danville, Kentucky

Ya'akov Meshorer
The Israel Museum, Jerusalem

Carol L. Meyers
Duke University, Durham, North Carolina

Eric M. Meyers
Duke University, Durham, North Carolina

Rebecca Martin Nagy
North Carolina Museum of Art, Raleigh

Joseph Naveh
The Hebrew University of Jerusalem

Ellen Reeder
Walters Art Gallery, Baltimore, Maryland

Leonard V. Rutgers
University of Utrecht, The Netherlands

Matthew W. Stolper
The Oriental Institute, University of Chicago

James F. Strange
University of South Florida at Tampa

Tsvika Tsuk
Israel National Parks Authority

Zeev Weiss
The Hebrew University of Jerusalem

Contents

Editors' Preface

AT THE OUTSET of planning for this publication we composed a list of colleagues whom we would invite to contribute essays on the history, religious traditions, culture, and art of Sepphoris and Galilee. To our amazement and delight, every one of them said yes. Our pleasure was deepened by the willingness of other colleagues to prepare catalogue entries on the individual objects in the exhibition. Launched in this auspicious manner, the project was destined to succeed. It is with great pleasure that we now see the cumulative work of these distinguished scholars, representing some twenty institutions in the United States, Israel, Ireland, and the Netherlands.

With numerous authors writing on a wide range of topics related to Sepphoris and Galilee, some differences in the interpretation of archaeological and literary evidence are to be expected. With respect for the scholarship and professionalism of the contributors, we acknowledge their varying interpretations and have made no attempt to impose a universal point of view.

Tremendous progress has been made in recovering the history and culture of Sepphoris as a result of the intense archaeological activity at the site since the mid-1980s. Only with the completion of these excavations and the publication of final reports, however, will a comprehensive interpretation of the evidence be possible. Until then, this volume will serve as a thorough and multifaceted presentation of the state of scholarship on Sepphoris and its place in Near Eastern antiquity.

It is our fervent hope that even after the exhibition has ended, and as excavations at the site continue, this publication will serve as a point of entry to the appreciation of the variety of peoples and cultures that have left their mark on Sepphoris.

Rebecca Martin Nagy
North Carolina Museum of Art

Eric M. Meyers
Duke University

Carol L. Meyers
Duke University

Zeev Weiss
The Hebrew University of Jerusalem

Introduction and Acknowledgments

IN THE SUMMER OF 1987 the discovery at Sepphoris of a beautiful, almost perfectly preserved mosaic with scenes from the life of the Greco-Roman god Dionysos was widely heralded by the media in Israel, the United States, and around the world. The hauntingly lovely face of a woman from the acanthus scroll border of the mosaic (the so-called Mona Lisa of Galilee) soon became the image most associated with the site. Responsible for the find were archaeologists from Duke University and from the Institute of Archaeology of the Hebrew University of Jerusalem, who were working together on the Joint Sepphoris Project under the direction of Eric M. Meyers, Ehud Netzer, and Carol L. Meyers.

When Eric and Carol Meyers returned from the field that summer to their work as professors in the Religion Department of Duke University, I invited them to participate in a symposium on biblical archaeology at the North Carolina Museum of Art. They spoke about their work at Sepphoris, particularly the discovery of the fabulous Dionysos mosaic. I shared with the Meyerses an idea I had nurtured since participating in the excavation of a medieval monastic complex at Psalmodi in southern France in 1987—to organize an archaeological exhibition that would bring together the work of scholars from various disciplines to illuminate the history of a particular site. Our conversations led to a proposal for an exhibition on Sepphoris, a site that seemed ideal for this kind of presentation. Archaeology was beginning to reveal the physical remains of this once-vibrant political, religious, and cultural center, whose importance was already well known from the literature of antiquity. The city had been home to Jews and Romans and, later, to Christians and Arabs, and it presented a wonderful opportunity to study how people of different religions and cultures had coexisted in an urban environment. Sepphoris was a Roman provincial capital and a major Jewish city, indeed, a leading center of rabbinical learning. Rabbi Judah Ha-Nasi (the Patriarch) lived the last years of his life there and, during that time, completed his compilation of the Mishnah (the first authoritative collection of postbiblical Jewish law and tradition). The city witnessed the gradual growth of Christianity in the early centuries of the common era, remained a place of religious pilgrimage for Jews and Christians for centuries, and a became a Crusader stronghold in the twelfth century. Its rich and colorful history could be revealed by drawing on the work of scholars in the fields of archaeology, history, religious studies, art history, numismatics, and the sciences.

The following summer the Museum sent me to Sepphoris to participate in the excavation and to explore further the idea of an exhibition on the art and archaeology of the ancient Galilean city. Although the time was not yet ripe in 1988 for such an undertaking, six years later circumstances would change in a dramatic way. In April 1994 Governor James B. Hunt, Jr., of North Carolina signed a memorandum of intent with the State of Israel establishing the North Carolina-Israel Cooperation Committee. The alliance was formalized in September 1995 with the goal of strengthening business, scientific, educational, and cultural ties between Israel and North Carolina. One of the stated objectives of the Committee is "to increase cultural awareness, promoting a deeper understanding of shared values through the arts, humanities, and education." To realize this goal, twenty-one of the state's leading arts institutions joined together under the auspices of the North Carolina Department of Cultural Resources to produce the Israel/North Carolina Cultural Exchange, a coordinated program of exhibitions, artists' residencies, concerts, and a film festival devoted to Israeli art, archaeology, and culture. As a result of Governor Hunt's initiative, the long-dreamed-of exhibition on Sepphoris could now be realized. Eric Meyers agreed to work with me to organize the exhibition. Serving with us on the board of editors for the exhibition catalogue would be Carol Meyers and Zeev Weiss, an archaeologist who originally participated in the Joint Sepphoris Project and who now directs the Hebrew University expedition at Sepphoris.

One of the Museum's principal goals in organizing the exhibition has been to include the work of the many archaeologists who have excavated at Sepphoris over the past ninety odd years. Thanks to the cooperation and assistance of many individuals and institutions, this goal has been realized. The earliest excavations at Sepphoris were conducted in 1908 by Prosper Viaud in and around the ruins of the Crusader Church of Saint Anne. The church had been acquired by the Franciscans in 1870 and still belongs to the Franciscan Custody of the Holy Land. Just north of the church, Viaud found a large fragment from a synagogue mosaic with a dedicatory inscription, the first physical evidence of a synagogue from the ancient city. Father Michele Piccirillo of the Studium Biblicum Franciscanum Museum in Jerusalem has been instrumental in arranging the loan of this mosaic from the Custody of the Holy Land.

In 1930 Eleazar L. Sukenik of the Hebrew University of Jerusalem conducted the first excavations of the burial caves at Sepphoris. Further tomb excavations were carried out by Adam Druks for the Israel Department of Antiquities (now the Israel Antiquities Authority) in 1980. The Roman-period mausoleum known as the Tomb of Jacob's Daughters was excavated by Nahman Avigad of the Hebrew University of Jerusalem. This aspect of archaeology at Sepphoris is represented in the exhi-

bition by three tomb inscriptions on loan from the Institute of Archaeology of the Hebrew University of Jerusalem and from the Israel Antiquities Authority.

The first systematic archaeological excavations at Sepphoris were conducted in 1931 by the University of Michigan expedition directed by Leroy Waterman. Waterman's team concentrated on the Roman theater on the northeastern summit and on another large public building or residence on the northwestern summit. The excavations brought to light many small objects from the Roman period. A glass bangle bracelet, bone hair pins, bone gaming pieces, and other small artifacts from the Waterman excavations have been loaned to the exhibition by the Kelsey Museum of Archaeology at the University of Michigan.

After conducting a systematic survey of the site in 1982, a team from the University of South Florida under the direction of James F. Strange began excavations in 1983 and 1984 on the western summit, adjacent to the Crusader/Ottoman citadel and the theater. After reopening the area of the large building first excavated by Waterman, this team has focused more recently on a large commercial building in the eastern lower city. Essays by Strange and Lucille A. Roussin explore the distinctive architectural features of this elaborate building and its extensive decorative mosaic floors. Included in the exhibition are several outstanding finds from the areas excavated by the South Florida team, including small bronze sculptures, gold jewelry, and a bronze amulet used for protection against illness.

The Joint Sepphoris Project, under the direction of Eric Meyers and Carol Meyers of Duke University and Ehud Netzer of the Hebrew University of Jerusalem, excavated for five seasons from 1985 to 1989, concentrating on the domestic areas of the western summit, the theater, and the large Roman residence on the eastern summit in which the Dionysos mosaic was discovered in 1987. Numerous objects in the exhibition, including bronze figurines, clay lamps, and a wide assortment of pottery vessels, come from this phase of the excavations. Because the Dionysos mosaic was restored and reinstalled in its original location at Sepphoris, where a building has been constructed to house it, the famous mosaic could not be included in the exhibition. However, the conservator who supervised the restoration of the mosaic, Joseph "Dodo" Shenhav, now retired from the Center for Restoration of the Israel Museum, created facsimiles of three scenes from the mosaic for the exhibition. Matched color for color and stone for stone, his replicas provide an excellent impression of the exceptional quality and beauty of the original. The mosaic is also the subject of an essay in this catalogue.

From 1990–94 under the direction of Ehud Netzer and Zeev Weiss, and since 1995 under the direction of Weiss, the Hebrew University has conducted extensive excavations at Sepphoris and has helped to develop the site for tourism. Essays by Weiss and Netzer on the history of Sepphoris in the Roman and Byzantine periods, as revealed by archaeology, provide an excellent overview of the work of this team as well as that of the other expeditions at Sepphoris. The Hebrew University team has continued to work on the summit, pursuing the excavation of the southern half of the Dionysos mosaic building and the theater and its vicinity. However, they have concentrated on the excavation of the lower eastern part of the city, where a clearer picture of the city's plan and construction during the Roman and Byzantine periods has emerged. Here they found the "Nile festival building" with stunning mythological mosaics on which Weiss and Netzer have written for this publication. Although most of the mosaics are being restored and prepared for exhibition at the site, one full-length, life-size mosaic of a hunter from the Nile festival building could be included in the exhibition. Another major building excavated by the Hebrew University team is the Byzantine-period synagogue at the northeast edge of the site. The synagogue mosaics are also the subject of a catalogue essay by the excavators.

The Duke University team was reorganized in 1993 as the Sepphoris Regional Project, with Kenneth G. Hoglund of Wake Forest University joining Eric Meyers and Carol Meyers to serve as field director. They have pursued further work on the domestic areas of the western summit, as detailed by Hoglund and Eric Meyers in a catalogue essay. Archaeologists from this team, under the field direction of J. P. Dessel, also have begun to explore a small nearby site known as Tel ʿEin Zippori. It is here that evidence for earlier periods of the history of the Sepphoris area is emerging, with significant finds from the Iron and Bronze ages. Discussed in an essay by Carol Meyers, the earliest periods represented in the history of the site are included in the exhibition by a selection of figurines, ceramic vessels, and objects of possible cultic significance.

Between 1975 and 1985, Tsvika Tsuk carried out systematic surveys of the water systems of Sepphoris and its surroundings. Then, between 1992 and 1995 under the sponsorship of the National Parks Authority and Tel Aviv University, he directed the excavation and preservation of the aqueducts, the vast subterranean reservoir, and the related structures that had supplied water to the city during the Roman and Byzantine periods. A selection of ceramic and bronze objects discovered by Tsuk and his team is included in the exhibition. In an essay Tsuk explains how the water systems functioned in antiquity.

In recognition of the historical and artistic importance of Sepphoris and the tremendous general interest in the finds there, the National Parks Authority of Israel opened the site to the public in October 1992 as Zippori National Park. During the planning and preparation of the exhibition, the executive director of the Zippori Project, Binyamin Shalev, has provided support and assistance. He has made available resources from the park, such as an interactive computer program, which includes segments on the mosaics of the Nile festival building as well as the water systems of Sepphoris. The development of the park and its remarkable growth and success are discussed here in an essay by Ehud Netzer and Shalev.

The story of Sepphoris is revealed in this catalogue through the contributions of a number of scholars whose fields of study intersect with that of archaeology. Special thanks are extended to the authors of essays on various aspects of the history of Sepphoris and Galilee. They have provided valuable insight into the meaning and significance of the objects in the exhibition and the archaeological evidence of the site. Thanks are due also to the authors of catalogue entries for their enlightening discussions of the objects and for their generosity in sharing information and insights along the way.

In addition to archaeological finds from Sepphoris, the exhibition includes works of art and artifacts from other locations in Galilee and neighboring regions, selected to help place Sepphoris in a broader historical and cultural context. The Museum is very grateful to all of the institutions that have made loans to the exhibition and to the individuals who assisted in making the loans possible. (Lenders to the exhibition are listed elsewhere in this catalogue.) Books related to the history of Sepphoris and its religious traditions also are included in the exhibition. We are especially grateful to Rabbi Jerry Schwarzbard, Curator of Special Collections at the Library of the Jewish Theological Seminary of America in New York. He was generous with his time and advice, and facilitated the loan of rare and important volumes for the exhibition.

The vision of Governor James B. Hunt, Jr., in initiating a broad-based engagement between the State of North Carolina and the State of Israel is gratefully acknowledged. Sincere thanks are extended to North Carolina Secretary of Cultural Resources Betty Ray McCain, Deputy Secretary of Cultural Resources Elizabeth F. Buford, and Professor Henry Levinson of the University of North Carolina at Greensboro for their unflagging enthusiasm and support in developing the Israel/North Carolina Cultural Exchange. As the coordinator for the visual arts projects of the Cultural Exchange, John Coffey, Chair of the Curatorial Department of the North Carolina Museum of Art, has accomplished a Herculean feat with good grace that is appreciated by all. Public relations for the Cultural Exchange was in the able hands of Anna Upchurch.

Financial support has been provided by the North Carolina Department of Cultural Resources, the Foreign Ministry of Israel, and the individual, foundation, and corporate donors who are listed elsewhere in this catalogue. The exhibition would not have been possible without the support and generosity of all of these contributors. Developmental coordination was provided by Ruth Cook, assisted by Paula Melhop.

The Museum is grateful also to the Honorable Uri Bar-Ner, Deputy Director General for Cultural Affairs in the Foreign Ministry of Israel, and to Arye Mekel, Consul-General of Israel to the Southeastern United States, who have provided support and encouragement throughout the project. In Jerusalem, Hava Katz, Acting Chief Curator of the Israel Antiquities Authority, has been responsible for the myriad of details necessary to make the exhibition possible. In the earliest stages, Ruth Peled, Chief Curator at the Israel Antiquities Authority, kindly extended her help and support. A very special debt of gratitude is owed to Avital Zitronblat, who served as special assistant to the exhibition at the Israel Antiquities Authority. The importance of her unfailing good cheer and her attention to detail cannot be exaggerated. At the Israel Museum, Yaᶜakov Meshorer, Tamar and Teddy Kollek Chief Curator of Archaeology, has contributed to the success of the project in many ways, as has Michal Dayagi-Mendels, Curator for the Israelite and Persian periods, who offered welcome advice and assistance during the planning of the exhibition. Shoshana Nitzan, Director of the Center for Restoration of the Israel Museum made arrangements for the production of replicas for the exhibition. At the Institute of Archaeology of the Hebrew University of Jerusalem, Curator Gila Hurvitz arranged the loan of two rare and important objects. Sincere appreciation is extended to these individuals and to their colleagues who have contributed to the exhibition in many and various ways.

In the summer of 1994, when the exhibition was in its inception, Renee Sivan, who designed the museum and information center in the citadel for Zippori National Park, sat with Eric Meyers and me in the garden at the W. F. Albright Institute of Archaeological Research in Jerusalem and freely shared her wonderful ideas for bringing Sepphoris to life for museumgoers. Seymour Gitin, Director of the Albright Institute, made facilities available there, and was helpful in numerous ways, as was his staff. Marva Balouka, Alysia Fischer, Kenneth Hoglund, Eric Lapp, Jonathan Reed, Leonard Rutgers, and other members of the Sepphoris Regional Project team spent hours patiently looking through materials from the excavations and offering suggestions for the exhibition. Lindsey Bute, architect for the Sepphoris Regional Project, has done exquisite work in the creation of scale models of the site and of major buildings, site plans, and reconstruction drawings. Cynthia Baker of the Department of Near Eastern Studies at Cornell University kindly agreed to construct a model loom and to serve as a consultant on women's and men's roles in the performance of domestic tasks.

All of my colleagues at the North Carolina Museum of Art have provided steady support and have helped out whenever and however they could. To Lawrence J. Wheeler, Director, and Joseph Covington, Director of Educational Services, special thanks are extended for providing the leadership and institutional support to make this exhibition possible. Stephanie Miller, Chief Designer at the North Carolina Museum of Art, has been a key member of the exhibition team, both in Israel and in Raleigh, contributing a designer's insight in the selection of objects and in the development of a creative and handsome installation. Carrie Hedrick, Museum Registrar, and her staff, have been enthusiastic and supportive partners in preparing the exhibition. As in every professional endeavor, I owe warm thanks to Carolyn B. Fitzgerald for all kinds of help. Three research interns made major contributions to the success of the exhibition. Laura H. Bryan conducted research on pilgrimage traditions related to Sepphoris and was instrumental in the selection of appropriate books and manuscripts to be included in the exhibition. Douglas B. Palmer provided essential administrative support and research assistance in the preparation of the catalogue. Vikas Patel planned and organized the "science and archaeology" section of the exhibition.

Working with Eric Meyers to organize the exhibition has been a delight from beginning to end. He has brought to the project boundless energy and enthusiasm. Working with him, with Carol Meyers, and with Zeev Weiss to edit the catalogue has also been a rewarding and enjoyable experience due to the exacting scholarship, dedication, and good will that each of them contributed to the effort. The editors owe a collective thanks, also, to Leslie Watkins, an excellent copyeditor who has made the completion of the catalogue an easier and more pleasant task than it might have been, and to Jennie Malcolm and Nancy Sears for the beautiful design of the publication.

Rebecca Martin Nagy
North Carolina Museum of Art
November 1996

*The History of Sepphoris
and the Archaeological Evidence*

Map of Ancient Palestine

This is a reference map of Palestine showing major sites from the Bronze Age through the Arab and Crusader periods. (Palestine is a name derived from a Greek adjective from the time of the historian Herodotus [5th century B.C.E.] meaning "the Philistine region" but was applied by ancient Latin writers to the entire Land of Israel.)

Chronology of Periods

Phases	Dates	Variants
Bronze	3400–1200 B.C.E.	
Iron	1200–520	Neo Babylonian/Iron III (586–539/520)
Persian	520–332	Second Temple (515 B.C.E.–70 C.E.)
Hellenistic	332–63	
Roman	63 B.C.E.–363 C.E.	Mishnaic and Talmudic (70–400)
Byzantine	363–638	
Early Arab	638–1099	
Crusader and Ayyubid	1099–1291	
Late Arab	1291–1516	
Ottoman	1516–1917	
British Mandate	1917–48	
Israel *(Modern Nation of)*	1948–present	

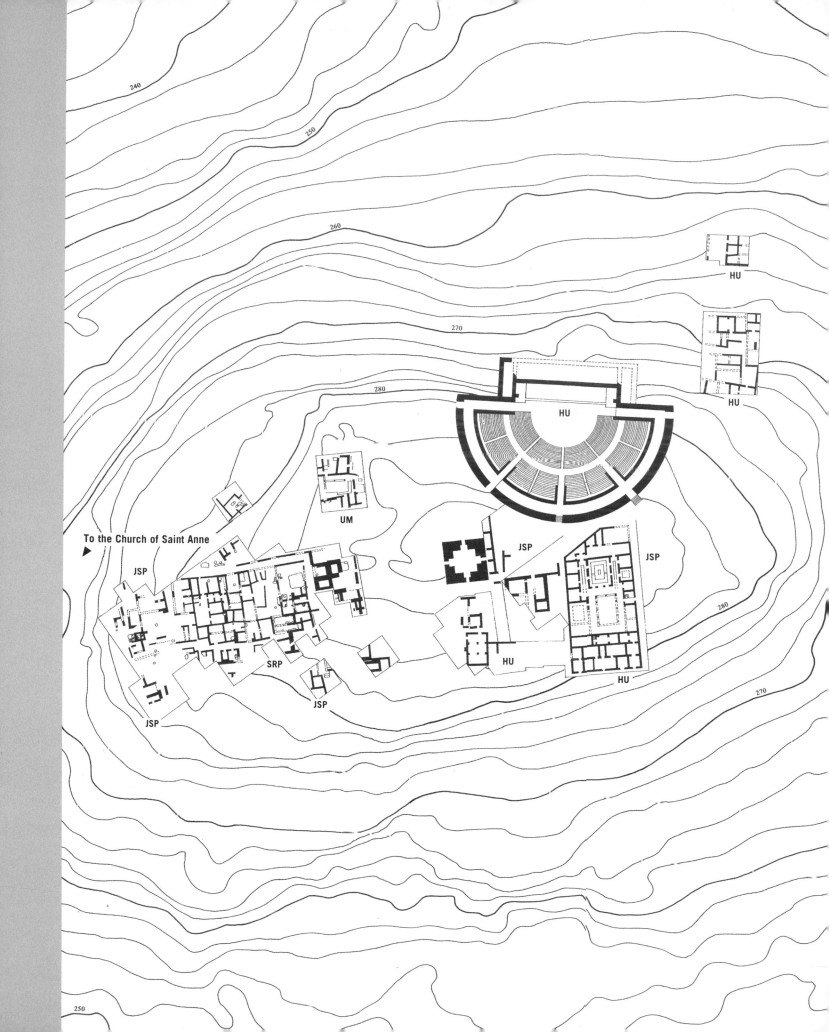

To the Church of Saint Anne

JSP

UM

JSP

JSP

SRP

JSP

JSP

HU

HU

HU

HU

HU

HU

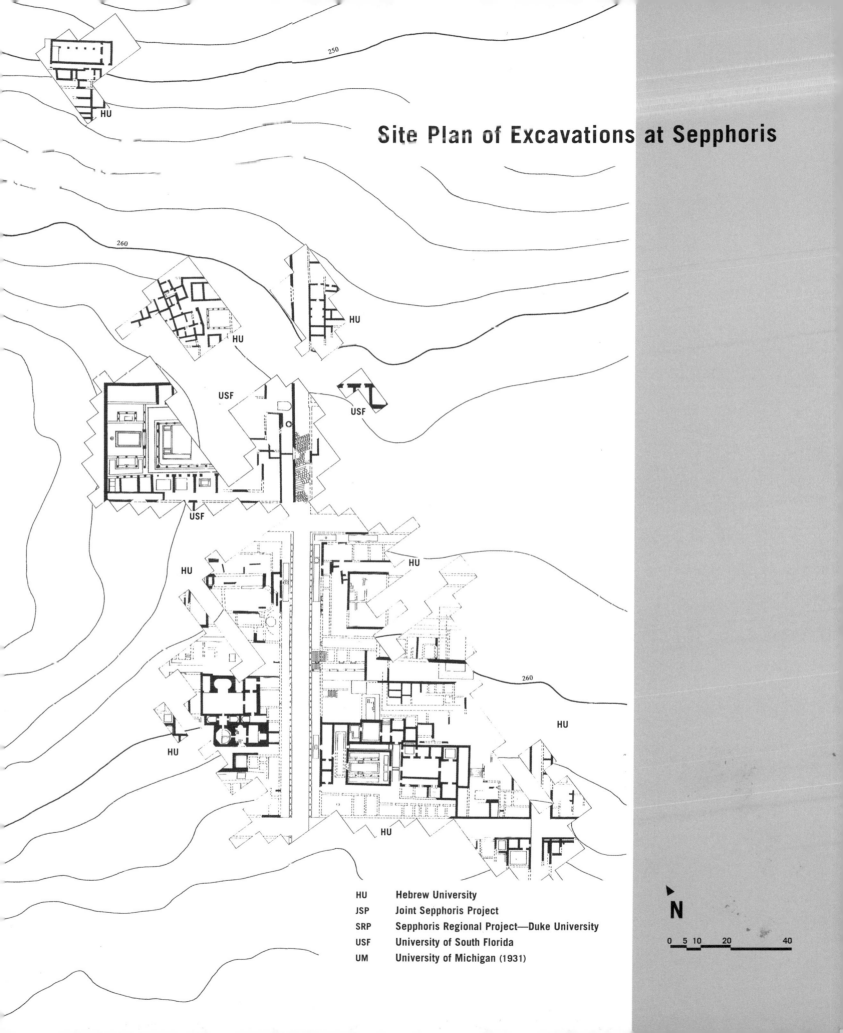

Site Plan of Excavations at Sepphoris

HU   Hebrew University
JSP   Joint Sepphoris Project
SRP   Sepphoris Regional Project—Duke University
USF   University of South Florida
UM   University of Michigan (1931)

N

0   5 10   20   40

Sepphoris and Lower Galilee

Earliest Times through the Persian Period

Carol L. Meyers

Sepphoris is perhaps the most centrally located site in a geographical region of Palestine known as Lower Galilee. The designation "lower" is fitting for the southern and lower portion of Galilee, the northern hill country of Israel stretching from the Lebanon border in the north to the broad sweep of the east-west Jezreel Valley in the south. Lower Galilee itself comprises three subregions or "units of landscape settlement," a phrase that involves archaeological data as well as geophysical conditions[1]: a *northern region* with rugged terrain and few water sources; an *eastern region* with hills and deep canyons; and a *southern region* with gentle topography and several excellent water sources.

The favorable environmental character of the southern region made it the most prominent unit in the long history of Galilee. The subregion's landforms and water supply were conducive to agricultural development and thus to the establishment of small village settlements and even some larger walled cities over the course of the many centuries that mark the presence of Israelites in ancient Palestine. The southern region itself has several distinct agricultural areas, the largest and most important being the two valleys of Naḥal Zippori and Beth Neṭofa. Located at the head of the former and on the edge

of the latter, Sepphoris lies in the heart of the richest area of Galilee and also along the major ancient road systems that wound through those valleys.

Human habitation in the Sepphoris area can be traced back from the prehistoric periods up to the present day. Unlike that of many other settlement sites in the eastern Mediterranean, the history of occupation at Sepphoris did not involve the repeated rebuilding and reoccupation of the same site over millennia. Thus the large truncated hill, or tel, characteristic of thousands of years of overlaying settlements at a particularly advantageous site did not develop at Sepphoris. Rather, an early Chalcolithic settlement, of the early fifth-millennium-B.C.E. Wadi Rabah culture, and also an Early Bronze settlement, known as Giba'at Rabi, can be identified on separate hills south of the main highway that leads from Nazareth to Haifa. Just north of that road lies a very small tel, known as Tel ᶜEin Zippori, which dates from the end of the Middle Bronze Age (if not earlier) through the Late Bronze Age, the Iron I period, and the early part of Iron II. Although the site was settled well before the Israelite period, it clearly was occupied during the time of Israelite beginnings in Palestine, which are known from traditions recorded in the Hebrew Bible. Settlement in the Sepphoris area apparently shifted a number of times from the fifth to the first millennium B.C.E., possibly with gaps in the early part of the Middle Bronze Age and for the later parts of the Iron Age.

fig. 1 This lead figurine of a nude female, discovered at Tel ᶜEin Zippori, is difficult to date, but may be as early as Late Bronze II, c. 1400–1200 B.C.E. See cat. no. 1.
Photo: Israel Antiquities Authority

The most recent excavations (1996) of the Sepphoris Regional Project suggest, however, that there may have been regional continuity throughout the Iron Age.

In any case, at some point toward the end of the Iron Age (sixth century B.C.E., if not before), and certainly by the Persian period (sixth to fourth centuries B.C.E.), settlement in the area shifted once again, from ᶜEin Zippori to a prominent hill, a few kilometers to the north, known in English as Sepphoris and in Hebrew as Zippori. Rising several hundred feet above the Neṭofian Valley to the north and the great Sepphoris plain, or Sahl el-Battuaf, to the south, Sepphoris was occupied almost continually from the Iron II or the Persian period until the 1948 war (Israel's War of Independence), when the sizable Arab village there, known as Saffuriyeh, came to an end. Shortly later a new Jewish collective settlement, or *moshav,* was founded just to the south of the Sepphoris hill. Indeed, the discovery of a Persian quadrilingual on a calcite vessel (cat. no. 11) and a very fine terracotta rhyton (cat. no. 8) from circa 400 B.C.E., along with sizable quantities of Persian-period pottery, indicate a substantial presence, perhaps of Persian officials and their retainers, in the fifth-fourth centuries. Both the rhyton and the inscribed vessel are precious sumptuary objects, their distribution reflecting the presence of political elites. The Persian officials were perhaps drawn to the site by a small existing settlement of the late Iron II period, although no architectural remains of that period (or of the Persian period, for that matter) have yet been identified.

However the question of when occupation at Sepphoris began—or when it ended— is resolved, it is certain that before the late Iron Age and after the Early Bronze Age, the major habitation of the area was at the small tel of ᶜEin Zippori, which means the "spring of Sepphoris," so named because it is located near a spring that still flows year-round and

fig. 2   The fertile landscape of Galilee as viewed from the Sepphoris acropolis.

was clearly a supply of good-quality water for the ancient inhabitants. The six distinct ancient strata of occupation thus far identified at ᶜEin Zippori by the excavations of the Sepphoris Regional Project[2] span the period from the seventeenth century B.C.E. (Middle Bronze III) through the ninth century B.C.E. (Iron IIB), with perhaps some squatters in the eighth century B.C.E. (also Iron IIB). To put it in ethnohistorical terms, ᶜEin Zippori was probably founded in the Canaanite period. Because the site lies within the district traditionally assigned to the tribe of Zebulun in a biblical listing (Josh. 19:10–16) that probably dates to the tenth century[3] but may reflect earlier settlement patterns,[4] it is often assumed that the site became Israelite at some point early in the Iron Age (Iron I). The distinction between Canaanite and Israelite sites, however, is often difficult to establish on the basis of material culture.[5] In the absence of textual references to ᶜEin Zippori— because its ancient name is unknown, it cannot be determined whether or not it is mentioned in the Hebrew Bible or in the Egyptian texts in which the names of many Canaanite cities are found[6]—it is difficult to determine when, if at all, the transition from Canaanite to Israelite occurred. Unlike most other Galilean sites of the Bronze and Iron ages, Tel ᶜEin Zippori was occupied in both the late Canaanite and early Israelite eras, with no break in between and no signs of the disruption or change that marks the large Canaanite urban sites apparently taken over by Israelites.

The problem of determining the ethnic identity of a site's inhabitants is particularly acute for Tel ᶜEin Zippori because it is a relatively small site, approximately one hectare (2.47 acres). Most of what is known about Canaanite and Israelite settlements comes from the investigation of larger sites, the walled cities or city-states of the Late Bronze and Iron ages. From the location and excavation of such sites, it is clear that Galilee as a whole was rather sparsely settled in the Late Bronze Age. Indeed, only a handful of sites can be identified for this period in all of Galilee, making the Late Bronze one of the most thinly settled epochs in Galilean history. In Lower Galilee itself only a few Late Bronze sites have been identified, all in favorable ecological settings, mainly in the southern region. Tel ᶜEin Zippori is one of these, but it is a rural village rather than an urban settlement.

The first glimmer of Middle Bronze settlement at the site was revealed by a tiny probe, or exploratory trench, dug below a Late Bronze I surface on the last day of the Sepphoris Regional Project's 1996 season. Thus the nature of the site in the Middle Bronze Age (Stratum VII) cannot yet be ascertained. Discussion of the settlement there can really begin only with the Late Bronze I (Stratum VI) period, for which a limited but significant exposure has been achieved by the current excavations. The cyclopean walls (walls made of very large irregular stone masonry) and beaten earth and plastered floors that have been uncovered are well made; and a fine assortment of pottery, at least nineteen vessels, includes imported vessels (Bichrome Ware and Cypriot White Slip I). This information, meager as it is, indicates a small agricultural settlement that included some rural elites rather than a village of peasant farmers alone. The presence of imported pottery, and of exceptionally wide (.90 m. to 1.10 m.) and strong walls, indicates a level of economic development allowing for the import of luxury wares that usually is not associated with subsistence agrarian activity.

Strata at Tel ᶜEin Zippori

Stratum I	modern period	
Stratum II	ninth century B.C.E.	(Iron IIB)
Stratum III	tenth century B.C.E.	(Iron IIA)
Stratum IV	c. 1200–1000 B.C.E.	(Iron I)
Stratum V	c. 1400–1200 B.C.E.	(Late Bronze IIA, B)
Stratum VI	c. 1550–1400 B.C.E.	(Late Bronze I)
Stratum VII	pre-1550 B.C.E.	(Middle Bronze III)

This settlement was apparently destroyed, with the subsequent Late Bronze II village (Stratum V) built in an entirely different orientation. Again, a sizable building along with imported wares, such as Base Ring II and White Slip II, indicate that the site was not an isolated farming community in Late Bronze II. Perhaps its location on the road system of Late Bronze Canaan had made this a way station and toll stop, with the resulting revenues evident in the prestige ceramics and perhaps also in the presence of a small female figurine (see cat. no. 1), although the date of that piece is difficult to determine.

The beginning of the Iron Age witnessed a burgeoning of settlements in the central hill country of Palestine, Galilee being no exception. In Lower Galilee, about twenty-five sites, most of them new ones in the southern region, are dated to the twelfth century. Tel ᶜEin Zippori was thus at the center of the rapidly expanding population of Galilee that usually is attributed to Israelite settlements. However, unlike most of the other early Iron Age sites, it was not newly founded in this period and thus cannot easily be identified with the villages of the Israelite settlers of the late thirteenth and early twelfth centuries. The various explanatory models of this greatly expanded settlement of the hill country are the subject of intense scholarly discussion with little consensus.[7] However one understands the emergence of Israel in Canaan, it is clear that the Canaanites and their culture persisted well into the Iron Age.

Because the substantial building of Late Bronze II ʿEin Zippori continued to be used, with some modification, in the Iron I period, it may well be that Canaanite elites maintained their control of this settlement into the twelfth century in the midst of an area dominated by Israelites. Traces of another building of this period may have been recovered in the form of a mudbrick wall on stone foundation courses. The architectural continuity with the Canaanite period is contrasted, however, with the presence of a particular kind of jar that is widely associated with Israelite settlements (see fig. no. 73). This large storage jar, averaging nearly five feet in height, is ovoid with a high narrow neck and sloping shoulders. The ridge, or collar, around the base of the neck gives it the common designation "collared-rim storejar." Although this jar type first appears in Canaanite strata of the Late Bronze Age, it is so ubiquitous at Israelite sites that often it is regarded as the hallmark of Israelite pottery traditions of the early Iron Age.[8] This may be so, but its presence in non-Israelite contexts should not be ignored.

In the late eleventh or the early tenth century, the period of the beginning of the Israelite monarchy, the settlement at ʿEin Zippori was rebuilt once more, this time with a different architectural layout,[9] although some continuity with the Iron I period is evident in one place where an Iron II wall follows the orientation of a preceding building. The Iron II settlement features a large (11 x 15 m.) rectangular building complex. Its size, the configuration of its rooms, and the relative dearth of ordinary household ceramics found in it suggest that it did not have an ordinary domestic function but, rather, a local administrative one. The plethora of stamped storejar handles from fills in this building (see cat. nos. 3, 4), and also from several contemporary structures on a lower terrace of the site, likewise indicates an administrative function. The appearance in tenth-century contexts of three cup-and-bowl vessels (see cat. nos. 5, 6), which may be specialized forms for the burning of incense, perhaps indicates a population able to secure expensive aromatics not locally available.

The large building of the late eleventh-early tenth century was permanently abandoned toward the middle of the tenth century, but there is evidence of renewed occupation later in that century in the form of a poorly constructed domestic structure with a silo. Occupation in the ninth century is clear in at least one part of the site, where a domestic building has been exposed. Its earthen floor was resurfaced at least four times, indicating continued habitation at ʿEin Zippori, apparently as a simple farming village, for a century or so before it was virtually abandoned in the late ninth century. There is also some evidence of squatters in the eighth century, about the time that significant amounts of potsherds begin to appear in fills at nearby Sepphoris.

The ethnicity of the inhabitants of ʿEin Zippori at any point in its history of well more than half a millennium cannot yet be determined. The earliest inhabitants were no doubt Canaanite, and it is likely that the latest ones were Israelite, but the transition from the former to the latter is difficult to distinguish. Given the overall continuity of occupation, it is possible that the emergence of an Israelite settlement did not result from new settlers founding—or conquering—a site, as apparently was the case throughout much of the hill country west of the Jordan River.

Rather, the process of Israelite state formation in the late eleventh and the early tenth century seems to have involved the establishment of regional centers, such as Hazor and Megiddo in Galilee, that in turn facilitated the superimposition of a state system over what had been a loosely affiliated network of rather independent villages and rural communities.[10] Under such a system, territories controlled at one level by local centers and at a higher level by the capital in Jerusalem were integrated into the political, economic, and religious domains of the central power. The centralized state was a new phenomenon on the Palestinian landscape, which previously had been characterized solely by relatively independent city-states. Centralization apparently succeeded to a great extent in imposing the state's cultural forms and hence ethnic identity upon the residents of all the

fig. 3 The eastern portion of a large tenth-century B.C.E. (Iron IIA) building complex at Tel ᶜEin Zippori.
Photo: Sepphoris Regional Project

settlements, rural villages as well as urban centers, that constituted the holdings of the Crown, initially the House of David and later, in the north, a succession of dynastic powers based in Samaria.

NOTES

1. Zvi Gal, *Lower Galilee in the Iron Age,* trans. Marcia Reines Josephy, American Schools of Oriental Research Dissertation Series, 8 (Winona Lake, 1992), 10.

2. J. P. Dessel, Eric M. Meyers, and Carol L. Meyers, "Tel ᶜEn Ṣippori, 1993, 1994," *Israel Exploration Journal* 45 (1995): 288–92.

3. Zvi Gal, "The Settlement of Issachar: Some New Observations," *Tel Aviv* 9 (1982): 85.

4. Carol Meyers, "Of Seasons and Soldiers: A Topological Appraisal of the Premonarchic Tribes of Galilee," *Bulletin of the American Schools of Oriental Research* 252 (1983): 52.

5. Amihai Mazar, *Archaeology of the Land of the Bible* (New York, 1990), 334, 353ff., and William G. Dever, "Cultural Continuity, Ethnicity in the Archaeological Record and the Question of Israelite Origins," *Eretz Israel* 24 (1993): 22*–33*.

6. Shmuel Aḥituv, *Canaanite Toponyms in Ancient Egyptian Documents* (Jerusalem, 1984).

7. See, for example, Robert B. Coote and Keith W. Whitelam, *The Emergence of Early Israel in Historical Perspective,* Social World of Biblical Antiquity Series, 5 (Sheffield, 1987); Israel Finkelstein, *The Archaeology of the Israelite Settlement* (Jerusalem, 1988); and Hershel Shanks, William G. Dever, Baruch Halpern, and P. Kyle McCarter, Jr., *The Rise of Ancient Israel* (Washington, 1992).

8. Amihai Mazar, "The Iron Age I," in *The Archaeology of Ancient Israel,* ed. Amnon Ben-Tor (New Haven, 1992), 290.

9. J. P. Dessel, "ᶜEin-Zippori, Tel," in *The Oxford Encyclopedia of Archaeology in the Near East,* vol. 2 (New York, 1996), 227–28.

10. Carol Meyers, "Kinship and Kingship: The Early Monarchy," chap. 6 of *The Oxford History of the Biblical World,* ed. Michael D. Coogan (New York, forthcoming).

Hellenistic and Roman Sepphoris

The Historical Evidence

Stuart S. Miller

Any discussion of Hellenistic and Roman Sepphoris should begin with the writings of Flavius Josephus, the first-century-C.E. Jewish historian who served as commander of the forces of Galilee during the First Jewish Revolt against Rome (66–70 C.E.). Josephus provides only a selective view of the city's past, one that encompasses little more than a century and a half (c. 103 B.C.E.–67 C.E.). Nevertheless, the information he supplies is critical for an appreciation of the development of the city in the years and centuries following the First Jewish Revolt.

The location of Sepphoris at the crossroads of Lower Galilee, connecting the coastal city of Akko (Greek: Ptolemaïs) with the fertile Jezreel and Beth-Shean valleys, provided it with strategic and commercial importance. The Hasmoneans (or "Maccabees"), the Jewish rulers (164–75 B.C.E.) who wrested the Land of Israel from Syrian domination and persecution, were aware of this importance. This can be inferred from Josephus's account of the failed attempt of Ptolemy Lathyrus, governor of Cyprus, to capture Sepphoris from the Hasmonean Alexander Jannaeus. By 103 B.C.E. it had become clear to Lathyrus that Jannaeus had no intention of helping him recover his throne after his mother, Cleopatra III, had deposed him. Instead, Jannaeus formed an alliance with Cleopatra. When Lathyrus went on the offensive, he was defeated by Jannaeus at Sepphoris,[1] which apparently had already been incorporated into the Hasmonean domains.

Events subsequent to Jannaeus's death in 76 B.C.E. provide further evidence of the regional significance of Sepphoris. Shortly after the Roman general Pompey conquered the Land of Israel in 63 B.C.E., Gabinius, the proconsul of Syria, attempted to limit Hasmonean rule in Jerusalem by decentralizing the administration. Sepphoris was one of five towns, the only one in Galilee, to be assigned a local, Jewish council.[2] Several decades later, around 39/38 B.C.E., the Parthians, a people who emanated from Persia, granted a royal title to Antigonus, the last Hasmonean ruler. This development did not sit well with Herod the Great, the Roman-appointed, client king of Judea, who set out to capture some of Antigonus's strongholds, including Sepphoris. After capturing the city in a snowstorm, Herod appears to have used it as his base of operations against the remaining supporters of the Hasmoneans.[3]

Subsequent events suggest that Herod's royal complex and arsenal at Sepphoris formed a fortification of sorts. In the rebellious climate that existed after the king's death in 4 B.C.E., a Galilean Jew named Judas the son of Ezekias attacked the city's royal palace and armory in order to obtain arms for

fig. 4 **This coin minted in Sepphoris, c. 211–17 C.E., features a portrait bust of Caracalla on the obverse and an inscription in Greek on the reverse that translates: "Diocaesarea the Holy, City Shelter, Autonomous, Loyal [a treaty of] Friendship and Alliance with the Romans." See cat. no. 50.**
Photo: Israel Museum

21

fig. 5 A view of the Sepphoris acropolis from Moshav Zippori showing the Crusader/Ottoman citadel and the reforestation of the site that has occurred since the 1950s. The hill rises some 115 meters (377 feet) above the surrounding plains. In the words of Rabbi Zeira, Sepphoris "is perched on a mountain like a bird." *Photo: Joint Sepphoris Project*

his large number of desperate followers.[4] Sepphoris would pay a high price for its participation in this insurrection. Josephus reports that Varus, the Roman legate of Syria, quelled the rebellion by burning the city and selling its inhabitants into slavery.[5] Josephus may have exaggerated the extent of Varus's retaliation, however, as the historian also informs us that the city recovered quickly.

Herod's son, Herod Antipas, who ruled Galilee from 4 B.C.E. to 39 C.E., fortified Sepphoris, renamed it "Autocratoris," and turned it into the "Ornament [*proschēma*] of all Galilee."[6] The name Autocratoris ("autonomous") alludes to either the sovereign emperor Augustus or to the independent status of the city. Josephus's use of *proschēma* to describe the city is significant because ancient authors generally reserved this term for impregnable cities, such as Sardis or Miletus in Asia Minor.[7] Evidently, as restored by Herod Antipas, Sepphoris had acquired a comparable reputation.

Josephus has little else to say about Sepphoris until the outbreak of the First Jewish Revolt against Rome in 66 C.E. Again impressed by the fortified nature of Sepphoris, he relates how the city eventually emerged as a stronghold whose residents

nonetheless had second thoughts about going to war. Thus when a Roman force was dispatched to subdue the region, it was received "with open arms" in Sepphoris, "the strongest city in Galilee."[8] Actually, Josephus is not entirely consistent in his portrayal of Sepphoris during the revolt. In *The Jewish War* he reports that the residents were so "eager for hostilities" that he, in his capacity as commander of the forces in Galilee, allowed them to erect their own walls.[9] Elsewhere in *War* he claims that he himself fortified Sepphoris "before it had abandoned the Galilean cause" and made peace with the Romans, which is precisely why, he maintains, he later was unable to capture the city.[10]

In his autobiographic *Life,* Josephus portrays Sepphoris as more consistently pro-Roman, a position that engendered the animosity of more revolutionary, rural Galileans. Josephus claims to have assaulted Sepphoris "twice by storm."[11] Josephus further asserts, perhaps in an expression of moderation as well as self-aggrandizement, that during the first of these attacks he prevented the Galileans from utterly destroying the city.[12] For their part, the Sepphoreans continued to press for aid from the Romans. After Sepphoris received some support from Rome, Josephus renewed his efforts to recapture the city but ultimately failed.[13] Josephus goes so far as to assert that the Sepphoreans refrained from sending assistance to Jerusalem when the capital was besieged by the Romans in order "to avoid all suspicion of having borne arms against the Romans."[14] Josephus may be exaggerating here. It is more likely that some elements in Sepphoris did at one time "bear arms" and that, as in Tiberias, Sepphorean society was characterized by factionalism that included anti-Roman elements. The more pacifistic elements, however, did gain the upper hand over time.[15] Thus after the Sepphoreans greeted the Roman general Vespasian when he arrived at Akko in the spring of 67 C.E., the town was granted a garrison that included some one thousand cavalry and six thousand infantry.[16] According to *War,* the Sepphoreans were "the only people of that province [Galilee] who displayed pacific sentiments."[17] These same sentiments were later advertised on coins minted at Sepphoris in 67/68 in honor of Nero. The legends of these coins refer to the city as "Neronias," in honor of Nero, and as "Eirenopolis," that is, "City of Peace."[18]

The pro-Roman position of Sepphoris seems to have hurt its relationship with Tiberias, located to the east on the western shore of the Sea of Galilee.

fig. 6　A coin minted in Sepphoris in 67/68 C.E. in honor of Nero refers to Sepphoris as "Eirenopolis," or "City of Peace." See cat. no. 43. *Photo: Israel Museum*

It seems that Sepphoris, upon submitting to Rome, replaced Tiberias as the first city of Galilee. No longer was Tiberias permitted to maintain a royal bank and archives; these were "dissolved," and the royal bank and archives of Sepphoris assumed expanded jurisdiction.[19] Sepphoris would continue as a leading city almost until the end of Roman rule in the Land of Israel. Tiberias would regain some of its earlier prestige by the third century, when it, like Sepphoris, emerged as an important rabbinic center. The earlier tensions between the two cities, the result of wartime differences, did not persist following the revolt. Indeed, the views of many contemporary scholars notwithstanding, the two cities seem to have enjoyed a harmonious relationship in ensuing centuries, when their Jewish populations had much in common.[20]

Surely Rome took advantage of its relationship with Sepphoris, especially after the revolt, when different security arrangements were required. Both the Romans and later the rabbis took note of the natural and artificial features that made Sepphoris a stronghold. Thus we hear Josephus proclaim that Vespasian was concerned about the possible loss of the city to the Jewish rebels, which would have been a "hazard greatly affecting the impending campaign,

as it was the largest city of Galilee, a fortress in an exceptionally strong position in the enemy's territory, and adapted to keep guard over the entire province."[21] For their part, the rabbis would preserve memories of the old fortification (*castra*) of Sepphoris, which likely was the walled acropolis or upper area of the city.[22] The explanation attributed to the third-century sage Rabbi Zeira that Sepphoris is called Zippori, from the Hebrew *zippor* ("bird"), because "it is perched on a mountain like a bird" undoubtedly has this area in mind. The allusion is clearly to the commanding strategic position of Sepphoris.[23]

Indeed, it is likely that the "old *castra* of Sepphoris" was the *Jewish* fortification at Sepphoris that *preceded* the arrival of the Romans in 67 C.E. The second-century-C.E. rabbis who used the expression "old *castra*" seem to be contrasting that institution with a contemporary, gentile establishment. The Romans probably maintained a limited force, perhaps a unit of cavalry or mounted constables under a prefect, within the walled acropolis at Sepphoris, as suggested by the following story preserved in rabbinic literature, which seems to have in mind a *castra* occupied by gentiles:[24]

> *If a gentile comes to extinguish [a fire on the Sabbath] they should not say to him, "Extinguish" or "Do not extinguish." It happened that a fire broke out in the courtyard of Joseph ben Simai of Shiḥin [Shikhin] and the men of the* castra *of Sepphoris came to extinguish it. But he did not permit them. A cloud descended and extinguished [the fire]. But the sages said, "He did not have to [prevent them from extinguishing].*

Little is known about the extent of the involvement of Galilee in the Second Jewish Revolt led by Bar Kokhba from 132 to 135 C.E. It is likely, however, that the Romans increased their presence in the city with the onset of hostilities in the south. It is noteworthy that coins with distinctly Jewish symbols were minted at Sepphoris during the reign of the emperor Trajan (98–117 C.E.). A milestone, however, indicates that the city received the Roman name "Diocaesarea" (Dio=Zeus; Caesar=Emperor) before

[handwritten margin note: Bar Kokhba]

fig. 7 During the reign of Trajan coins minted at Sepphoris bore the emperor's portrait on one side and distinctively Jewish symbols on the other. The middle coin, for example, shows a palm tree with a Greek inscription that translates: "of the people of Sepphoris." See cat. nos. 45, 46, 47.
Photo: Israel Museum

the Bar Kokhba revolt.[25] With the stationing of a legion some sixteen miles to the south, it was inevitable that Sepphoris would be incorporated into the defense line of the Romans, however small the regiment stationed at the *castra*.[26] In any event, coins issued within just a few years of the fall of Bar Kokhba bear the legend "Diocaesarea, the Sacred, City of Shelter and Autonomous" and include images of the goddess Hera holding a patera and of a temple of the Capitoline Triad (Jupiter, Juno, and Minerva).[27]

Whatever role Rome played at Sepphoris between the First and the Second Jewish Revolt, it was precisely in the post-Bar Kokhba Revolt years, when the Jewish population shifted northward, that Sepphoris emerged as a rabbinic center that attracted prominent sages from throughout the land. Toward the end of the second century c.e., Rabbi Judah Ha-Nasi (the Patriarch) moved to Sepphoris from Beth-She‘arim, a move undoubtedly prompted, at least to some extent, by the prominence that the city had achieved both as a rabbinic and as an administrative center. Legends preserved in rabbinic literature concerning the ongoing relationship of one "Antoninus" (often assumed to be the Roman emperor Caracalla, who ruled in the early third century) and Rabbi Judah enhance the impression that the city maintained a positive relationship with Rome. Coins minted during the early third century, when Rabbi Judah is likely to have lived at Sepphoris, indicate that the city wanted to capitalize on its earlier asso-

ciation with Rome, as their inscriptions boast that the Sepphoreans were "friends and allies" of the senate and of the Roman people.[28]

The predominance of Jews, and especially of members of the rabbinic class, in the city accounts for the fact that, despite its Hellenistic veneer and the periodic presence of Roman troops, Sepphoris was largely regarded as a Jewish city. Many prominent sages who would make important contributions to rabbinic literature resided there. Some of these sages called attention to noteworthy aspects of the city's urban life and society, noting such prominent institutions as the *castra*, the archives,[29] and the thoroughfare[30] and, from time to time, alluding to the city's commercial importance. That the city would have an upper and a lower market should come as no surprise.[31] Sepphoris was located within a highly fertile area of Lower Galilee, and its location along one of the major transportation arteries of the region made it economically as well as strategically important. This was not lost on the rabbis. One third-century rabbi was said to have commented that the milk and honey of Sepphoris "flowed for sixteen square miles."[32] A report assigned to Rabbi Yose ben Halafta, the leading sage of mid-second-century Sepphoris, alludes to the city's burgeoning meat markets.[33] Within a century, the expertise of the local butchers would be widely recognized.[34] Moreover, the weights, measures, and even coins of Sepphoris would become recognized standards.[35]

The Roman presence also would continue to be noted by the rabbis, if only in offhand remarks that give the impression that it was of limited interest to them, no more than a passing annoyance. A handful of notices concerning this presence has sometimes been used as corroborating evidence of an insurrection centered at Sepphoris (Diocaesarea) under

Gallus circa 351 C.E. For example, we hear of the presence of a *numerus*, or military unit of varying size, during the time of Rabbi Mana[36] and of Sepphoreans who appear to have been "sought after" by the Romans in the "days of Ursicinus the king."[37]

Church chronographers writing as late as the fourteenth century speak more directly of an insurrection. Their reports seem to be based upon information provided by the church father Jerome, writing circa 380, and by the chronographer Socrates (c. 380–450), who writes:

> . . . *there came to pass with respect to the East another internal war. For the Jews in Diocaesarea [Sepphoris] of Palestine raised up arms against the Romans and laid waste near those places. But then Gallus . . . whom the Emperor appointed Caesar and sent to the East, dispatched a force which prevailed against them. And their city, Diocaesarea, he ordered to be razed to the ground.*[38]

The extent of the "revolt" has been seriously called into question in recent years.[39] Whatever the impact of the Gallus Revolt, it must be regarded as a brief and exceptional interlude in the history of a city that was once regarded as a "City of Peace." Roman Sepphoris probably suffered greater destruction from the earthquake of 363 C.E. Even so, the city continued to have a Jewish presence in the late fourth century.[40]

NOTES

1. *Jewish Antiquities* 13.337–38. Translations of Josephus follow *Josephus,* in nine volumes, trans. H. St. J. Thackeray, Loeb Classical Library (Cambridge, Mass., and London, 1967).

2. *Antiquities* 14.91; see also, Josephus, *The Jewish War* 1.170. These councils, whose powers are unclear, did not rule for very long, however.

3. *Antiquities* 14.414–15.

4. *Antiquities* 17.271; *War* 2.56.

5. *Antiquities* 17.289; *War* 2.68–69.

6. *Antiquities* 18.27.

7. For a discussion of Autocratoris and *proschēma,* see Stuart S. Miller, *Studies in the History and Traditions of Sepphoris* (Leiden, 1984), 2, 57.

8. *War* 2.510–11.

9. *War* 2.574–75.

10. *War* 3.61–62.

11. *Life* 82.

12. *Life* 373–80.

13. *Life* 394–97.

14. *Life* 348.

15. See the discussion of Josephus and Sepphoris in my (tentatively titled) "Ancient Sepphoris and Historical Memory" (in preparation).

16. *Life* 411.

17. *War* 3.30–31.

18. See Ya'akov Meshorer, "Sepphoris and Rome," in *Greek Numismatics and Archaeology: Essays in Honor of Margaret Thompson* (Wetteren, 1979), 159–71, and his entries on coins in this catalogue; also see Miller,

"Intercity Relations in Roman Palestine: The Case of Sepphoris and Tiberias," *Association for Jewish Studies Review* 12 (1987): 6, esp. n. 30

19. See *Life* 36–39. Also see Miller, *Studies,* 54f., where I maintain that Sepphoris did not necessarily take over the royal bank and archives of Tiberias.

20. See Miller, "Intercity Relations," and my article on Jewish Sepphoris in this catalogue.

21. *War* 3.34.

22. See Miller, *Studies,* 28–30.

23. See Babylonian Talmud, *Megillah* 6a, and Miller, *Studies,* 25–29. On the elevation of Sepphoris, also see Babylonian Talmud, *Ketubot* 103b.

24. Tosefta, *Shabbat* 13:9. For parallels and discussion, see Miller, *Studies,* 31–45.

25. See Benjamin Isaac and Israël Roll, "Judaea in the Early Years of Hadrian's Reign," *Latomus* 38 (1979): 56f. The name Diocaesarea presumably would have honored the emperor Hadrian, who had adopted the title Zeus Olympius, which was equivalent to the divine "Dio."

26. See Miller, *Studies,* 40–45, 58.

27. On the coins, see Meshorer, "Sepphoris and Rome," 163–65, and his catalogue entries on coins in this publication.

28. See Miller, "Intercity Relations," 7, and "Those Cantankerous Sepphoreans Revisited," in the festschrift for Baruch A. Levine, to be published by Eisenbrauns. For another view of the coins, see Meshorer's entries in this catalogue.

29. Mishnah, *Qiddushin* 4:5; compare *Numbers Rabbah* 9:7.

30. Tosefta, *Hullin* 2:24; *Ecclesiastes Rabbah* 1:8; Jerusalem Talmud, *Ta'anit* 7, 25d; compare *Ecclesiastes Rabbah* 7:7 and Jerusalem Talmud, *Ta'anit* 4, 68a.

31. Babylonian Talmud, *Erubin* 54b and *Yoma'* 11a.

32. Babylonian Talmud, *Megillah* 6a and *Ketubot* 11b; compare Jerusalem Talmud, *Bikkurim* 1, 64b.

33. Babylonian Talmud, *Baba' Batra'* 75b.

34. Babylonian Talmud, *Baba' Qamma'* 99b. For a full discussion, see my "Those Cantankerous Sepphoreans Revisited."

35. For the *litra* of Sepphoris see Midrash Tanna'im 32:13; Sifre Deuteronomy, *Ha'azinu* 317; Jerusalem Talmud, *Pe'ah* 7, 20a; and Babylonian Talmud, *Ketubot* 11b. For a lead weight with the word "half-*litra*" found at Sepphoris, see Eric M. Meyers, Ehud Netzer, and Carol L. Meyers, "Sepphoris, 'Ornament of All Galilee,'" *Biblical Archaeologist* 49 (1986): 16–17; also see cat. no. 67 in this publication. For measures see Babylonian Talmud, *Pesaḥim* 109a; Jerusalem Talmud, *Shabbat* 8, 11a and *Pesaḥim* 10, 37c. For money see Tosefta, *Ma'aser Sheni* 4:13, and Babylonian Talmud, *Berakhot* 53b.

36. Jerusalem Talmud, *Pesaḥim* 4, 31b. See Miller, *Studies*, 43f.

37. Jerusalem Talmud, *Yevamot* 16, 15c and *Sotah* 9, 23c.

38. *Ecclesiastical History* 2.33, following translation of Barbara Geller Nathanson, "Jews, Christians, and the Gallus Revolt in Fourth-Century Palestine," *Biblical Archaeologist* 49 (1986): 33.

39. See especially, Nathanson, "Jews, Christians, and the Gallus Revolt," 34, and Peter Schäfer, "Der Aufstand gegen Gallus Caesar," in *Tradition and Re-Interpretation in Jewish and Early Christian Literature: Essays in Honour of Jurgen C. H. Lebram*, ed. J. W. Van Henten et al. (Leiden, 1986), 184–201.

40. Theodoret, *Ecclesiastical History* 4.22, writes with reference to events of 373 C.E. that Diocaesarea was "inhabited by Jews." It would appear that Rabbi Mana and Rabbi Ḥanina *De-Zipporin*, both leading sages at Sepphoris, lived at the end of the century; see my discussion of Jewish Sepphoris in this catalogue.

Hellenistic and Roman Sepphoris
The Archaeological Evidence

Zeev Weiss and Ehud Netzer

Even though archaeological excavations at Sepphoris have not included all parts of the city that date from the Second Temple period and the period of the Mishnah and the Talmud (that is, the Hellenistic and Roman periods), there is ample evidence to conclude that initially in this time span the city centered around the top of the hill and on its slopes.[1] The ancient city of Sepphoris had occupied the southern slope, where much of the twentieth-century Arab village of Saffuriyeh was situated, but it also extended over the remaining, somewhat less accessible, western, northern and eastern slopes. The initial Hellenistic core of the city presumably covered an area of about 2.5 hectares, the so-called acropolis extending over the entire summit of the hill. Because the summit had the advantages of being relatively flat and surrounded by fairly steep slopes, it was easy to defend and also was exposed to pleasant breezes during the summer months.

It is still difficult to summarize the urban structure of the acropolis at the end of the Hellenistic period and the begining of the Roman era because important parts of it have not yet been exposed, but the evidence of intensive construction revealed thus far indicates a continuity of settlement from the Hellenistic period up to the Early Arab period. The layout of houses and narrow streets on the western summit was maintained, without any significant changes, until the earthquake of 363 C.E. This densely built-up western area had a predominantly residential character. The average house measured 15 x 15 meters and included several rooms built around an inner courtyard that was not much larger than the rooms themselves. Houses were accessed via alleys that apparently were parallel and perpendicular to each other, their general direction being dictated by the topography. An east-west street paved with stone slabs was built along the northern edge of the acropolis. There are also signs of a drainage channel that would have run under the road of a parallel street, along its southern edge. Nonetheless, the general impression is that in the earliest stages of occupation the acropolis lacked a well-planned layout.

During the early stages of urbanization, from the Hellenistic period up to the second century C.E., it appears that the city's water was supplied to the city primarily through the storage of rainwater in subterranean cisterns. Water was needed not only for daily usage (drinking, cooking, and washing) but also for religious purification purposes, as indicated by the many ritual baths (*miqva'ot*) located on all parts of the hill. It may also have been required for certain "industrial" operations. The average annual

fig. 8 The Greek inscription on this lead market weight from Sepphoris is framed by two rows of columns. They may refer to the city's colonnaded streets, which were constructed during the Roman period and remained in continuous use for more than 500 years. See cat. no. 67.
Photo: Israel Antiquities Authority

fig. 9 The Roman theater against the backdrop of the Crusader/ Ottoman citadel on the summit of the Sepphoris acropolis. Constructed at the end of the first century c.e. or later, the theater could seat around 4,500 spectators.
Photo: Ehud Netzer

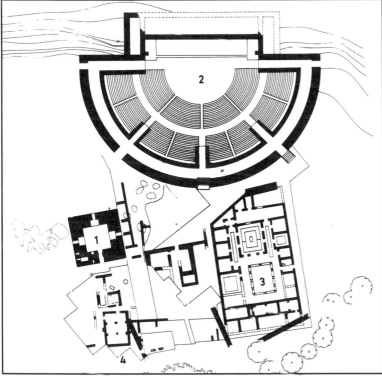

fig. 10 Plan of the eastern side of the acropolis showing:
1) the citadel; 2) the theater; 3) the Dionysos mosaic building; and 4) the storehouse.
Courtesy: The Hebrew University Expedition

rainfall in Sepphoris is about 550 millimeters, of which about 220 millimeters per dunam (0.1 hectare) could presumably be stored. Rainwater alone was thus able to fill all of the numerous water cisterns on the hill. However, it should be mentioned that in the days of Herod and his son Antipas, the city's water supply was supplemented by means of an aqueduct that led water from a spring some miles to the east, close to the present-day village of Mashad.[2]

The urban layout at the center of the acropolis and on its eastern side is very unclear. On the eastern edge of the aforementioned residential area, the Duke University expedition has uncovered a building from the Hellenistic period that was perhaps used as a barracks.[3] Not far from that structure, in the center of the acropolis, the University of South Florida expedition exposed a building that contains bathing facilities, either public or private ones. There are also signs of the presence of public facilities to the east, close to the Crusader citadel. To the south of the citadel the Hebrew University expedition revealed various water installations, some of which might be dated to the early stages of the city. Southeast of the citadel, the foundations of what seems to have been a public building were uncovered. To the east of it are the remains of a luxurious mansion constructed in the third century c.e., which is referred to here as the Dionysos mosaic building because of its magnificent mosaic carpet featuring scenes from the Greek god's life.[4] The remains of domiciles were found beneath this building.

An analysis of the literary sources suggests that a market building existed on the summit.[5] It, together with other public buildings, might have been located on the southern slope. In any event, there probably were shops on the acropolis flanking some of its streets. The only shops excavated so far were exposed in the basement of the Dionysos mosaic building. These shops were adjacent to the street that apparently ran along the southern edge of the acropolis, part of which has been excavated by the Duke University expedition in the westernmost area of the residential quarter.

According to first-century historian Flavius Josephus, a palatial building existed at Sepphoris in the days of Herod the Great, but the remains of such have not been discovered.[6] However, fragments of frescoes from fills beneath the Dionysos mosaic building suggest that such a palatial structure could have stood not far from there. The civic center of the early city probably was located in the middle of the acropolis or slightly to its east. In any case, access to the acropolis was easier from this direction than from the steeper western slope.

From the acropolis, the city expanded over the slopes of the hill in every direction. It appears that this process occurred first on the southern slope, which was more amenable to construction. Only limited areas on the hill's slopes have been exposed: several soundings were taken on the southern slope by the Joint Sepphoris Project; a few were taken on the northern slop by the South Florida team; and others were taken by the Hebrew University expedition, some under the theater situated along the steep northern slope and some to the northeast of it. The general character of the buildings in that area (including many water cisterns and ritual baths) is comparable to that on the western portion of the acropolis. The remains of buildings uncovered below the theater serve as the best examples of how the residents of Sepphoris coped with the steep slopes of the hill. Future excavations may help to clarify the character of the areas of the city on the hill slopes. Presumably urban growth was gradual, without overall planning, and the slopes were utilized mainly for residential purposes. However, some public buildings, such as synagogues, shops, and perhaps even markets, may also have been constructed on them.

It is noteworthy that no fortifications have yet been found around the acropolis or anywhere else in Sepphoris.[7] From a topographic standpoint it would have been easy to surround the acropolis with a defensive barrier, either a freestanding wall or a line of houses, raised on solid foundations, immediately adjacent to one another.[8] The latter type of fortification was implemented in medium-sized cities throughout Galilee during this period.[9]

An important development in the layout of Sepphoris occurred during the first half of the second century c.e. By this time the top of the hill and all of its slopes had been completely built up, yet an increase in the population—and a higher standard of living —necessitated an extension of the city limits. The fairly level area to the east of the summit, with its gentle slope toward the south, was suitable for this purpose, and the expansion was well planned. It has not been determined whether this area had been used solely for agricultural purposes or if it already featured some buildings, but in any event, an area of at least five hectares was marked out and a street grid was constructed, giving rise to a series of *insulae*, or organized blocks of space.

The new streets east of the acropolis were linked to both the existing ones on the top of the hill and to those leading to the surrounding fields as well as to the nearby intercity roads. The general direction of the new grid, about 30 degrees off north, probably was dictated by the topography as well as by the position of the above-mentioned streets on the hill. The initiative for the new, planned urban development apparently was taken by the city council, the *boulē* of Sepphoris, which in the past had consisted primarily of Jewish members (see cat. nos. 45–48). The development of this area not only extended the city limits; it also facilitated the building of a new civic center that catered to the needs of a rapidly growing city. The various buildings were constructed between the streets, within the *insulae*. These *insulae* were not equal in size, as in some Roman cities; they varied, the smaller ones measuring about 70 x 40 meters, the larger ones roughly 90 x 70 meters.

Rapid development made it no longer possible for the city to rely solely on the collection of rainwater in cisterns. Thus an aqueduct system, extending from the springs of the present-day village of Raineh to the east of Sepphoris, was built in this period. The most significant operation was the quarrying of a 200-meter-long subterranean reservoir, 1.5 kilometers away from the city. This reservoir was connected to the aqueduct and was intended for water storage either overnight or for longer periods during the winter season. From the reservoir toward the city the aqueduct began as a tunnel and continued as a channel. This elaborate water installation was apparently built at the same time as the new civic center to the east of the summit. How water was distributed within the built-up area is not yet known. However, the discovery of sections of channels and lead pipes from different periods indicates the existence of a supply system.[10]

At the time of the construction of this new water system, efforts were also made to improve the water supply to the top of the hill. At this stage a large reservoir, measuring 13 x 8 meters, was quarried at the center of the acropolis. This cistern, which today is located south of the Crusader citadel, probably provided water to the entire summit, or at least to its southern slope. This assumption is based on the discovery of a tunnel-conduit that directed water toward the southern slope. If this reservoir was supplied by the new water system, water was brought to the top of the hill either by pack animals or by some other means of transport.

The theater at Sepphoris was apparently built while the new development to the east of the acropolis was underway. In this period new theaters were built throughout the Roman world, many as free standing structures based on arches and vaults. For practical reasons, however, in the Land of Israel theaters were built mainly on natural slopes.[11] As alluded to previously, the construction of this theater required the demolition of some houses that already existed here. A large portion of the auditorium was hewn out of the bedrock, and the rest of it was built with large field stones. On the basis of historical background, some scholars have attributed construction of the theater to the reign of Herod Antipas (4 B.C.E.–39 C.E.), who made Sepphoris his capital.[12] The archaeologial evidence, however, suggests that this large edifice was not erected before the end of the first century C.E.[13]

The new civic center featured two colonnaded streets: the *decumanus*, running from east to west, and the *cardo*, running from north to south. These two main streets were paved with hard rectangular limestone slabs laid in rows across the width of the street at a slight angle to the sidewalks. Noteworthy is the high quality of work that went into laying these two streets, which were used continually, almost without repairs, for more than 500 years! Limestone stylobates (continuous pavements supporting rows of columns) separated the streets proper from the sidewalks. Very few of the original columns

that once stood on these stylobates have survived, and it is difficult to determine whether those few belong to the original stage of construction. However, it seems that the floors of the sidewalks were paved with mosaics from the outset. On both sides of these colonnaded streets, close to their intersection, were shops, evidence of the intensive commercial activity that took place in this newly developed sector of Sepphoris.

The overall width of both the *decumanus* and the *cardo*, including their colonnades (each of which was approximately 3.5 meters wide), reached 13 meters. No signs of a drainage system have yet been revealed under these streets, but it appears that the natural gradient facilitated the rapid drainage of rainwater from this area. This runoff was apparently preferable to an underground system that would have been expensive and difficult to maintain.

Altogether, three north-south streets and three east-west streets have been exposed thus far in the area to the east of the summit. The westernmost street, on the flank of the hill about 65 meters to the west of the *cardo*, was at least partially paved with rectangular stone slabs. It probably continued beyond the city limits, toward the important road that led from Akko (Greek: Ptolemaïs) to Tiberias. (In the Byzantine period, a synagogue was built next to this street, north of the well-planned eastern sector.[14]) Unlike this street, the *cardo* did not extend northward beyond the limits of the eastern sector; rather it ran southward into what appears to have been an extensive agricultural area, as indicated both by an analysis of the topography and by the clearly visible ruts of wagon wheels on the paving stones. The easternmost street, located about 75 meters to the east of the *cardo*, probably was paved from the outset with plaster. Over the years the level of this street was raised repeatedly, as indicated by the several layers of plaster.

The northernmost street, located about 50 meters north of the *decumanus*, was apparently also paved with plaster and not stones. It was situated on the northern side of the large public building that occupied an entire *insula* excavated by the South Florida expedition. This street also ran along a second structure that tentatively can be identified as a public building occupying the next *insula* to the east of the *cardo* (see below). On the northern side of that *insula* is evidence of the existence of shops with barrel-vaulted ceilings, which faced the northernmost street. Based on the architectural evidence as well as on the topography in this part of the building, these shops probably had a second floor, access to which was gained from within the *insula*. This street continued westward along the base of the hill's northern slope, passing the rear side of the theater, but there is no evidence of its extension eastward beyond the limits of the new sector.

The *decumanus* was undoubtedly one of the most important streets of Sepphoris, as it served as the principal link between the summit of the hill and the newly developed area. It linked up almost rectilinearly with the narrow street at the northern edge of the acropolis, and it bordered on the southern, rounded side of the theater, thereby serving as an important access to this large public edifice.

The southernmost street, revealed about 90 meters south of the *decumanus*, was paved with stone slabs and, like the *cardo*, bears marks of wagon wheels. To the west, this street apparently continued to the built-up, southern slope of the hill. To the east, it must have continued beyond the expansion of the city into the agricultural fields in the nearby valleys. This street seems to have been flanked mainly by residential buildings, many of which incorporated agricultural facilities.

The new urban framework apparently included a few other streets, one or two of which probably ran north-south on the eastern side of the newly developed area; possibly there was also a street that ran east-west on the southern side. Topographic conditions discouraged the construction of another east-west street farther to the north, but such a street might have been built at the end of the Roman period or, more probably, in the Byzantine period.

There is no reason to assume that at this stage, or later, the extended city was surrounded by any sort of fortifications. Still, on its outskirts, along the main roads that led into the city, gates similar to the monumental ones found at Gerasa (modern Jerash), Tiberias, and Beth-Shean might have been erected.

fig. 11 The intersection of the *cardo* (north-south street) and the *decumanus* (east-west street) viewed from the north.
Photo: Gabi Laron

Two reasons can be offered for the eastward spread of the city: to increase the residential area in order to accommodate the growing population—which by the second century C.E. might have numbered around 10,000 to 12,000—and to erect an up-to-date civic center to serve that population. The many shops lining the *cardo* and the *decumanus* indicate a new, bustling civic center, as do the public building at the intersection of these two streets and the building to the south of the *decumanus*, of which only the foundations have survived (see below). Despite extensive excavations in this area, large parts of this building have still not been exposed; thus information regarding the civic center remains incomplete.

The structure excavated by the University of South Florida expedition near the main intersection is known as the basilical building.[15] Its main entrance was apparently on the east, from the *cardo*, although there were possibly other entrances. This edifice, which measures about 70 x 95 meters, features a high standard of architecture and probably was built at the

Agora/basilica (handwritten margin note)

same time as the new streets. This building may have served as an *agora* (forum) or a basilica, or it may have had some other function yet to be disclosed.

Another possible public building stood in the *insula* east of the one mentioned previously, on the other side of the *cardo*. Most of this *insula* has not yet been exposed, but the row of barrel-vaulted shops(?) also mentioned previously is situated on its northern side. We can therefore assume that this was a public and not a private edifice. It is possible that the central market (*macellum*) of Sepphoris mentioned in the Jewish sources might have been located here. This possibility is bolstered by the lead weight discovered on the acropolis by the Joint Sepphoris Project. The weight (see cat. no. 67) bears a Greek inscription that mentions Simon son of Aianos (no doubt a Jew) as the city's *agoranomos*, the official responsible for its markets. Also depicted on this lead weight are two parallel rows of columns, which possibly represent either a market building or one of the city's colonnaded streets.

The importance of the *decumanus* as a main thoroughfare is demonstrated by its location. On the one hand, it is aligned with the water system leading to the civic center from the east; on the other hand, it served as a major link to the acropolis. Other public buildings existed south of the *decumanus* and the two aforementioned *insulae*. Along the *decumanus*, about 45 meters from its intersection with the *cardo*, the Hebrew University expedition uncovered the foundations of a building measuring about 23 x 12 meters that probably was surrounded by a *temenos* (sacred place) and may have been used as a pagan temple or even a synagogue. During the Byzantine period building activity took place on both sides of the *cardo*, adjacent to the *decumanus*. To the south of the latter, foundations of buildings, probably churches, have been found, but it is still not possible to define the character of the Roman buildings that preceded them.

Baths (handwritten margin note)

Two public bathhouses were exposed south of the *decumanus*, on either side of the *cardo*. The first (from the first or early second century C.E.) is situated to the east of the *cardo*; the second, which is larger, more elaborate, and dates from the third or

fig. 12   The remains of a public bathhouse from the third or fourth century C.E. located west of the *cardo*.
Photo: Gabi Laron

fourth century C.E., is to its west. The smaller bathhouse included a long, narrow hot room (*caldarium*) flanked by rooms that are only partly preserved. Small sections of mosaic floors and a stepped pool also were revealed nearby. Many details of this bathhouse resemble those in bathhouses uncovered at other sites in the country, mostly from the Herodian period.[16] The stepped pool, like those in the Herodian bathhouses, might have served as a ritual bath. It has been theorized that this bathhouse preceded the system of well-planned streets and *insulae*; it is hoped that future excavations will clarify this matter.

The later, larger bathhouse measured 27 x 26 meters (excluding service areas, furnaces, etc.). Planned in the best Roman tradition, it had two perpendicular axes of symmetry. The east-west axis, on the south side of the building, passed through three adjacent hot rooms (*caldaria*), the westernmost one of which was octagonal in shape. The second axis of symmetry bisected the central courtyard, the warm room (*tepidarium*), and the central hot room (*caldarium*). Two cold rooms (*frigidaria*) containing pools for bathing were exposed on either side of the *tepidarium*. The main entrance of this bathhouse was at its northeastern corner, directly from the *cardo*. Most of the rooms were paved with mosaics, some having simple designs (such as alternating rows of white and black triangles), others having elaborate geometric ones.

South of this bathhouse excavators uncovered the remains of a structure consisting of a group of elongated basements, possibly the foundations of a large building. Drums of columns were revealed in some of these basements. The building's proximity to the bathhouse and its architectural details suggest that it had a public function.

Because the civic center of the Roman period has only been partially excavated, and because major changes were introduced here during the Byzantine period, not much is known about the associated residential structures that existed in this area. Some of the exposed ritual baths may have belonged to domiciles. There is scattered evidence of some residential buildings, as in the remains to the west of the *cardo* of the *triclinium* of a luxurious building decorated with an elaborate mosaic floor. The floor displays three scenes from everyday life and one depicting Orpheus charming animals with his lute playing. On a street corner southeast of this building, a large section of another elaborate domicile that dates to the end of the Roman period and to the beginning of the Byzantine period was revealed. During both periods its rooms were covered with decorative mosaic floors. A few other houses, some of which contained various agricultural installations, were exposed in this vicinity as well. The proximity of some of these private dwellings to the public buildings hints at the public/private mix of urban life in lower Sepphoris at this time. Some of the *insulae* probably contained both public and private buildings.

One can assume that the city continued to develop during the Middle and Late Roman periods (second century through the second half of the fourth century c.e.). Important evidence of this is found in the previously mentioned Dionysos mosaic building on the east of the acropolis. Probably built at the beginning of the third century c.e., this structure, which is 48 x 23 meters, spread across the entire width of the acropolis between two streets, the one on the north being the continuation of the *decumanus*. This elaborate structure, erected around a peristyle (colonnaded) courtyard, apparently had two floors aside from a basement under its southern part. This luxurious building is noted for its outstanding mosaic floors; the best-preserved and most widely known mosaic depicts scenes from the life and cult of Dionysos. It is difficult to determine the ethnic background and occupation of the house's ini-

tial owner, but there is no doubt that he was wealthy and held a distinguished position in the community. The Dionysos mosaic building was not the only *domus* from the Roman period exposed on the acropolis. Another such house built around a peristyle courtyard was revealed in 1931 by Leroy Waterman, who erroneously termed it a basilica.[17] Such dwellings presumably existed not only on the acropolis and around the civic center but also throughout the city, in particular on its periphery. Some of these dwellings, incorporating agricultural installations—*villae* in the true sense of the term—were perhaps located in the surrounding fields.

Archaeological research has revealed only scant evidence of the cemeteries of Sepphoris, although the various burial caves discovered to date suggest that they were spread over the hills close to the city. The location of these caves helps define the boundaries of the city during the Roman and Byzantine periods because in antiquity there was a clear separation between an inhabited area and its burial grounds. Some of these burial caves, especially the more elaborate ones, were hewn out of the rock

fig. 13   A tomb in one of the burial caves of Sepphoris. *Photo: Oren Gutfeld*

along the sides of the main roads leading to the city, as was customary in the Roman world.[18] They consisted of a few chambers of various sizes with *loculi* carved into their walls, sometimes on two levels. This system of burial began in the Second Temple period and continued into the first centuries of the common era.

Other burial caves featured *arcosolia* (arched shelves with one or several rectangular burials cut lengthwise into the wall of the tomb) hewn out of the walls or stone coffins (sarcophagi) that were placed within the burial chambers. Such sarcophagi were incorporated, in secondary use, in the corners of the Crusader citadel on the summit of the hill. A few of them were decorated with flowers or wreaths of leaves. In addition, a mausoleum, built of stone, was found north of the city. Here too *loculi* (a burial shaft cut perpendicularly into the wall of the tomb) were used for the internment of the deceased.[19]

Inscriptions in Aramaic and Greek that mention the names of the deceased were found in some of the burial caves at Sepphoris; they were carved on the tomb walls as well as on marble and stone slabs (see cat. nos. 32, 33, 34). The following are two examples: "Hoshea, son of Tanhum from Tiberias" and "This grave is of Nachum and Yaᶜakov, sons of Rabbi Hosochi, may his soul rest in peace." The cemetery of Sepphoris, one of the most important and central cities in the Galilee, was perhaps no less rich and elaborate than that of Beth-Sheᶜarim.[20]

It thus appears that in the late Roman period Sepphoris was a well-laid-out and a well-maintained city. Its boundaries have yet to be clearly defined, but the city probably spread over an area of approximately 35 hectares and had between 14,000 and 18,000 inhabitants. The expanding development to the east is representative of the growth that many cities experienced at this time in the Land of Israel. Sepphoris, however, is one of the most beautiful examples of this process.

NOTES

1. The information presented here is based primarily on excavations conducted during the years 1990–96 under the directorship of the authors on behalf of the Institute of Archaeology, the Hebrew University of Jerusalem. For previous publications see Ehud Netzer and Zeev Weiss, "Sepphoris," *Israel Exploration Journal* 43 (1993): 190–96; Weiss, "Sepphoris," in *The New Encyclopedia of Archaeological Excavations in the Holy Land*, vol. 4 (Jerusalem, 1993), 1324–28; Netzer and Weiss, *Zippori* (Jerusalem, 1994); and Weiss, "Sepphoris during the Roman and Byzantine Periods in Light of Archaeological Finds," in *Proceedings of the Eleventh World Congress of Jewish Studies* (Jerusalem, 1994), 47–53 (in Hebrew).

2. For details on the water system of Sepphoris, see Tsvika Tsuk's article in this catalogue.

3. Eric M. Meyers, Carol L. Meyers, and Kenneth G. Hoglund, "Sepphoris (Ṣippori), 1994," *Israel Exploration Journal* 45 (1995): 68–71. Also see Kenneth G. Hoglund and Eric M. Meyers's article on the residential quarter in this catalogue.

4. See the detailed discussion of the Dionysos mosaic in this catalogue.

5. See, for example, Babylonian Talmud, *Yoma'* 11a and *Erubin* 54b.

6. Josephus, *Jewish Antiquities* 17.271–72; all translations of Josephus follow that of H. St. J. Thackeray, Loeb Classical Library (Cambridge, Mass., and London, 1967).

7. According to Josephus, the city was fortified with walls during the First Jewish Revolt before taking a pro-Roman stand; see *Jewish War* 2.574 and 3.61.

8. According to the Mishnah, the houses in the old *castra* of Sepphoris (presumably the acropolis) were all lined up and actually formed the city wall; see Mishnah, *ᶜArakhin* 9, 6. Also see Stuart S. Miller, *Studies in the History and Traditions of Sepphoris* (Leiden, 1984), 15–30, and his article on Hellenistic and Roman Sepphoris in this catalogue.

9. Zeev Yeivin, "On the Medium-sized City," *Eretz Israel* 19 (1987): 57–71 (in Hebrew).

10. See Tsuk's discussion of these issues in his article on the water systems of Sepphoris in this catalogue.

11. On the theaters of the Land of Israel and their construction see Zeev Weiss, "Roman Leisure Culture and Its Influence on the Jewish Population in the Land of Israel," *Qadmoniot* 28 (1995): 2–19 (in Hebrew), and "Buildings for Entertainment," in *The Cities of Roman Palestine*, ed. Daniel Sperber (in press).

12. Shmuel Yeivin, "Historical and Archaeological Notes," in Leroy Waterman et al., *Preliminary Report of the University of Michigan Excavations at Sepphoris, Palestine, in 1931* (Ann Arbor, 1937), 29–30, and Arthur Segal, "Theaters in Eretz-Israel in the Roman Period," in *Greece and Rome in Eretz-Israel*, ed. A. Kasher et al. (Jerusalem, 1989), 532 (in Hebrew).

13. This evidence raised doubts regarding Richard Batey's theory concerning the term *hippocritis* (meaning an actor), which appears several times in the New Testament, as proof of Jesus' visits to the theater at Sepphoris; see Richard Batey, "Jesus and the Theatre," *New Testament Studies* 30 (1984): 563–74; for a full discussion of the issues raised by Batey, see E. P. Sanders's article about Jesus' relationship to Sepphoris in this catalogue.

14. For more information on this synagogue, see our accompanying article on Sepphoris in the Byzantine period in this catalogue.

15. See James F. Strange's article on the basilical building in this catalogue; also see Strange et al., "Zippori," *Excavations and Surveys in Israel* 13 (1993): 29–30.

16. See, for example, Ehud Netzer, "Cypros," *Qadmoniot* 8 (1975): 54–61 (in Hebrew), and "Recent Discoveries in the Winter Palaces of Second Temple Times at Jericho," *Qadmoniot* 15 (1982): 22–28 (in Hebrew).

17. Waterman believed that this was an early church, but Michael Avi-Yonah correctly identified the structure as a Roman mansion; see Waterman et al., *Preliminary Report of the University of Michigan Excavations*, 4–6, and Avi-Yonah, "Sepphoris," in *Encyclopedia of Archaeological Excavations in the Holy Land*, vol. 4 (Jerusalem 1978), 1053–4. This conclusion is reinforced by the University of South Florida team that reexcavated the building; see

James F. Strange, "Six Campaigns at Sepphoris: The University of South Florida Excavations, 1983–1989," in *The Galilee in Late Antiquity*, ed. Lee I. Levine (New York and Jerusalem, 1992), 344–51.

18. For more details regarding cemeteries in Roman Galilee see Zeev Weiss, "The Location of Jewish Cemeteries in the Galilee in the Mishnaic and Talmudic Periods," in *Graves and Burial Practices in Israel in the Ancient Period*, ed. I. Singer (Jerusalem, 1994), 230–40 (in Hebrew).

19. Nahman Avigad, "The 'Tomb of Jacob's Daughters' near Sepphoris," *Eretz Israel* 11 (1973): 41–44.

20. This is based on an unpublished survey conducted recently in the necropolis of Sepphoris. For Beth-She͑arim see Benjamin Mazar, *Beth-She͑arim*, 1 (Jerusalem, 1973), and Nahman Avigad, *Beth-She͑arim*, 111 (Jerusalem, 1976).

The Residential Quarter

on the Western Summit

Kenneth G. Hoglund and Eric M. Meyers

Along the northern edge of the upper city, or acropolis, is an area that has been excavated almost continuously since 1985. Numerous successive phases of occupation have been recovered in this area, and all suggest that for most of the area's history it served a domestic purpose, thus its designation as the residential quarter.

The earliest signs of occupation have been recovered from deep crevices in the bedrock of the ridge on which the Roman city stood. The materials from this phase, mainly fragments of ceramic cooking pots and other simple vessels, are distributed in a manner consistent with water-borne sediments and are similar to sherds from Stratum II (Iron IIB) at nearby Tel ᶜEin Zippori, suggesting that the western summit may have first been settled in the ninth century B.C.E. or slightly later.[1] However, as with the succeeding Persian-period (539–330 B.C.E.) occupation, attested mainly by numerous ceramic remains, including some imported Attic black-glazed wares typical of the fifth century B.C.E., the possible Iron Age phase cannot be associated with any architectural remains yet uncovered at the summit.

The earliest structures in the residential quarter date from the Hellenistic period (332–63 B.C.E.), for which there is substantial evidence of human habita-tion. The signs of extensive quarrying activities can be seen in several places, and some cisterns and underground storage chambers have been uncovered. The most notable structure from this period is a monumental building situated at the far southeastern end of the area. Still under excavation, the building extends for more than 20 meters along one side, and in some places its walls are more than 2 meters thick. The function of the structure has yet to be deter-mined, but the thickness of its walls suggests a mili-tary citadel or barracks. The surviving walls presumably were the foundations for a superstructure that has since disappeared. Only three identifiable rooms of this building have been recovered. One of them contained the remains of a large *tabun* or bread oven. Another room featured a corbeled opening to a large underground cistern built into one of the walls, apparently a primary source of water for the resi-dents. Among the few remains that can be associated with the last occupation of the building are more than 100 coins from the reign of the Hasmonean ruler Alexander Jannaeus (104–78 B.C.E.). However, because the architectural form does not match any known Hasmonean fortification, it may well have been constructed before the time of Jannaeus.

At the beginning of the Early Roman period (63 B.C.E.–135 C.E.), many bedrock structures were shaped to accommodate a gradual growth in popula-tion and a change in the layout and expansion of the town. Numerous rock-cut *miqva'ot* (ritual baths)

---

fig. 14 **These bronze statuettes of Prometheus and Pan, dating to the second or third century C.E., were found in the residential area on the western summit of the Sepphoris acropolis. See cat. nos. 17, 18.** *Photos: Israel Antiquities Authority*

fig. 15 **Remains of dwellings from the Hellenistic, Roman, and Byzantine periods in the residential area on the western summit.** *Photo: Sepphoris Regional Project*

fig. 16 **One of the many *miqva'ot* (ritual baths) excavated in the western residential area of Sepphoris. These stepped pools were used for ritual bathing, which became a common Jewish practice around the first century C.E.** *Photo: Sepphoris Regional Project*

excavated in the western summit areas and many subterranean cavities may be assigned to this period. The presence of *miqva'ot* at the outset of this period and an increased number of them at the end probably indicates a growing Jewish community mindful of the biblical laws of purity. Steady urban growth in the residential quarter in the first century C.E. resulted, late in the Early Roman period, in the building of the two east-west streets that mark the *insulae* in the area. The construction of a large public building and/or open square and subsequent structures, including several *miqva'ot*, necessitated the filling in and elimination of the earlier Hellenistic structures sometime in the Early Roman period. Because some of these building activities may be dated to the first half of the first century B.C.E., this phase can be called Late Hellenistic-Early Roman transitional—perhaps the period when the domestic area was first systematically planned.

Clear evidence of at least two fairly distinct phases of the Early Roman period can be discerned in the residential quarter. The earlier phase, which overlaps with the transitional period just mentioned, may be dated from about 50 B.C.E. to 70 C.E. and includes, most notably, a fairly complete house (Insula II). Only a few rooms from the Early Roman period remained unaltered. A well-built stairway led down to an equally well-formed entryway through which visitors would have entered a richly decorated

reception or dining room. Fragments of painted frescoes depicting a vegetative decorative scheme were found here. A layer of fine ash, bearing the hallmarks of an intense fire, covered the room's plastered floor. An adjacent room, probably a kitchen or storage area, yielded an extensive collection of household wares. Just to the side of the kitchen was a room with a *miqveh*. The incorporation of *miqva'ot* and corroborating ceramic evidence from this domicile, as well as the absence of pig bones from this period, may reflect concern with issues of purity associated with Second Temple Judaism, possibly evident also in the rock-cut *miqva'ot* elsewhere at the site.

Expanded urban planning doubtless took place closer to the end of the period, circa 100 C.E., when the theater, the *cardo* (the north-south commerical street) in the lower city, and the great water reservoir were constructed.[2] After circa 100 C.E., many of the earlier-occupied structures in the residential quarter were altered slightly or modified. One of the most significant features of this later phase of the Early Roman period is the beautifully paved roadway that runs along the northern edge of the area. Heading east, this roadway led to the summit of the acropolis area until terminating at the point where an artificial level was created as a result of the extensive filling

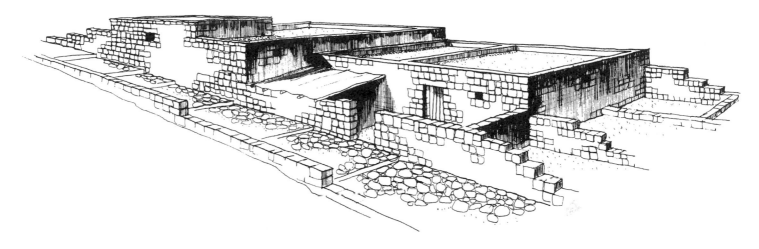

fig. 17 Reconstruction of a large Roman house of the third and fourth centuries c.e. in the residential quarter on the western summit, area 84.1. *Drawing: Lindsey Bute*

over of the monumental structure from the Hellenistic period. Whatever was situated on this level during this phase of occupation has yet to be recovered, and stones from any architectural remains may well have been taken for use during later phases of occupation. The extensive filling operation that was undertaken to create the level surface on the summit points to a major concern with public spaces in both this area and this phase of the city's existence.

The subsequent Middle Roman period (135–250 c.e.) is one of the more elusive periods of occupation in the residential quarter. Several areas, including a sealed-off cistern, have provided an extensive collection of domestic housewares unparalleled in Galilee, yet little associated architecture has been found. That few of the structures in the residential quarter may be dated to this period—undoubtedly a substantial occupational era in the city's history—is a seeming anomaly that is the result both of elaborate rebuilding conducted in the fourth century and of the destruction caused by the earthquake of 363 c.e. This conclusion is based in part on the fact that the Early and Late Roman levels, but not the Middle Roman level, are well preserved. The magnificent building with Dionysos mosaic on the eastern summit, which can be firmly dated to the early third century c.e., is

suggestive of more extensive building activities in this period.[3] Extensive modifications to the smaller domiciles farther to the west, and the adaption of spaces there to new uses, usually are dated to the Late Roman era. Certainly alterations to and modifications of internal spaces were made in the Middle Roman period as well, but such evidence has been difficult to isolate, especially because of the regular reuse of bedrock in the construction of floors and walls in many areas.

Among the finds from the Late Roman period (250–363 c.e.) is a particularly well-preserved domicile situated along the northern edge of the residential quarter (Insula IV). A well-defined entryway led traffic from the adjacent northern roadway into what may have been an enclosed courtyard. Just inside the doorway are two *miqva'ot*, one of which is large enough to be used by a person for bathing; the other is too shallow for this purpose and may have functioned instead as a pool for cleansing vessels being brought into the household or for purifying vessels made out of glass or metal, as per rabbinic law. An open-air courtyard further into the interior of the building may have been used for food preparation, washing, and other household tasks. Three chambers opened out onto this courtyard; the one farthest to the south featured a gracefully executed arch over a large opening to a water cistern. A series of steps led from the floor level of this chamber up over the arch and ended on a level of the main living areas of the owners.

A doorway from the transverse roadway of the residential quarter opened into an entry courtyard surfaced with stone tesserae. Off the courtyard, an entry led to series of rooms, the back rooms situated on wooden flooring extending over the chambers adjacent to the courtyard. The debris recovered in the spaces underneath these rooms suggest that they were the homeowner's private chambers. The architectural form of the building, and the extensive depth of ashy debris uncovered in many rooms, strongly point to the prior existence of a wooden floor extending over many of the surviving spaces. Along the southern edge of the building, a small paved courtyard led to a *miqveh* cut into a bedrock ledge, the remains of earlier quarrying activity.

Ceramic and numismatic evidence suggests that the domicile was occupied by a wealthy family of some status. Although the inhabitants' apparent concern for matters of ritual purity may indicate that they were Jewish (and perhaps pious Jews at that), the domicile also yielded examples of Roman decorative art, namely the fine small bronze statues of Pan and Prometheus (see cat. nos. 17, 18), though both were recovered from an underground dump of an earlier period. The presence of such artifacts may be indicative of the asesthetic tastes rather than any pagan inclinations of the household.

The Late Roman phase of the residential quarter ended decisively with the earthquake of 363 C.E., as evidenced by the extensive tumble of wall stones and other building elements encountered in every Late Roman living space. Coins as well as ceramic materials recovered on the floors of these structures provide a certain date for this destruction. This major earthquake, which left almost no major city of the Near East untouched, must have been devastating for the inhabitants of Sepphoris.

The subsequent Byzantine phases (363–c. 650 C.E.) of the residential quarter are preserved largely along its southern edge. Buildings constructed after the utter destruction of 363 C.E. were erected at a

slightly different (by a few degrees) orientation from the prevailing grid that was used throughout the Roman periods. Several small household industries and shops featuring a variety of trades were apparently established in the area. One of the more notable structures from this period is a series of small stalls built over the remains of an east-west, Roman-period roadway that ran between the northern and southern access roads. Several of the stalls yielded evidence of light metallurgy: for example, an intact iron plow tip that perhaps had been in the shop for repairs. Both the material remains and the faunal evidence suggest a mixed population in the city at this time. An increased percentage of pig bones as well as the presence of fine wares with stamped crosses on them indicate Christian and/or Roman inhabitants (see cat. no. 85).

The evidence from the later Byzantine period seems to reflect a gradual transition into the subsequent Early Arabic period (early seventh to the ninth century C.E.), though there are indications of some disruption by burning, perhaps the result of another documented earthquake in the mid-eighth century. One of the more certain indications of Early Arabic occupation during this time is the appearance of a distinctive white pottery known as Khirbet Mefjar ware, of which several outstanding pieces have been recovered (see cat. no. 89). (Many fine examples have been found in the lower city in the east as well.) From the limited evidence it appears that the residential quarter prospered during the latter centuries of the Byzantine and Early Arabic periods and that its inhabitants endured the major cultural shifts that took place around them with relative ease. However, in comparison with the level of both public and private buildings in the lower city at this time, the western summit did not sustain the quality it had enjoyed in the Roman period. Civic attention focused more on the lower city to the east, and only parts of the acropolis in the west were renovated after the enormous collapse caused by 363–C.E. earthquake.

There are scattered remains from even later periods of the history of the Land of Israel in the residential quarter, but these were badly disturbed as a result of their proximity to the modern living surfaces of the inhabitants of the Arab village of Saffuriyeh. The history of Sepphoris as told from the archaeological perspective of its artifacts ends with the Early Arabic period, though literary sources reveal aspects of the city's history for centuries after this point. For the Crusader period the elegant Church of Saint Anne and the lower part of the present-day citadel provide eloquent testimony.[4]

NOTES

1. For a fuller discussion of the Iron Age and Persian remains, see Carol Meyers's article on Sepphoris and Lower Galilee in this catalogue.

2. More detailed information on these Roman building activities, as well as the aqueducts at Sepphoris, is presented in related articles by Zeev Weiss and Ehud Netzer, Tsvika Tsuk, and James F. Strange in this catalogue.

3. See the discussion of the Dionysos mosaic in this catalogue.

4. The Crusader Church of Saint Anne at Sepphoris is the focus of an article by Jaroslav Folda in this catalogue.

The Aqueducts of Sepphoris

Tsvika Tsuk

Rabbi Judah observed: "It actually happened with the aqueduct, which flowed from Abel to Sepphoris, that water was drawn from it on the Sabbath on the authority of the Elders" (Babylonian Talmud, *Erubin* 87a).

The aqueducts that supplied water to large urban populations were among the most remarkable engineering achievements of the Roman period. As a major urban center in Galilee in Roman and Byzantine times, Sepphoris was served by two aqueducts that carried water to the city from the Nazareth hills.

These aqueducts were first surveyed in modern times in 1872 by the Palestine Exploration Fund, whose researchers discovered in a valley northwest of Mount Yonah the sources of water for one of the aqueducts, the Amitai and Genona springs.[1] Southwest of the village of Mashad they located a section of the aqueduct system, which they were able to trace for approximately two kilometers. They also identified a collapsed tunnel that had carried the aqueduct through a long ridge, a section of raised wall, and the subterranean reservoir near the city.

In 1931 the aqueducts were surveyed by an expedition from the University of Michigan.[2] This team traced the aqueducts for only a half mile east of the city to Mount Yedaya and observed in their report that the remains of the waterworks system was located to the east of Sepphoris. They examined the remains of the subterranean reservoir and also discovered in the vicinity of Sepphoris a pool that was fed by one of the aqueducts.[3]

Azriel Zigelman, while conducting a survey in 1966 for the Israel Department of Antiquities (now the Israel Antiquities Authority),[4] identified another section of the aqueduct south of the village of Mashad. Zigelman also located remains of a second aqueduct near the village of Raineh, which he mistakenly concluded did not lead to Sepphoris.

In the most recent survey, carried out from 1975 to 1990, the water sources, aqueducts, and reservoir of Sepphoris were comprehensively studied by Tsvika Tsuk from Tel Aviv University.[5] Previously unknown sections of the aqueducts were discovered so that it is now possible to determine the course of the aqueducts and to map out their progress from their sources down to the city. This survey examined all components of the aqueduct system of Sepphoris, which had a total length of 13.5 kilometers and included channels hewn from bedrock, shallow aboveground channels constructed of stone and roofed with stone slabs, and a vast subterranean reservoir. Evidence suggests that one of the aqueducts was carried across a wadi (dry stream bed) val-

fig. 18   The subterranean reservoir of Sepphoris after restoration. Hewn from bedrock, the reservoir could store up to 4,300 cubic meters of water. *Photo: Tsvika Tsuk*

ley on an arched stone bridge. Apparently the water system even included a swimming pool close to the city.

The oldest Sepphoris aqueduct began at the Amitai and Genona springs at the north foot of Mount Yedaya near the village of Mashad. It can be dated to the first century C.E. based on several observations. Although the springs that fed this aqueduct do not supply a great deal of water, they are located in the hills at an elevation that provided the necessary slope downward toward the city. (By contrast, the springs that fed the second, later aqueduct are at a considerably lower elevation. However, a sufficient grade downward to Sepphoris allowed for the successful channeling of water.) In two places the Mashad aqueduct was excavated directly into the bedrock, which is now badly eroded. Originally, the walls of the channel were surfaced with a type of gray plaster made of ash mixed with lime. This gray plaster was widely used in Israel from the first century B.C.E. through the first century C.E.[6]

A second aqueduct began at the El-Qanah spring, which today is in the village of Raineh, and collected water from several springs along its route. It was constructed in the second century C.E., when the builders of the water systems recognized that the elevation was sufficient to make an aqueduct from this source feasible. These abundant springs supplied nine times more water to the Sepphoris reservoir than had the springs that supplied the older Mashad aqueduct. The source of the El-Qanah spring is located inside a subterranean structure built of large stones. Although sections of this aqueduct have been located, most of it was obliterated by agricultural development in the twentieth century. Apparently this aqueduct once crossed the stream bed of Nahal Zippori on an arched bridge before becoming a tunnel again on the other side of the valley. In fact, the local name of the valley, Wadi el-Gisser (Valley of the Bridge), reinforces this theory.[7] Closer to Sepphoris the aqueduct joined with the Mashad aqueduct into a single channel. Then east of Mount

fig. 19   **The remains of a Roman-period swimming pool at Sepphoris.** *Photo: Tsvika Tsuk*

Yedaya, some 1.5 kilometers outside the city, the combined aqueducts branched again into two above-ground channels.

One channel, its stone roof slabs still partially preserved, continued for about one kilometer to end in an open pool some 21 meters long and 14.5 meters wide, with a depth of at least 2.2 meters. The proximity of this pool to the city, its size, and the remains of its plastered surfaces suggest that it was a swimming pool for use by residents of Sepphoris in the warmer months of the year when there was abundant water from the springs. It can be dated to the second century C.E. Swimming pools from the Roman period and of comparable size, or even larger, have been identified at Susita, Jericho, and Herodium.[8] The other channel continued to a huge reservoir about a kilometer east of the city. Sections of this channel are well preserved, providing evidence of the building methods used in construction of the aqueduct system.

The subterranean reservoir is the most interesting and impressive installation of the entire water supply system of ancient Sepphoris. In 1993–94 the reservoir was extensively excavated and restored under the auspices of the National Parks Authority of Israel and the Archaeological Institute of Tel Aviv University.[9] In the summer of 1995 the reservoir was opened to the public and became one of the premier attractions at Zippori National Park.

Long, narrow, and sausagelike in shape, the reservoir, on average, is 260 meters long, 10 meters high, and 3 meters wide. Its function was to store

fig. 21 A tortuous tunnel runs some 55 meters from the reservoir to terminate at this wall, into which is fitted a lead pipe 10.5 centimeters in diameter and 5.8 meters long. The pipe, when opened, provided the sole egress for water leaving the reservoir to continue toward the city.
Photo: Tsvika Tsuk

fig. 20 This section of the water conduit west of the reservoir on the way to Sepphoris is one of the best preserved. Constructed above ground, it was roofed with stone slabs.
Photo: Tsvika Tsuk

first layer can be dated to the second century C.E.[11] The second layer, applied over fourth-century-C.E. pottery fragments, may be indicative of repairs after the earthquake that devastated Galilee in 363 C.E.

Four supporting vaults extended across the width of the reservoir between the north and south walls. Of the three originally constructed barrel vaults, two are still intact, as is a fourth vault hewn directly from the rock. In the ceiling of the reservoir were nine openings for different purposes, including primary rock cutting, removal of hewn material, access to the interior, maintenance, and the drawing of water. Of the nine openings, seven had flights of stairs, two of which descended to water level in order to provide access for the purpose of cleaning the reservoir.

The exit for water from the reservoir was discovered below one flight of stairs. From an opening on the floor of the reservoir a tortuous tunnel runs some 55 meters to terminate at a wall into which a lead pipe 10.5 centimeters in diameter and 5.8 meters long was inserted, providing the sole egress for water from the reservoir. Mathematical calculation of the flow rate of water in the pipe has demonstrated that in order to store water in the reservoir, it was necessary to close off the exit port; otherwise all the water entering the reservoir would not accumulate inside the cavity but would immediately run out through the lead pipe.

The pipe led into another section of the tunnel with a plastered channel through which water continued to flow for another 235 meters toward Sepphoris. Six angled shafts, each with a carved stairway, led into the tunnel and originally were used for its construction. The first shaft descended to the end of the lead pipe, near which a metal lug was discovered, solidly fastened into the floor. The lug sug-

water and regulate its flow to the city. The volume of water that could be stored has been calculated at 4,300 cubic meters. The reservoir was hewn from bedrock, a soft, chalky native limestone (*kirton* in Hebrew), whereas the north wall is supported by hard limestone bedrock. The reservoir was constructed at the closest point to the city where *kirton* bedrock of the appropriate height could be found. Water approached the reservoir on the east side through a chute that fed into a sedimentation basin about 2 meters square and some 5 meters deep. A large number of ceramic vessels, which can be dated to the end of the Byzantine period (seventh century C.E.), were found on the floor of the basin, from which water flowed directly into the reservoir.[10]

Along the entire length of the reservoir two distinct layers of plaster are recognizable, with the second layer very well preserved in many places. The

gests that a gate valve or stopcock, which was opened and closed as required for filling the reservoir and supplying the needs of the town, was once here. It probably resembled the bronze stopcock discovered in South Jordan in 1988.[12] Thus a worker would have descended the stairs to the tunnel to turn the stopcock, adjusting the supply of water flowing through the lead pipe and on through the tunnel to the city.

The construction of this shaft tunnel is typical for the Roman rock-digging technique.[13] The shafts were cut at a steep angle that reflects a compromise between ease of descent and the need to raise the hewn material nearly vertically. From the bottom of each shaft the diggers tunneled in two directions in order to meet other workers cutting their way toward them from the adjacent shafts. Four places where the cutters met were clearly evident from the deviations they made in order to correct their cumulative directional error. In addition to these visible marks of their working methods, the laborers who constructed the Sepphoris water systems left behind material traces. Many niches for oil lamps, as well as some clay lamps, were found along the length of the walls.

To the west of the tunnel, the water conduit emerges to the surface, where its channel is constructed on a shallow foundation of natural rock. Here the stone slabs covering the conduit survive in their entirety. From this point, the water conduit continues in the direction of Sepphoris and may be traced for another 400 meters to a distance of some 400 meters from the city, beyond which it is covered with earth and cannot be seen. From here it apparently continued to the residential quarter on the slopes of the Sepphoris hill. Inside the city, near the fifth-century-c.e. building with Nilotic mosaics excavated by the Hebrew University team,[14] many small water channels have been located as has one section of lead pipe, the remains of an elaborate system to supply water to the city.

From the time of their construction in the first and second centuries c.e., the Sepphoris aqueducts continued in use throughout the Byzantine period, having been repaired after the earthquake of 363 c.e. However, in the early period of Muslim rule, beginning in the seventh century, the city declined in importance and size, and water apparently stopped flowing in the aqueducts of Sepphoris.

NOTES

1. C. R. Conder and H. H. Kitchener, *The Survey of Western Palestine*, vol. 1, *Galilee* (London, 1881), 330–34.

2. Leroy Waterman et al., *Preliminary Report of the University of Michigan Excavations at Sepphoris, Palestine, in 1931* (Ann Arbor, 1937), 14–16.

3. As an excuse for stopping their work, the team related the following incident: "A number of cisterns on the Tell were cleaned with the hope of finding some connection between them and the aqueduct. There was a promising one with steps cut leading down to it. After considerable trouble work on it had to be abandoned when a serpent fell into it and the men were too frightened to continue the excavation" (Waterman et al., *Preliminary Report,* 15).

4. Azriel Zigelman, "Identification of the Location of the City of Avel," *Nofim* 5 (1976): 50–53 (in Hebrew).

5. Tsvika Tsuk, "The Aqueducts to Sepphoris" (M.A. thesis, Tel Aviv University, 1985; in Hebrew with an English summary).

6. Yosef Porath, "Lime Plaster in Aqueducts—A New Chronological Indicator," *Mitteilungen* 82 (1984): 1–16.

7. The aqueduct from the Aruv springs to Solomon's pools crosses a tributary of Naḥal Teqo'a via a bridge. This tributary, too, is named Wadi el-Gisser; see Amihai Mazar, "The Ancient Aqueducts to Jerusalem," *Qadmoniot* 5 (1972): 120–24 (in Hebrew).

8. For more on these pools see Zeev Meshel, Henning Fahlbush, Tsvika Tsuk, and Yehuda Peleg, *The Water Supply System of Susita* (Tel Aviv, 1996), 20. Also see Ehud Netzer, "Herodium" and "Jericho," both in *The New Encyclopedia of Archaeological Excavations in the Holy Land,* vol. 2 (Jerusalem, 1993), 622–23 and 684–85.

9. Tsvika Tsuk, Arik Rosenberger, and Martin Peilstocker, *The Ancient Reservoir of Zippori, Excavations 1993–1994* (Tel Aviv, 1996) (in Hebrew).

10. See Tsuk, "The Aqueducts to Sepphoris," 34–36.

11. Porath, "Lime Plaster in Aqueducts," 1–16.

12. J. P. Oleson, "Nabatean and Roman Water Use in Edom: The Humayma Hydraulic Survey, 1987," *Echoes du Monde Classique/Classical Views* 32, no. 7 (1988): 117–29.

13. Klaus Grewe, "Zur Geschichte des Wasserleitungstunnels," *Antike Welt* (1986): 65–76.

14. For a full discussion of this building and its mosaic floors, see Zeev Weiss and Ehud Netzer's articles on the archaeology of Sepphoris in the Byzantine period and on the mosaics of the Nile festival building in this catalogue.

Daily Life in Galilee and Sepphoris

Isaiah Gafni

Our knowledge of daily life in Galilee in the first five centuries of the Common Era derives primarily from literary sources, to which a wealth of archaeological evidence has been added over the past century. Most of these literary sources were not produced with any intention of preserving historical information or depicting the daily life and contexts of the contemporary scene. Nevertheless, the nature of these sources is such that although the "facts" or "events" described in them can rarely be substantiated, the assumed lifestyles to which they relate, their *Sitz-im-Leben*, necessarily reflect the realities of the times. Only then would the stories and parables contained in these works be understandable and immediate in the eyes of their intended audience, and only under such conditions would the legal portions of these works be meaningful to anyone who desired to keep the life-embracing strictures layed down in them. This holds true for early Christian literature produced in the Land of Israel as well as for the complete corpus of rabbinic literature produced in the first six centuries. Because these sources reflect much of the lifestyles of their day, they also provide a general context for examining and understanding the wealth of archaeological material discovered in Galilee and dating from the Roman and Byzantine periods.

fig. 22 This basalt mortar with lug handles was probably used to crush grain into flour for baking bread. See cat. no. 131.
Photo: Kelsey Museum of Archaeology

Demographics

Throughout the Roman and Byzantine periods Galilee was home to a variegated population: Jews, Christians, elements of the Greco-Roman pagan society of the East, as well as the indigenous groups of the Near East who frequently made their way into Galilee either as itinerant travelers or as residents. Nevertheless, we can safely assume that until the fifth century, the Jews represented the predominant portion of the Galilean population. In fact, in the aftermath of the Bar Kokhba uprising (132–35 C.E.), with its devastating consequences for southern portions of Judea, Galilee emerged as the major center of Jewish life in Palestine and remained so throughout late antiquity and into the Middle Ages. Jewish and Christian sources alike project a Jewish majority in Galilee for the talmudic period (3d–5th centuries). The consensus in rabbinic literature, for instance, is that if one found a slaughtered animal "between Tiberias and Sepphoris," the animal may be eaten by a Jew (Babylonian Talmud, *Baba' Mezia'* 24b). A legal determination of this sort assumes a preponderance of Jews and thus of Jewish ritual slaughterers in Galilee. The noted third-century sage Rabbi Yoḥanan similarly declares that "if an [unidentified] person was killed between Tiberias and Sepphoris, we assume that person was Jewish" (Palestinian Talmud, *Sanhedrin* 5:1, 22c). These texts inform the statement of Joseph of Scythopolis, a fourth-century Jewish convert to Christianity, who was granted permission by Emperor Constantine to establish churches "in the cities and villages of the Jews . . . where there is not among them a pagan or a Samaritan or a Christian . . . and they are most particular about this in Tiberias and Diocaesarea [Byzantine Sepphoris] and Nazareth and Capernaum, where no gentile can be found among them" (*Panarion* 30.11.9–10).[1]

The Galilean population in general was divided into two major categories: those who dwelled in the two major cities, Tiberias and Sepphoris, and the majority of the population, which was dispersed among scores of smaller towns and villages that dotted the countryside. This distinction is crucial for any analysis of the cultural influences that shaped the lives and thoughts of Galilean Jews: those who lived in the major cities were in regular contact with the Hellenistic-Roman manifestations of pagan culture and, later, also with Christian practices and beliefs. On the other hand, those Jews who lived in the smaller towns and villages, while not immune to a variety of non-Jewish cultural influences, probably led more isolated lives and may have felt less threatened by the growing non-Jewish presence in Galilee. The important point, in any case, is that the vast majority of Jews in Galilee lived in villages and small towns rather than in the two great cities (*poleis*).

How large were these towns and villages, and what were their distinguishing characteristics? Rabbinic literature supplies us, *en passant*, with some interesting information and provides an excellent example of how aspects of daily life were preserved unintentionally by the formulators of rabbinic law. The Mishnah (Tractate *Taʿanit* 3:4) lists a variety of imminent local catastrophes that might lead Jewish officials to proclaim an extraordinary fast day as a means of arousing repentance and thereby warding off God's apparent wrath. Among these is "pestilence," which is understood as an inordinate number of deaths in a particular city on three successive days. The Mishnah declares: "If in a city that can furnish five hundred foot soldiers three men die on each of three consecutive days—this is a pestilence." "Foot soldiers" in this context would probably be males from the age of approximately seventeen to fifty[2];

working under a common anthropological assumption that this group represents about one-fifth of the general population,[3] we have before us a "city" numbering approximately twenty-five hundred residents. In the Babylonian Talmud text on this mishnah (*Taʿanit* 21a), such a city is considered a "small city," whereas a city that can furnish fifteen hundred soldiers (that is, approximately seventy-five hundred residents) is a "big city." Clearly these numbers for the local populations in Galilee do not reflect the reality in the large *poleis*, such as Tiberias or Sepphoris, but instead supply us with an average population for what today would be defined as a town or village but which was called by the Mishnah a city (*ir*), as distinct from a major metropolis, referred to by the rabbis as *kerakh*.

Archaeological Evidence

The circumference of town walls where such exist (most smaller towns do not seem to have had defensive walls surrounding them) as well as the density of housing in those Galilean villages where sufficient evidence has been uncovered (for example, the town of Chorazin, near Capernaum) tend to support these figures for the average population of local towns and villages.[4] In rabbinic eyes, however, it was not so much the population figures that served as a criterion for distinguishing between a city and a village but rather the religious self-sufficiency of a town. If a Galilean community could support all the requisite religious functions incumbent on Jewish life without having to turn to a nearby city for practical assistance, that community was deemed a city. If, however, the community required outside support (for example, a reader of the *Megillah* [= Book of Esther] on Purim, a circumciser for newborn babies, and so on), it, in effect, was not self-sufficient and thus was deemed a village.

Local Officials and Institutions

An interesting talmudic source lists the functions that ideally should exist in every local community (Babylonian Talmud, *Sanhedrin* 17b). The list includes a local judiciary, an organized framework for charity, a synagogue, a bath, a public convenience, a doctor, a bloodletter, a scribe, and an elementary schoolteacher. This list may be more a *desideratum* than a reflection of reality, yet it certainly suggests the type of offices and institutions that an average Galilean Jew would encounter throughout life. Noteworthy is that alongside religious items are more secular ones: a doctor, a bloodletter, a bath (which in this context does not necessarily mean a ritual bath, or *miqveh*), and even a public convenience. Moreover, rabbinic sources imply that the local community, rather than the individual, was held responsible for maintaining many of these institutions as part of the public domain even though the benefactors would be private citizens. Thus, for instance, local towns were required to pay a salary to the elementary schoolteacher, and a special tax was levied by the community for this purpose.[5] This is striking in light of the fact that throughout most of the Greco-Roman world (with only a few exceptions) elementary education was normally provided only to the children of those parents who would privately hire a tutor. The tax for hiring a teacher in the local Jewish community created some interesting legal problems, such as whether a bachelor was required to contribute to this particular fund. The answer was affirmative, with God—according to the sages—promising to reward said bachelor in time with offspring of his own.

The Greek *polis* is renowned for having cultivated among its residents a deeply felt sense of "belonging" to the city through the framework of "citizenship." Jewish towns also developed a sense of citizenship, and various stipulations spell out when a person was recognized as being "one of the city." Whereas Greek citizenship was primarily a function of pedigree and social class, citizenship in the Jewish town was based on length of residence in a community. The Mishnah stipulates: "How long must he be in the city to be considered one of the city? Twelve months; if he purchased a residence therein, he is one of the city immediately" (*Baba' Batra'* 1:5). Such citizenship bestowed upon the resident an impressive list of both requirements and privileges: After three months of residency a person would contribute to (and—if necessary—receive food from) the free kitchen; after six months one was required to pay

into the local charity fund, after nine months, to contribute to burial expenses; upon completing the twelve-month period of residency, to assume payment of all other city taxes (Tosefta, *Pe'ah* 4:9; Babylonian Talmud, *Baba' Batra'* 8a; Palestinian Talmud, *Baba' Batra'* 1:6, 12d).

Attaining citizenship should be understood as becoming something of a partner in the common property of the city, and this also had some interesting implications. For example, if someone was caught stealing some bit of public property—the Talmud mentions the stealing of a scroll of Torah!—the thief could not be judged before a local tribunal inasmuch as the judges were considered to be part owners of the stolen property; the trial would thus require a change of venue (Babylonian Talmud, *Baba' Batra'* 43a). In sum, while the members of the various religious communities in Galilee probably evinced a certain common bond with their fellow believers, loyalties also were expressed vis-à-vis the local village or city in which one resided, to which one was expected to pay a considerable range of taxes but consequently also could expect to be provided by that town with a wide array of services.

Economic Life

While the vast majority of Galilean residents were probably involved in some sort of agricultural activity, whether as farmers or as merchants of agricultural produce and its derivatives, it would be fair to assume that there were some differences between city dwellers and their village counterparts. As might be expected, a far greater range of income sources was available to those who lived in the larger cities, such as Tiberias and Sepphoris, than to the residents of villages. In Tiberias, for instance, fishing as well as agriculture was a major industry, and this should remind us that fish—rather than meat from domesticated animals—was the Sabbath-meal staple for most Jews in Roman Palestine.[6]

Other industries included weaving, tanning, smelting and refining, pottery, manufacturing of glass and copper utensils, and clothing production. In addition, the texts mention the providers of various services: launderers, barbers, various bathhouse

fig. 23 Three commonware vessels from the pottery manufacturing center of Kefar Shiḥin recovered from the residential quarter at Sepphoris. See cat. nos. 73, 74, 76.
Photo: Mariana Salzburger for the Israel Antiquities Authority

functionaries, and scribes as well as purveyors of a variety of therapeutic services, such as doctors and bloodletters. Some villages also had a local constabulary responsible for the prevention of crime and the apprehension of criminals and also for the implementation of various local bylaws, such as the opening and closing of the marketplace at fixed hours. Some cities—most probably the larger ones—appointed special overseers for the market. The function of these overseers, known in rabbinic sources by their Greek title, *agoranomos*, was to examine weights and measures and in certain cases also to regulate prices and prevent either price fixing or hoarding, as evidenced by the lead market weight uncovered at Sepphoris (see cat. no. 67).

Large cities such as Tiberias and Sepphoris had more than one marketplace (hence the "upper market" and "lower market" in both cities), and in certain cases there were separate markets—or sections in the market—for each type of product or service. Thus we find the "market of basket weavers," the "market of potters," and so on. Certain Galilean villages specialized in particular industries. For exam-

ple, the main center for pottery production was in Kefar Ḥananyah, on the border between Upper and Lower Galilee and situated today on the road from Safed to Acre (Akko).[7] The products of these local industries apparently found their way to the marketplaces of a variety of cities in a manner similar to that of agricultural produce, as we hear that the pottery of Kefar Ḥananyah and Kefar Shihin (Shikhin, near Sepphoris) was sold in the marketplace of Tiberias. The major markets of Galilee at times probably competed with one another in an attempt to attract customers; thus we hear of different prices for certain produce in the different markets: "A man gave his friend eight dinarii to buy wheat for him in Tiberias. [The friend] bought it [instead] from Sepphoris. [The man] told [his friend]: Had you bought [the wheat] in Tiberias, I would have twenty-five modii; now that you bought it in Sepphoris I have only twenty modii" (Palestinian Talmud, *Baba' Qamma'* 9:5, 6d–7a).[8]

The Local Village: Private and Public Domain

Daily life in Galilee can be described along lines that run parallel to the physical division evident in most ancient (and modern) settlements, that is, the division between the private and public domains through which most people passed on a daily basis. Galilean settlements of all sizes contained two physical domains: that of the private individual and family and that of the public sector. The private domain was that portion containing the dwelling places of the local inhabitants. The public portion of the settlement might have two or three major components, depending on the size and self-sufficiency of the community. Three public areas of most Jewish settlements would be the synagogue, the ritual bathhouse (*miqveh*), and some sort of public thoroughfare, possibly also containing a marketplace. Indeed, the synagogue was probably the only major structure in many smaller towns and therefore is frequently the only archaeological remnant of that town.

Although the rabbis had no intention of preserving historical information in their texts, rabbinic sources nevertheless contain considerable information on the private house. The sages were required to

fig. 24 Detail from the third-century C.E. birds and fishes mosaic in the eastern basilical building at Sepphoris. Fish was the Sabbath meal staple for most Jews in Roman Palestine. *Photo: Gabi Laron*

define and describe the attributes of a house for a variety of legal purposes, such as tithing, the building of a *sukkah* (a booth for the Festival of Tabernacles), the establishment of a *mezuzah* at the entrance to and in the rooms of a domicile, and even in connection with certain laws of ritual purity. Furthermore, the laws of Sabbath (in particular those that pertain to carrying effects from the public to the private domain and vice versa) required a definition of what constitutes a person's private domain, and here too the sages can be found describing, *en passant*, the dwelling quarters of the common village of their day.

Archaeologists recently have tried to relate these bits of literary information with the remains of excavated houses. Perhaps the best example to date of such an examination is Yizhar Hirschfeld's *The Palestinian Dwelling in the Roman-Byzantine Period* (Jerusalem, 1995). One of Hirschfeld's main conclusions is that, regional differences notwithstanding, the Roman-Byzantine period marks the end of one stage in the nature of the private dwelling in Palestine and the Arab period marks the ushering in of a new model.

The Roman-Byzantine house comprised a number of rooms, each with a designated function. One room was used for sleeping, and it was set off from the other room(s), which served as the place(s) for receiving guests and eating. A third area—either another room or a courtyard adjacent to the house—served as a repository for food, supplies, and various utensils. In most cases these functional rooms were clearly set apart from the sleeping area, a division sometimes effected by erecting two floors: a lower floor devoted to various household functions—at times even to housing animals—and an upper floor reserved for sleeping. The adjacent courtyard, which commonly was shared by several surrounding houses, was an extension of the functional part of the house; it was the place where daily activities such as cooking and baking, laundering, and so on were carried out. Animals might be allotted a particular part of the courtyard, in which case their fodder would be stored there as well. The courtyard fulfilled yet another function; it served to delineate the boundary between the private domain of the family and the public area of the village. Preserving a sense of privacy was a highly regarded tradition in these villages and frequently was linked with religious notions of modesty.[9]

References in rabbinic literature to the private dwelling constitute yet another example of the acculturation of the sages themselves into the surrounding Hellenistic-Roman environment of Palestine. The very terms that the rabbis used to describe various portions of the house, such as the *kiton* (bedroom), *traklin* (entertaining room), and *exedra* (portico), indicate that the spiritual leaders of the Jewish Galilean community—the very leaders who at times might have frowned on Jews visiting the theater—were nevertheless part of their cultural surroundings and so employed the same Greek terms used by their neighbors. Thus, although Jews, Christians, and pagans all embraced particular religious beliefs and tenets, daily life linked every element of Galilean society and thereby rendered the various lifestyles therein far more similar to one another than the individual groups may have realized.

Treat Talmudic sources critically?

NOTES

1. For an English translation of the entire *Panarion*, see *The Panarion of Epiphanius of Salamis,* trans. Frank Williams, Nag Hammadi Studies, vols. 35 and 36 (Leiden, 1987).

2. This age span is not intended as that for the conscription of soldiers into a standing army but rather the ages of those males who might have been expected to take on some active duty in the face of an impending danger to the local community. The years cited constitute roughly the same age span for males serving in the Israeli army today.

3. In these calculations I have followed, with slight emendations, the figures suggested by Zeev Safrai in his recent work *The Jewish Community in the Talmudic Period* (Jerusalem, 1995), 41 (in Hebrew). On the rabbinic terminology for the classification of settlements into cities, towns, and villages, see Safrai's *The Economy of Roman Palestine* (London and New York, 1994), 17–19; compare *The Jewish Community,* 41–42, for Safrai's population calculations.

4. Much of the fieldwork in determining these figures was done by Zeev Ycivin and presented in his doctoral dissertation, "A Survey of Settlements in Galilee and Golan in the Mishnah and Talmud Period in the Light of the Sources" (Hebrew University, Jerusalem, 1971; in Hebrew). For his work on Chorazin see "Excavations at Khorazin," *Eretz Israel* 11 (1973): 144–57; "Ancient Chorazin Comes Back to Life," *Biblical Archaeology Review* 13 (1987): 23–36; and "Chorazin," in *The New Encyclopedia of Archaeological Excavations in the Holy Land,* vol. 2 (Jerusalem, 1993), 774–79. For questions of population density and the size of Jewish cities, see Yeivin, "On the 'Medium-Sized' City," *Eretz Israel* 19 (1987): 59–71 (in Hebrew).

5. While most sources assume that teachers were hired to teach Torah primarily to young boys, at least a few rabbinic statements suggest, *en passant,* that teachers were hired for girls as well; for example, see Mishnah *Nedarim* 4:2–3. It is important to note, in any case, that every talmudic discussion about the requirement to hire teachers revolves solely around the various levels of a Torah education; matters involving a secular "career" and earning a livelihood were taken up within the family and were not part of any organized school system.

6. The Tannaitic halakha is that normally a poor person is provided with charity sufficient for two daily meals but on Sabbath is given enough for three meals, with the stipulation that this include a small fish (Tosefta, *Pe'ah* 4:8); compare Safrai, *The Economy,* 105ff., for the standard diet in Roman Palestine.

7. See David Adan-Bayewitz, *Common Pottery in Roman Palestine: A Study of Local Trade* (Ramat Gan, 1993).

8. For a description of the regional markets and fairs see Safrai, *The Economy,* 239ff.

9. These basic distinctions between the functions of various parts of the dwelling were blurred considerably in the Arab period; indeed, according to Hirschfeld, the Arab dwelling is noted precisely by its lack of distinction between the areas set aside for sleeping, eating, storage—even the sheltering of animals; compare Hirschfeld, *The Palestinian Dwelling,* 18–19, 293.

Jewish Sepphoris

A Great City of Scholars and Scribes

Stuart S. Miller

Both Jewish and non-Jewish literary sources testify that Sepphoris was by and large regarded as a Jewish city. This is especially true of the writings of the early rabbis (loosely called "talmudic literature"), but Flavius Josephus and even some Christian writers shared this view.[1] Both Josephus and the rabbis were very much aware of the presence of Romans, but in their eyes the city was almost exclusively Jewish. The rabbis in particular provide much insight into their own class as well as occasional glimpses of other Jews who resided at Sepphoris.

The rabbis did not chronicle the day to day history of Sepphoris, or that of any of its inhabitants, but the hundreds of references to the city in talmudic literature make it an invaluable resource for gaining an appreciation of Sepphorean society during their time. To be sure, the information provided is casually conveyed, that is, relayed within a larger discussion of Jewish law or the beliefs and theological perspectives of the rabbis. In addition, it is often difficult to determine the precise dating of an institution or incident reported to have taken place at Sepphoris. Because of these and other critical issues, the use of talmudic literature for historical reconstruction poses quite a challenge, though one worthy of pursuit.[2]

Many of the sages who lived at Sepphoris at one time or another contributed greatly to and, in some instances, helped formulate many of the writings included in talmudic literature. Prominent rabbis lived at Sepphoris from the late first century on. Rabbi Ḥalafta, a leading sage of that era, resided in the city and was the progenitor of a family of sages that played an important role in the city into the third century. His son Rabbi Yose (ben Ḥalafta), a central figure in Jewish life during the mid-second century, is responsible for many observations about life in Sepphoris. Yose's connection to the city is often revealed in sayings attributed to him. For example, he reportedly said, "May it be my lot to be among those who welcome the Sabbath in Tiberias and among those who dismiss the Sabbath at Sepphoris."[3] The saying is intended to emphasize the beauty of the Sabbath. This Yose does by indicating that he would not mind extending the Sabbath, which begins at sunset on Friday and ends Saturday night, by beginning it in the lowlands of Tiberias (where the sun appears to set early) and ending it in the mountainous region of Sepphoris (where the sun appears to set late). Yose also relates various traditions, perhaps preserved within his family and passed on to him by his father, about the period before the destruction of the Temple by the Romans in 70 C.E.[4]

Yose's historical interests were not limited to Sepphoris—he is reputed to have been the author of the rabbinic chronology known as *Seder Olam Rabbah*[5]—but literally hundreds of legal and

fig. 25 A seven-branched *menorah* (lampstand) is depicted in molded relief on the discus of this Late Roman lamp fragment discovered at Sepphoris. See cat. no. 117.
Photo: Israel Antiquities Authority

homiletic views are assigned to him throughout talmudic literature. His considerable contribution to the legal compendium known as the Mishnah is especially noteworthy, as Yose is one of the most-quoted authorities in that work.

By the end of the second century, Sepphoris had already become, much to the credit of Rabbi Yose, a well-established center of rabbinic learning. Indeed, the Babylonian Talmud includes the court of Yose at Sepphoris among those where the pursuit of justice as urged in Deuteronomy 16:20, "Justice, Justice shall you pursue," was promoted.[6] This in turn must have been a primary consideration in the decision of Rabbi Judah Ha-Nasi (the Patriarch) to move from Beth-She'arim to Sepphoris. True, "Rabbi," as this leader was known, was said to have moved to Sepphoris on account of the city's air, which was more conducive to his health than was that of the Beth-She'arim region.[7] Nevertheless, the long-established rabbinic presence in the town and its prominence as an administrative center certainly must have influenced his decision.[8] At any rate, it was at Sepphoris that Rabbi Ishmael ben Yose, son of Yose ben Halafta, became part of the Patriarch's inner circle and served as an important conveyer of his father's traditions.[9] It is indeed probable that he facilitated the inclusion of his father's traditions into the Mishnah of Rabbi Judah, which became the authoritative compilation of Jewish law upon which the two Talmuds, that of Babylonia and that of the Land of Israel (called the Jerusalem or Palestinian Talmud), are based.

Although little is known about Rabbi Judah's activities at Sepphoris, because relatively few talmudic reports can definitively be assigned to his time in the city, it is likely that he completed his work on the Mishnah during his remaining seventeen years there. The patriarchal house (the court of the leading representative of the Jews) was usually responsible for declaring fast days, appointing judges, authorizing the pronouncement of leap years, supervising taxation, and, in general, overseeing all legal concerns of a communal nature,[10] yet very few talmudic passages refer to Rabbi Judah's involvement in these matters at Sepphoris per se. This is not to say that he had

limited influence within the city, only that not much is known about his precise activities there.

The patriarchal house would remain at Sepphoris for some time after Judah's death before it was moved to Tiberias, another city of Lower Galilee.[11] By then, however, the legacy of learning fostered by the Halafta family and by Rabbi Judah had become well entrenched. One of the most outstanding of Judah's disciples, Rabbi Hanina bar Hama (the Babylonian), would, in fact, become the pivotal figure at Sepphoris after the demise of the Patriarch.[12] Hanina's circle would include Rabbi Yohanan and Rabbi Simeon ben Laqish ("Resh Laqish"), two authorities who in the latter half of the third century would be largely responsible for turning Tiberias into a great center of learning. Other disciples of Hanina, referred to simply as "Sepphoreans," interpreted Hanina's decisions and transmitted them to other academies, including that of Tiberias.[13] Among the many opinions and sayings attributed to Rabbi Hanina, one in particular stands out, as it is used to close several treatises of the Babylonian Talmud and is included in prayerbooks of Jews the world over: "Scholars increase well-being [*shalom*] in the world."[14]

Hanina's reputation would ultimately secure him a place in rabbinic history as a larger-than-life figure, as a holy man with wonder-working abilities. When a town was faced with calamity, such as pestilence or drought, it was to scholars such as Hanina that the people turned for help and guidance. So efficacious were Hanina's prayers believed to be that when his efforts failed to bring relief, the people expressed bewilderment—even antagonism.[15] Such tensions should not be seen as characteristic of relations between the sages and their neighbors at Sepphoris. Rabbis of the stature of Hanina could not help but engender criticism from time to time.[16]

Talmudic literature also provides insights into the Jewish community at Sepphoris as a whole. Already in the last century before the destruction of the Temple by the Romans in 70 C.E., residents of Sepphoris, including those belonging to priestly families, had made their way to Jerusalem to worship at the Temple.[17] It is also known that the descendants

fig. 26 This Greek inscription found at Sepphoris, tentatively dated to the fifth century C.E., mentions Judah, the *archisynagōgos* (leader of a synagogue) of Sidon, and Severianus Afrus, the *archisynagōgos* of Tyre.
Courtesy: Biblical Archaeologist

of a priestly course (*mishmar*), one of the designated families of priests that took turns officiating at the Temple, settled at Sepphoris during the third century, when the twenty-three other *mishmarot* had consolidated and made their way to destinations in Galilee.[18] However, although it is tempting to regard the population of Sepphoris as largely composed of members of the upper-class aristocracy, more likely the residents represented the full social spectrum and not only the priests and "great men of Sepphoris" who are occasionally referred to in the sources.[19] Rabbinic sources also speak of bakers, tailors, weavers, fullers, bathhouse owners, butchers, millers, and grist makers, in addition to the farmers who very likely lived in the city and worked in the surrounding fields.[20]

The Jewish residents of Sepphoris had diverse geographic origins as well. By the third century, Cappadocians (from Asia Minor), Babylonians, and émigrés from the Judean town of Gofnah had all made Sepphoris their home. The Babylonians and Gofneans even established their own synagogues in the city. That of the Babylonians was regarded as a local landmark.[21] An inscription found at Sepphoris and dated tentatively to the fifth century mentions Judah, the *archisynagōgos* (leader of a synagogue) of Sidon, and Severianus Afrus, the "illustrious" *archisynagōgos* of Tyre. These figures may have been leaders of a local synagogue established by Jews from their hometowns.[22]

The varied backgrounds and classes represented at Sepphoris, combined with its location at the crossroads of Lower Galilee, may have something to do with the diverse, non-rabbinic, religious ideas that were found there. These were primarily individual expressions, however, and not those of organized groups with distinct ideologies. Thus we hear that *minim*, or "heretics," appeared in the city at one time or another. The sages designated all sorts of individuals as *minim*, including Jews who espoused Gnostic (esoteric knowledge of God) and Christian views, believed in "two powers in heaven," denied the future resurrection of body and soul or the existence of a future world, or who practiced in a manner contrary to rabbinic law. Four passages specifically place *minim* at Sepphoris. One passage tells of a *visiting* Jewish Christian during the early second century; another relates the magical practice of a *min* (singular) of the third century who, like the Jewish Christian, appears on "the road of Sepphoris"; a third may involve a second-century (Jewish?) Gnostic, Epicurean, or, more simply, a "heretic" who denied corporeal resurrection; and the last recounts how a disrespectful *min* once challenged Rabbi Yoḥanan's interpretation of a scriptural verse and, consequently, his authority to teach.[23] None of these *minim* represent larger, well-defined groups of Christians (of any type), Gnostics, magicians, or, for that matter, impudent students, but they do attest to the variety of alternative religious expressions that undoubtedly

fig. 27 A synagogue mosaic from Sepphoris, late 4th-5th century C.E., with Aramaic dedicatory inscription: "Remembered . . . for good, Rabbi Yudan, . . . son of Tanḥum, son of . . . who gave one [dinar?]." See cat. no. 25. *Photo: Custody of the Holy Land*

existed *within* Jewish society in Sepphoris and Galilee.[24]

It must be remembered that even when they recognized the presence of Romans and other gentiles, the rabbis thought of Sepphoris and its environs as primarily Jewish. Rabbi Yose ben Ḥalafta is credited with referring to his hometown as a "great city of sages and of scribes."[25] Certainly it was that. Many, if not most, of the prominent authorities of Galilee and the Land of Israel made their way to Sepphoris to study, teach, or visit. Rabbinic sources especially note the ongoing relationship between the rabbis of

Sepphoris and Tiberias even after the patriarchate and the high court moved from the former city to the latter.[26] Moreover, traditions assigned to Sepphorean sages were incorporated into the Jerusalem and the Babylonian Talmud as well as into midrashic literature (rabbinic writings devoted to explicating Hebrew Scripture).

The Jewish and rabbinic presence would persist at Sepphoris well into the fourth century, when the church writer Epiphanius emphasized the Jewish character of the city.[27] Among the noteworthy sages of this period was Rabbi Huna *Rova* ("the Great") of the late third century, who is credited with composing a prayer that would be included in the Eighteen Benedictions of the Ninth of Ab, on the Jewish calendar the day of mourning for the destruction of both the First and the Second Temples. In the late fourth century, Rabbi Ḥanina *De-Zipporin* ("of Sepphoris"), another highly regarded sage, stepped aside and permitted his eminent colleague Rabbi Mana to assume the leadership of the academy at Sepphoris.[28]

A city with such a rich Jewish past could hardly have escaped the attention of later Jewish writers and pilgrims. The strong association of the patriarchal house with Sepphoris well into the late third century and perhaps later evidently played into the mistaken notion, so prevalent in the medieval Jewish Diaspora, that Rabbi Judah was buried at Sepphoris.[29] Ancient Sepphoris also appears as a great rabbinic center in the classic of Jewish mysticism, *Sefer Ha-Zohar*, which traditionally is ascribed to the second-century sage Rabbi Simeon bar Yoḥai but which, according to scholarly opinion, is actually the work of the thirteenth-century Moses de León of Spain. Especially noteworthy are the Zohar's accounts of scholars who engage in discussions of Torah while traveling from Tiberias to Sepphoris, which clearly are modeled after similar travel accounts preserved in talmudic literature.[30] Rabbis who lived in the medieval and later Diaspora who responded in writing to questions pertaining to community taxation and to sensitive personal matters frequently resorted to the use of "Sepphoris," oftentimes along with "Tiberias," to disguise the intended venue. Of the many important *talmudic* sites in the Land of Israel and in Babylonia, Sepphoris and Tiberias are most frequently referred to by these rabbis—this despite the fact that Babylonian talmudic centers such as Sura and Pumbedita rivaled the ancient centers of the Land of Israel and (at least in the case of Sepphoris) survived long after.[31] These continued recollections of Jewish Sepphoris testify not only to the ongoing importance of the Land of Israel in the psyches of Jews throughout the medieval and later Diaspora but also to the enduring legacy of one of its most important, ancient talmudic centers.

NOTES

1. Josephus's view is self-evident. See my discussion of Hellenistic and Roman Sepphoris in this catalogue. For later, fourth-century Christian views, see *Panarion* 30.11.9–10 (*The Panarion of Epiphanius of Salamis*, trans. Frank Williams, Nag Hammadi Studies, vols. 35 and 36 [Leiden, 1987]) and compare Stuart S. Miller, "The *Minim* of Sepphoris Reconsidered," *Harvard Theological Review* 86, no. 4 (1994): 400, n. 90, and Theodoret, *Ecclesiastical History* 4.22.

2. See Miller, *Studies in the History and Traditions of Sepphoris* (Leiden, 1984), 6–12, for an examination of the relevant issues regarding the reconstruction of urban history.

3. Babylonian Talmud, *Shabbat* 118b.

4. For some of these traditions see Miller, *Studies*, 46–51 and 63–88.

5. Babylonian Talmud, *Yevamot* 82b and *Niddah* 46b.

6. Babylonian Talmud, *Sanhedrin* 32b.

7. Babylonian Talmud, *Ketubot* 103b.

8. Compare Aharon Oppenheimer, *Galilee in the Mishnaic Period* (Jerusalem, 1991), 68f. (in Hebrew).

9. See Jacob Neusner, "An Aristocrat of the Intellect," in his *History and Torah: Essays on Jewish Learning* (New York, 1965), 103–21.

10. See Lee Levine, "The Jewish Patriarch (Nasi) in Third Century Palestine," *Aufsteig und Niedergang der römischen Welt*, II, 19.2 (1979), 663–80.

11. The exact date of the transfer to Tiberias is not clear, although a third-century date seems likely. See Y. Cohen, "Did the Patriarchate Move to Tiberias and [if so] When?" *Zion* 39 (1974): 114–22. Sepphoris nonetheless continued to be associated with members of the patriarchal house.

12. See Miller, "R. Ḥanina bar Ḥama at Sepphoris," in *The Galilee in Late Antiquity*, ed. Lee I. Levine (New York and Jerusalem, 1992), 175–200.

13. See Miller, "R. Ḥanina bar Ḥama," 177–99; compare Miller, "*Zippora'ei, Tibera'ei* and *Deroma'ei*: Their Origins, Interests and Relationship," in *Proceedings of the Tenth World Congress of Jewish Studies*, Division B, vol. 2 (Jerusalem, 1990), 15–22.

14. Babylonian Talmud, *Yevamot* 122b and *Nazir* 66b; and ed. Vilna of Babylonian Talmud, *Keritot* 28b.

15. Jerusalem Talmud, *Ta'anit* 3, 66c.

16. Miller, "R. Ḥanina bar Ḥama," 192–200.

17. See Miller, *Studies*, 46–51 and 63–88.

18. For a full discussion of priests at Sepphoris, see Miller, *Studies*, 62–102. Also see Daliah Trifon, "Did the Priestly Courses Move from Judea to Galilee after the Bar Kokhba Revolt?" *Tarbiz* 59 (1990): 77–93 (in Hebrew).

19. Moreover, not all priests should be thought of as wealthy. On the "great men of Sepphoris" see Adolph Büchler, *The Political and Social Leaders of the Jewish Community of Sepphoris in the Second and Third Centuries* (London, 1909), 7–17; on both of these matters see Miller, "Those Cantankerous Sepphoreans Revisited," in the festschrift for Baruch A. Levine, to be published by Eisenbrauns.

20. On bakers see Jerusalem Talmud, *Sanhedrin* 3, 21b; tailors, *Ecclesiastes Rabbah* 6:12; weavers, Jerusalem Talmud, *Baba' Batra'* 2, 13b; fullers, Jerusalem Talmud, *Kil'ayim* 9, 32b; bathhouse owners, Mishnah, *Baba' Mezia'* 8:8; Babylonian Talmud, *Baba' Mezia'* 102b; butchers, Jerusalem Talmud, *Sheqalim* 7, 50c; *Leviticus Rabbah* 5:6; Tosefta, *Ḥullin* 3:2; Babylonian Talmud, *Ḥullin* 50b; millers, *Pesiqta' Rabbati* 23; grist makers, Jerusalem Talmud, *Mo'ed Qatan* 2, 81b and *Pesaḥim* 4, 30d; Babylonian Talmud, *Baba' Qamma'* 99b; farmers, Tosefta, *Makhshirin* 3:5; Jerusalem Talmud, *Shevi'it* 6, 37a and 7, 37b; for the agricultural interests of the residents of Sepphoris see Miller (tentative title), "Ancient Sepphoris and Historical Memory" (in preparation). Daily life in Sepphoris and Galilee is also the focus of the article by Isaiah Gafni in this catalogue.

21. On the Cappadocians see Jerusalem Talmud, *Shevi'it* 9, 39a; Babylonians, *Genesis Rabbah* 33:3 and 52:3; Jerusalem Talmud, *Berakhot* 5, 9a, *Shabbat* 6, 8a, *Sanhedrin* 10, 28a; Gofneans, Jerusalem Talmud, *Berakhot* 3, 6a, and compare Miller, *Studies*, 119f.

22. See Lea Roth–Gerson, *The Greek Inscriptions from the Synagogues in Eretz Israel* (Jerusalem, 1987), 107f. (in Hebrew). There is also an Aramaic inscription, apparently from the same synagogue, that refers to one R. Yudan bar Tanḥum; see Miller, *Studies*, 6 and cat. no. 25 in this publication.

23. See Tosefta, *Hullin* 2:24; *Genesis Rabbah* 14:7; Jerusalem Talmud, *Sanhedrin* 7, 25d; and *Pesiqta' de-Rav Kahana*, 18.

24. See Miller, "The *Minim* of Sepphoris Reconsidered," 377–402, and "Further Thoughts on the *Minim* of Sepphoris," *Proceedings of the Eleventh World Congress of Jewish Studies*, Division B, vol. 1 (Jerusalem, 1994), 1–8.

25. *Mekhilta' de Rabbi Shimeon ben Yohai*, ed. Hoffman, p. 98.

26. See Miller, "Intercity Relations in Roman Palestine: The Case of Sepphoris and Tiberias," *Association for Jewish Studies Review* 12 (1987): 1–24.

27. See n. 1.

28. Jerusalem Talmud, *Pesahim* 6, 33a.

29. Talmudic accounts of funerals at Sepphoris for members of the patriarchal house who postdated Judah may have influenced this association. See Miller, *Studies*, 116–20.

30. *Sefer Ha-Zohar* II, *Shemot* 13a; *Pequdei* 225a; compare *Ki Tissa'* 187b. Also see Miller, "Sepphoris and the Diaspora: The Lasting Influence of a Galilean Talmudic Center," to be published in Hebrew and English by the Zalman Shazar Center.

31. See Eliezer Bashan, "The Names of Cities of the Land of Israel as Designations for Cities of the Diaspora in the Responsa Literature of the Ottoman Period," *Bar Ilan Annual* 12 (1974), 137–65 (in Hebrew), and Miller, "Sepphoris and the Diaspora."

Christianity in Sepphoris and in Galilee

Sean Freyne

[handwritten: – Maximalist reading of Talmud ± Epiphanius!]

The renewal movement initiated by Jesus of Nazareth was rapidly transformed after his death by the transition from its rural base in Galilee to urban centers throughout the Mediterranean region. To the extent that in the first century Galilee was beginning to experience the effects of urbanization emanating from Sepphoris and its rival city, Tiberias, as well as from the older cities on its perimeter, one might have expected that Christianity would have found a ready acceptance there also. Yet unambiguous evidence is lacking for the immediate post-Resurrection period, despite the portrayals in the Gospels of the enthusiastic reception of Jesus by the Galilean crowds. In the Acts of the Apostles, Luke depicts the progress of the Christian mission northward from Jerusalem to Antioch, concentrating largely on the cities of the coastal plain, mentioning Galilee only in passing (Acts 9:31). This suggests that he had no real evidence on which to rely, in sharp contrast to his detailed treatment of the missionary activity of Philip and the apostles in Samaria (Acts 8:4–25).

A growing body of scholarly opinion ascribes the earliest gospel, a putative collection of sayings of Jesus called Q (from the German *Quelle* for souce),

which may have undergone more than one edition before being utilized subsequently by both Matthew and Luke in their gospels, to a Galilean context.[1] *[handwritten: "Q" in Galilee]* Even if this were the case, however, the rejection experienced by the prophets of the Q Gospel at various Galilean centers as reflected in the source itself (QMatt. 10:19–20, 11:21–24; QLuke 10:13–15, 12:11–12) suggests that these missionaries were not likely to have subsequently formed the nucleus of a permanently settled community of Christians, at least not in Galilee. Mark's gospel also has been ascribed to a *[handwritten: Mk]* Galilean setting,[2] particularly in view of the instruction by Jesus to the disciples to return to Galilee after the crucifixion (Mark 14:28, 16:7), but in the absence of definite criteria such claims are at best inconclusive.[3] Nothing in either Matthew's or Luke's gospel *[handwritten: not Mt or Lk]* suggests that either was directed to Galilean Christian communities.[4] John's gospel has a Jerusalem rather than a Galilean focus for the ministry of Jesus, though his special association with Cana in Galilee (John 2:1–11, 4:46, 21:2) rather than with Capernaum, as in the earlier gospels, could possibly be interpreted as reflecting a community of Christians there at an early stage.[5]

If the Gospels are at best inconclusive with *[handwritten: the minim]* regard to Galilean Christianity, the evidence from rabbinic sources raises different interpretative problems. That there were some followers of Jesus among the *minim*, or heretics, mentioned in various texts seems certain, especially in light of the traditions

---

fig. 28 **Fragment of a redware vessel with a stamped cross from the late fourth or early fifth century C.E. See cat. no. 85. The earliest archaeological evidence suggesting the presence of Christians at Sepphoris is pottery decorated with crosses.** *Photo: Israel Antiquities Authority*

concerning Jacob of Kefar Sekhanyah (Siknin), who is described as a disciple (*thalmid*) of "Yeshua ben Pantera" (or Yeshua *ha-Nozri*, "the Nazorean," in the parallel account). Clearly this is a reference to Jesus of Nazareth, as we know from other sources of a contemporary report claiming that Jesus was the child of an illicit union between his mother and a Roman soldier named Pantera (Origen, *Contra Celsum* 1.32).[6] Jacob is known as a healer in Yeshua's name (Tosefta, *Ḥullin* 2:22f.; Palestinian Talmud, *Shabbat* 1, 14b; Babylonian Talmud, *Abodah Zarah* 27b) and, by rabbinic standards, as a teacher of unorthodox views (Tosefta, *Ḥullin* 2:24; Babylonian Talmud, *Abodah Zarah* 16b–17a). In the first instance his healing powers are rejected by the authorities; in the second, the influential Rabbi Eliezer (teacher of Rabbi Akiba) was reported to the governor for having agreed with Jacob on a point of religious law when they encountered each other in the upper market at Sepphoris. Dates of rabbinic stories are notoriously difficult to pinpoint, even when they refer to named sages, but the stories themselves indicate that at the time of the final editing of the various writings (third to fifth century C.E.), Jewish followers of Jesus were operating within the orbit of the rabbinic schools of Lower Galilee and that they were less than popular with the Jewish authorities there. Part of the reason may have been fear of the Romans, but primarily it was because of theological differences on various issues, including the messianic status of Jesus. Despite the fact that direct reference to Christians, even under such designations as *minim* ("heretics") or *nozrim* ("Nazarenes"), are infrequent in the rabbinic sources, literary evidence does suggest a larger and more influential presence of Jewish Christians in Galilee and Sepphoris than might be assumed. Such discussions as those concerning "the curse on the heretics" (whether this deals with Jewish Christians only or has a wider reference) and expelling them from participation in the synagogue worship,[7] as well as various doctrinal debates among the rabbis, offer glimpses of the issues that were at stake for Jews and Christians even after the so-called parting of the ways of the two faiths in the second century.[8]

Among early Christian writers on heresy, Epiphanius (315–403 C.E.), the Palestinian-born bishop of Salamis, appears to have had relevant, firsthand information about a group of Jewish Christians called Nazarenes, even if his rigid orthodoxy colors his account.[9] Along with other writers (Jerome, for example), he locates these Nazarenes in Beroea, Pella, and Cocabe in Transjordan (modern Golan and Hauran), yet definite similarities with the Galilean *minim/nozrim* from Sepphoris and Kefar Sekhanyah are apparent: an orthodox belief in Jesus born of the Virgin combined with a strict observance of the Jewish law, including circumcision, giving rise to hatred from the Jewish authorities (*Panarion* 29.6,7).[10] Recent analysis of pottery finds at various sites in the Golan indicates the presence of considerable amounts of Galilean ware.[11] These finds presuppose some trading links between the two regions, thereby facilitating contacts between adherents of similar groups. A migration of Nazarenes from Galilee is not, therefore, improbable in the wake of their isolation from both fellow Jews and gentile Christians in the fourth century.[12] Jerome, while acknowledging their orthodox views on the nature and person of Christ, remarked in an epistle that "though they wish to be both Jews and Christians, they are neither Jews nor Christians" (Ep. 112, 13; see *Corpus Scriptorum Ecclesiasticorum Latinorum* 55, 382).

The literary evidence leaves many unanswered questions about Christians in Galilee: the origins and subsequent history of the *nozrim* in Sepphoris; their possible relations with the followers of James, the brother of Jesus, who, according to early church historian Eusebius (*Ecclesiastical History* 3.5.4), fled Jerusalem in 62 C.E. after James's violent death and settled in Pella (one of the sites in Transjordan associated with the Nazarenes, according to Epiphanius); the influence, if any, of gentile Christianity before the conversion of Roman emperor Constantine in 312 C.E.; and the fate of the Q missionaries in the turbulent years leading up to the First Jewish Revolt, if in fact they continued to operate in Galilee until 66 C.E. Archaeological investigation of Christian remains can throw light on some of these questions, particularly in view of more recent advances in relating data from stratified digs at particular sites to the wider,

fig. 29
Ostracon with Maria (?) Graffito

Sepphoris; Joint Sepphoris
Project
Early Byzantine, c. 4th–6th
centuries c.e.
Ceramic
Excavation #84.4061.5X
Photo: Israel Antiquities
Authority

Found in an underground installation in a residential area of Sepphoris, this scratched inscription on a blackware pottery fragment (maximum width 6 cm.), apparently made by an unskilled writer, is both messy and poorly spelled. So the decipherment is uncertain, but, tantalizingly, one plausible reading is "Hail Mary" in Greek (uppercase letters): XAIPE MAPIA. This phrase is based on the account, in the Gospel of Luke (1:26–28), of the angel Gabriel announcing the future birth of Jesus. Mary is spelled both as MAPIA and MAPIAM in the Greek New Testament. Here the lower word reads MAAΠHA, which in any case is a misspelling, but phonetically (as m_r_a ?) it resembles the name. The upper word is even less clear, but it appears to begin with X (chi). A somewhat similar graffito, scratched in plaster and reading XE MAPIA (the first word an abbreviation), has been found in Nazareth (Bagatti, 1967: 150–52). Legends of the childhood of Mary place her not only in Sepphoris but also in Nazareth (according to John of Würzburg, writing in 1165, in Crusader times) and in Jerusalem (according to the second-century text the Proto-gospel of James). Although the historicity of some of these stories may be doubtful, they indicate that by the Byzantine period, and probably earlier, devotion to Mary was clearly a part of the life of many Christians.—S G

REFERENCE

Bagatti, Bellarmino. Gli Scavi di Nazaret. Studium Biblicum

regional surveys, thereby enabling more general conclusions to be drawn on the social and cultural environment.[13]

It is only with the beginning of the Byzantine era (from the middle of the fourth century C.E.) that clear evidence of a distinctive Christian architecture and iconography begins to emerge. The Jewish population of Galilee had increased considerably in the wake of the Bar Kokhba-led war against Rome (132–35 C.E.), and on the basis of the number of settlements where synagogue remains have been recovered, this trend continued in subsequent centuries. These settlements appear to follow a clear pattern of concentration in eastern Upper Galilee and western Golan.[14] Once this Christian presence begins to be discernible in the material culture, very few, if any traces of it are to be found in the Jewish areas, whereas in western Galilee (both Upper and Lower), bordering the territories of the cities of Tyre and Akko (Greek: Ptolemaïs), a considerable number of remains of Christian churches and burial places have come to light.[15] A similar pattern can be discerned to the north and east of the Jewish territories where remains of Christian churches have been uncovered in the Hermon region and in eastern Golan.[16] On the basis of this evidence it would seem that Christianity entered Galilee by way of the territories of the surrounding cities and that it made little if any inroads in the traditional Jewish regions. The beginnings of such a development may have occurred by the second and third centuries, though there is no datable architectural evidence to prove this. Only very gradually does evidence of a Jewish presence in the Christian areas of western Galilee emerge, in the sixth and seventh centuries.[17]

Most scholarly attention has been devoted to those areas of Galilee where evidence of both a Jewish and a Christian presence has been uncovered. Epiphanius relates that a Jewish convert to Christianity, Joseph of Scythopolis (Beth-Shean), was deputed by the Emperor Constantine (ruled from 306 to 337 C.E.) to build "churches of Christ in the cities and villages of the Jews where no one had ever been able to put churches, since there were no pagans, Samaritans, or Christians in them.

Especially in Tiberias, Diocaesarea, also called Sepphoris, Nazareth, and Capernaum they take care to have no foreigners living among them" (*Panarion* 30.11.9–10). While his statement clearly is not accurate for Sepphoris and Tiberias, given their mixed populations from at least the first century, this account nevertheless supports the suggestion of separate Jewish and non-Jewish areas, and it confirms that the building of churches in the wake of the Constantinian takeover also occurred in Galilee.

This process of establishing a visible Christian presence raises the issue of the relationship between the fourth-century developments and the earlier traces of a Jewish Christianity in rabbinic and other literary sources. According to Epiphanius, Count Joseph attempted to transform a temple to Hadrian (emperor from 117 to 138 C.E.) in Tiberias into a Christian church but encountered difficulties with the project. The architectural remains of fifth-century churches at both Nazareth and Capernaum have been interpreted as evidence of a similar pattern of transformation of previously existing structures, though in these cases, belonging to Jewish Christians. At Nazareth, the remains of a small, pre-Constantinian church "on the plan of a synagogue," with a baptismal font as well as mosaics and graffiti attributed to Jewish Christians, were found under the mosaics of the later Byzantine church.[18] Earlier than that, pottery and plaster remains from three caves that had been in ordinary domestic use from the early Iron Age suggest that the caves were transformed into sacred grottos with Christian inscriptions and drawings.[19] The Byzantine church, the remains of which were uncovered in the excavations in preparation for the building of the present basilica, is attested also by the anonymous Christian pilgrim from Piacenza (c. 570 C.E.), who states that the house of Mary is a basilica. A similar three-stage process has been suggested for Capernaum: a house church (again with Jewish-Christian graffiti) from the first century C.E.; over that an extended *insula sacra,* or sacred precinct, surrounded by a wall in the fourth century (also mentioned by Egeria as the house of Peter); and over that an octagonal-shaped basilica built in the fifth century.[20]

70

Thus far, it has not yet been possible to trace fully a similar trajectory for Christians at Sepphoris. A dedicatory inscription, probably from the Byzantine period, which frequently had been taken as a *chi-rho* sign with reference to the Jewish Christians in the city,[21] has now been interpreted as an abbreviation rather than as a Christian symbol.[22] Likewise, an inscription discovered in 1959, which initially was thought to refer to the restoration of a church in the time of Marcellinus (518 C.E.),[23] is now considered to be associated with a municipal building.[24] Also discovered, however, are the remains of a Byzantine church that archaeologists have attributed to Bishop Eutropius (late fifth or early sixth century C.E.) because of its proximity to the main streets, which were renovated in the bishop's time; in addition, he is honored by the city in a nearby Greek inscription that describes him as "our most saintly father, Eutropius, the Episcopus."[25] That this Christian bishop is associated with the renovation of the city as well as the building of a Christian basilica is consonant with the generally increasing civic importance of the Greek-speaking Christian church in the Byzantine period. In view of the literary evidence about the Jewish Christians at Sepphoris, it would come as no surprise if further archaeological evidence should come to light, either at this location or elsewhere at the site, that confirms the pattern of transition from a Jewish-to a gentile-Christian church, as exhibited at Nazareth and Capernaum, even though Sepphoris, unlike those two cities, lacks a clear association with the earthly life of Jesus. The tradition linking the city with Anna and Joachim, the parents of the Virgin Mary, is preserved in the Crusader Church of Saint Anne, but the legend itself, first recorded circa 570 C.E. by the pilgrim of Piacenza, was often repeated by subsequent pilgrims.[26]

The process of transition from a Jewish-Christian to a gentile-Christian church in Palestine can be seen as a gradual and peaceful transformation analogous with what, according to Eusebius (*Ecclesiastical History* 4.5.1–3), occurred at Jerusalem.[27] Alternatively, taking a cue from the Christian writers who treated all Jewish Christians—even the Nazarenes with their orthodox views about Christ—

as heretics, the development may also be understood as a new beginning after Constantine, one that signaled large-scale demographic changes as well.[28] Unlike at Jerusalem, where the transition is clear (Eusebius lists every pre-Constantinian Jewish-Christian bishop there), no Galilean bishop is mentioned in the list of those who attended the first church council, held at Nicea in 323 C.E.; the first such references are to the bishop of Tiberias, at the Council of Ephesus in 449 C.E., and the bishop of Diocaesarea (Sepphoris), at the Council of Jerusalem in 519 C.E. Furthermore, in view of the widening gulf between mainline Christians and Jews in Palestine, especially after the abortive Jewish revolt against Rome under Gallus (351–52 C.E.), it is difficult to imagine how Jewish Christians could possibly have been accommodated among an increasingly gentile population in Lower Galilee.[29] The likelihood is that they, like their more orthodox Jewish counterparts, migrated from Lower Galilee to a more congenial environment, possibly to eastern Golan.[30]

Neither the Christian nor the Jewish presence in Palestine ended with the Muslim conquest of 634–40 C.E., as both churches and synagogues continued to be built throughout the seventh and into the eight century C.E.[31] Many Christian churches had already been destroyed during the Persian invasion earlier in the seventh century.[32] The evidence from coins and pottery suggests a gradual turning toward the East, in terms of economic links, and the consequent cutting of ties with the West for Palestinian Jews and Christians alike. Pilgrimages to the holy places, including those in Galilee, continued until Jerusalem was captured by the Seljuk Turks in 1071 C.E., an event that gave rise to the Christian Crusades. But that is a very different story.

71

NOTES

1. John Kloppenborg, "Literary Convention, Self-Evidence and the Social History of the Q People," in *Early Christianity, Q and Jesus*, ed. John Kloppenborg and Leif Vaage, Semeia, 55 (Atlanta, 1991), 81–88; Burton Mack, *The Lost Gospel: The Book of Q and Christian Origins* (New York and San Francisco, 1993), 51–68; and Jonathan Reed, "Places in Early Christianity: Galilee, Archaeology, Urbanization, and Q" (Ph.D. diss., Claremont Graduate School, 1994), 125–45.

2. Ernst Lohmeyer, *Galiläa und Jerusalem*, Forschungen zur Religion und Literatur des Alten und Neuen Testaments, 34 (Göttingen, 1936), 37, and Willi Marxsen, *Der Evangelist Markus: Studien zur Redaktionsgeschichte des Evangeliums*, Forschungen zur Religion und Literatur des Alten und Neuen Testaments, 67 (Göttingen, 1955), 66–77.

3. Elizabeth Struthers-Malbon, "Galilee and Jerusalem: History and Literature in Markan Interpretation," *Catholic Biblical Quarterly* 44 (1982): 242–55.

4. Sean Freyne, *Galilee from Alexander the Great to Hadrian: A Study in Second Temple Judaism* (Wilmington, Del., 1980), 360–72.

5. Wayne Meeks, "Galilee and Jerusalem in the Fourth Gospel," *Journal of Biblical Literature* 85 (1966): 159–69, and Jouette M. Bassler, "The Galileans: A Neglected Factor in Johannine Community Research," *Catholic Biblical Quarterly* 43 (1981): 243–57.

6. See Henry Chadwick, trans., *Origin: Contra Celsum* (Cambridge, England, 1953).

7. Reuben Kimelman, "*Birkat Ha-Minim* and the Lack of Evidence for a Christian Jewish Prayer in Late Antiquity," in *Jewish and Christian Self-Definition*, vol. 2, ed. E. P. Sanders, A. I. Baumgarten, and Alan Mendelson (London, 1981), 226–44, and William Horbury, "The Benediction of the *Minim* and Early Jewish-Christian Controversy," *Journal of Theological Studies* 33 (1982): 19–61.

8. Marcel Simon, *Verus Israel: A Study of Relations between Christians and Jews in the Roman Empire* (Oxford, 1986), 183–96.

9. Ray A. Pritz, *Nazarene Jewish Christianity* (Leiden, 1988), 29–47.

10. Translations of Epiphanius follow Philip R. Amidon, trans., *The Panarion of St. Epiphanius, Bishop of Salamis, Selected Passages* (New York and Oxford, 1990).

11. David Adan-Bayewitz, *Common Pottery in Roman Galilee: A Study in Local Trade* (Ramat Gan, 1993), 166–71, 211–19.

12. Claudine Dauphin, "Farj en Gaulanitide: Refuge judéo-chrétien?" *Proche Orient Chrétien* 34 (1984): 233–45.

13. Eric Meyers, "Early Judaism and Christianity in the Light of Archaeology," *Biblical Archaeologist* 51 (1988): 69–79, and "The Challenge of Hellenism for Early Judaism and Christianity," *Biblical Archaeologist* 55 (1992): 84–91.

14. Eric Meyers, James Strange, and Dennis Groh, "The Meiron Excavation Project: Archaeological Survey in Galilee and Golan," *Bulletin of the American Schools of Oriental Research* 230 (1978): 20; Dan Urman, *The Golan: A Profile of a Region in the Roman and Byzantine Periods*, British Archaeology Reports International Series, 269 (Oxford, 1985), 75–140; Zvi Ilan, "Galilee, Survey of Synagogues," *Excavations and Surveys of Israel* 5 (1986–87): 35–37; and Yoram Tsafrir, Leah di Segni, and Judith Green, *Tabula Imperii Romani. Iudaea-Palestina. Maps and Gazetteer* (Jerusalem, 1994), maps of churches and synagogues.

15. Mordechai Aviam, "Galilee: The Hellenistic and Byzantine Periods," in *The New Encyclopedia of Archaeological Excavations in the Holy Land*, vol. 2 (Jerusalem, 1993), 455–58, and Claudine Dauphin, *La Palestine Byzantine du IVe au VII Siècle ap. J.-C.*, vol. 3, *Peuplement* (Paris, 1994), figs. 43, 57, 74.

16. Zvi Maᶜoz, "Comments on Jewish and Christian Communities in Byzantine Palestine," *Palestine Exploration Quarterly* 117 (1985): 65f.

17. Dauphin, *La Palestine Byzantine*, figs. 91 and 93.

18. Bellarmino Bagatti and Vassilios Tzaferis, "Nazareth," in *The New Encyclopedia of Archaeological Excavations in the Holy Land,* vol. 3 (Jerusalem, 1993), 1103–5, and Virgilio Corbo, "La chiesa-sinagoga dell' Annunziata a Nazaret," *Liber Annuus* 37 (1987): 333–48.

19. Bellarmino Bagatti, *Excavations in Nazareth,* vol. 1, *From the Beginning Until the Twelfth Century,* trans. E. Hoade (Jerusalem, 1969), 174–218,

20. Virgilio Corbo, *Cafarnao. I: Gli edifici della citta* (Jerusalem, 1975), 26–58, and "The Church of the House of St. Peter at Capernaum," in *Ancient Churches Revealed,* ed. Yoram Tsafrir (Jerusalem and Washington, 1993), 71–76, for summary.

21. Meyers, "Early Judaism and Christianity in the Light of Archaeology," 71.

22. Lea Roth-Gerson, *The Greek Inscriptions from the Synagogues in Eretz Israel* (Jerusalem, 1987), 106 (in Hebrew).

23. Michael Avi-Yonah, "A Sixth-Century Inscription from Sepphoris," *Israel Exploration Journal* 11 (1961): 184–87, and Zeev Weiss, "Sepphoris," in *The New Encyclopedia of Archaeological Excavations in the Holy Land,* vol. 4 (Jerusalem, 1993), 1327.

24. Ehud Netzer and Zeev Weiss, "New Evidence for Late-Roman and Byzantine Sepphoris," in *The Roman and Byzantine Near East: Some Recent Archaeological Research,* ed. John H. Humphrey, Journal of Roman Archaeology, Supplementary Series, 14 (Ann Arbor, 1995), 170.

25. Netzer and Weiss, "New Evidence for Late-Roman and Byzantine Sepphoris," 171–73; also see their article on Sepphoris during the Byzantine period in this catalogue.

26. See Jaroslav Folda's article on the Church of Saint Anne in this catalogue and Stuart S. Miller, "Sepphoris: The Well Remembered City," *Biblical Archaeologist* 55 (1992): 80f.

27. Meyers, "Early Judaism and Christianity in the Light of Archaeology," 71, and Dauphin, "De l'Église de la Circoncision à l'Église de la Gentilité. Sur une nouvelle voie hors de l'impasse," *Liber Annuus* 43 (1993): 240–42.

28. Robert L. Wilken, *The Land Called Holy: Palestine in Christian History and Thought* (New Haven, 1992), 85, and Joan Taylor, *Christians and the Holy Places: The Myth of Jewish-Christian Origins* (Oxford, 1993), 18–42.

29. Barbara Geller Nathanson, "Jews, Christians, and the Gallus Revolt in Fourth-Century Palestine," *Biblical Archaeologist* 49 (1986): 34.

30. Claudine Dauphin, "Jewish and Christian Communities in the Roman and Byzantine Gaulanitis: A Study of Evidence from Archaeological Surveys," *Palestine Exploration Quarterly* 114 (1982): 137, and "Encore des judéo-chrétiens au Golan?" in *Early Christianity in Context: Monuments and Documents,* ed. F. Manns and E. Alliata (Jersualem, 1993): 69–84.

31. Dennis Groh, "The Religion of the Empire: Christianity from Constantine to the Arab Conquest," in *Christianity and Rabbinic Judaism,* ed. Hershel Shanks (Washington, 1992), 302f.

32. Claudine Dauphin and Gershon Edelstein, "The Byzantine Church at Nahariya," in *Ancient Churches Revealed,* ed. Yoram Tsafrir (Jerusalem and Washington, 1993), 53, and Mordechai Aviam, "Horvat Hesheq: A Church in the Upper Galilee," in *Ancient Churches Revealed,* 65.

Jesus' Relation to Sepphoris

E. P. Sanders

Because Sepphoris is only about four miles from Nazareth, where Jesus grew up, there is a strong presumption that he was acquainted with the city. According to the Gospels, both Jesus and his father were artisans (Mark 6:3; Matt. 13:55).[1] In 1926, Shirley Jackson Case combined these two points and proposed that both Jesus and his father worked in Sepphoris during Herod Antipas's rebuilding of the city.[2] More recently Richard Batey renewed this proposal and developed it in several publications.[3]

Sepphoris is not mentioned in the New Testament, which contains the only direct information about Jesus. As a consequence, arguments about Jesus' relation to the city are actually speculations based partly on Nazareth's proximity to Sepphoris and partly on the assumption that ancient villages were like modern suburbs and that villagers commuted to work in cities. Both of these premises are general and vague, and the second is also intrinsically unlikely. Thus, although it is not impossible that Jesus commuted to work in Sepphoris, there is no reason to think that he did so. The discussion might end at this point, but the recent proposals do raise some issues that merit comment: the dates of the rebuilding of Sepphoris and the period during which it was the major city in Antipas's realm; whether or not Sepphoris was a Hellenistic or Roman city that

spread Greco-Roman culture to the surrounding area; and Jesus' relationship to the cities of Galilee.

Sepphoris was destroyed or partly destroyed during a period of unrest that followed the death of Herod the Great in 4 B.C.E.[4] When Herod's son Antipas was appointed ruler of Galilee, he immediately began rebuilding the city and made it his major city, probably the capital.[5] This work most likely began in 3 or 2 B.C.E. Some time later, between the years 17 and 23 C.E., Antipas founded Tiberias as his new capital.[6] Since it is unlikely that he could have carried on two major building projects at the same time, most of the construction in Sepphoris was probably done prior to 20, and possibly before 17 C.E. Jesus was born shortly before the death of Herod the Great, probably between 6 and 4 B.C.E.[7] This means that he grew up while Sepphoris was being rebuilt and could have worked there as a teenager. During all or most of his adulthood, however, Sepphoris was not the capital city, and it did not house Antipas's court (as Batey proposes).[8]

Some of the more striking aspects of Batey's view of the significance of Sepphoris for the ministry of Jesus depend on his opinion that during Jesus' lifetime Galilee in general and Sepphoris in particular were very strongly influenced by the cultures of Greece and Rome. He thinks that Galilee was occupied by the Roman army, which built roads[9] and assisted in the construction of gymnasia and other buildings that were necessary for Greco-Roman

fig. 30 As viewed from Nazareth, the prominent hill of Sepphoris on the edge of the Neṭofian Valley is marked by the Crusader/Ottoman citadel. *Photo: Joint Sepphoris Project*

political and cultural activities.[10] Besides Roman soldiers, in Batey's view, there were Roman officials and administrators in Galilee[11]; there were also gentile scribes and learned men[12]; and they all had to be served in the accustomed ways. He believes there was a theater in Sepphoris in which performances were given in Greek and a pagan temple "dedicated to Augustus and to Rome."[13] He also argues that local farmers raised pigs for Roman appetites and sacrifices and that workmen used mules—practices that are forbidden by Jewish law.[14] As a consequence of this overwhelming Roman presence in the city where Jesus worked, Batey concludes, he and his hearers spoke Greek: Greek plays were performed in the supposed theater.[15]

It is surprising that many of these beliefs are shared by other scholars. Howard Kee imagines that in Jesus' day Sepphoris was an "important Roman cultural and administrative center."[16] He also believes that Sepphoris was the home of gentile temples.[17] According to another scholar, "Galilee was in fact an epitome of Hellenistic culture,"[18] whereas others maintain that "life in lower Galilee in the first century was as urbanized and urbane as anywhere else in the empire."[19] Thus, the argument continues, Jesus and his contemporaries were deeply affected by the "all-pervasive" influence of "Roman urbanization"[20] and even were acquainted with Cynic philosophy.[21]

Most of these views rest on a basic mistake about Rome and Galilee. Batey, Kee, and others think that when Gabinius appointed five regional councils, called *synedria*, to administer Jewish Palestine (c. 57 B.C.E.),[22] he installed Roman governors and Roman bureaucrats.[23] Apparently they then suppose that these Roman officials were permanent, remaining in the city through Julius Caesar's reorganization of the country (47 B.C.E.), the remainder of the Hasmonean period (through 37 B.C.E.), the Parthian invasion (40 B.C.E.), and the reign of Herod the Great (37–4 B.C.E.). Further, they believe that the Romans were still in place when Antipas was ruler of Galilee.[24]

None of this is true. The administrative officials appointed by Gabinius were Jewish.[25] Subsequently, as even a cursory reading of Palestinian history will show, Rome did not govern Galilee directly. Julius Caesar appointed as ethnarch ("ruler of the nation," a lesser title than "king") Hyrcanus II, a member of the royal and high-priestly Hasmonean family whose rule over Jewish Palestine stretched back into the second century B.C.E. Hyrcanus was supported by an Idumaean strong man, Antipater, father of Herod the Great. Herod and his brother, Phasael, governed main parts of Hyrcanus's ethnarchy. In 40 B.C.E. they were routed by the Parthian invasion of the Near East; the Parthians installed another Hasmonean, Antigonus, as king and high priest. He, in turn, was supplanted by Herod in 37 B.C.E. Roman troops assisted Herod in the conquest of his domain, but then they left. Herod ruled with an iron hand, and without Roman help, until his death in 4 B.C.E. After Herod died, Antipas governed Galilee as his father had governed all of Jewish Palestine—without Roman soldiers and administrators. He, like his father before him, was an ally of Rome. When an Arab ruler, Aretas, invaded Galilee, his army defeated Antipas's army, not a Roman army. The Roman legions in Syria began a punitive expedition against Aretas in support of their ally Antipas; and, when the Roman army moved, Aretas fled. If proof were still needed, this would show decisively that there were no Roman administrators or soldiers in Antipas's Galilee. Roman troops did not reside in Galilee until after the Second Jewish Revolt against Rome (that is, after 135 C.E.).[26]

It now appears that the theater that features so prominently in some theories about Jesus was not built until at least fifty years after his death. Had it existed, the available entertainment would have been mostly pantomimes and farces, not classical comedy and drama. The audience would not have needed much Greek.[27]

The upshot is that during Jesus' lifetime the situation in Galilee was vastly different from that envisaged by Batey, Kee and others. Presumably there were some gentiles in Antipas's realm, and Antipas probably made use of gentile architects and construction engineers. But one of the probable purposes of the construction projects was to employ Jewish laborers, not imported gentiles. This consideration certainly figured in the plans of Herod the Great, and all the rulers of Palestine were aware of the political and social unrest produced by large bodies of unemployed men.[28] In short, Antipas's Galilee was mostly Jewish. Scythopolis (Beth-Shean), south of Sepphoris, was a major gentile city in geographical Galilee, but it was politically independent. We do not know what the relations were between Scythopolis and the surrounding Jewish areas. In any case, Batey and others have greatly exaggerated the pagan influence in Galilee during Jesus' lifetime.

Finally, one of the most striking aspects of the ministry of Jesus as recorded in the Gospels is that they never place Jesus in a Jewish city other than Jerusalem. They describe journeys into the territory of gentile cities, though they indicate that Jesus did not enter the cities themselves (Mark 5:1, 7:24; Matt. 8:28, 15:21). In view of this silence about cities, it is improbable that Jesus carried out a substantive ministry in the cities of Galilee. We may only speculate as to the reasons for this. The most likely explanation is simply that the world Jesus knew was that of the small towns and villages of Galilee, and he directed his mission to the men and women who shared that world with him.

1. No Roman rule in Galilee until after Antipas, even after 135.

2. Theatre built post 80 CE + not Greek.

3. No city in Gospels except Jerusalem.

NOTES

1. The Greek word is *tekton,* which can refer to a carpenter, woodworker, builder, or craftsman.

2. Shirley Jackson Case, "Jesus and Sepphoris," *Journal of Biblical Literature* 45 (1926): 14–22.

3. R. A. Batey, "'Is Not This the Carpenter?'" *New Testament Studies* 30 (1984): 249–58; "Jesus and the Theatre," *New Testament Studies* 30 (1984): 563–74; *Jesus and the Forgotten City: New Light on Sepphoris and the Urban World of Jesus* (Grand Rapids, 1991). For a generally supportive review of *Forgotten City,* see Richard Oster in the *Critical Review of Books in Religion* 6 (1993): 201–4. A sharply critical review is that by Lawrence Schiffman, *Biblical Archaeologist* 55 (1992): 105–6, to which are appended some equally critical remarks by Eric Meyers, 106–7.

4. Josephus, *The Jewish War* 2.68. Translations of Josephus follow *Josephus,* in nine volumes, trans. H. St. J. Thackeray, Loeb Classical Library (Cambridge, Mass., and London, 1967).

5. Josephus, *Jewish Antiquities* 18.27.

6. Josephus, *Antiquities* 18.36–38. On Sepphoris and Tiberias, see Emil Schürer, *The History of the Jewish People in the Age of Jesus Christ,* revised by Geza Vermes and Fergus Millar, vol. 2 (Edinburgh, 1979), pp. 172–76, 178–82. On the date of the founding of Tiberias by Antipas, see also Harold W. Hoehner, *Herod Antipas. A Contemporary of Jesus Christ,* repr. ed. (Grand Rapids, 1980), pp. 93–95.

7. E. P. Sanders, *The Historical Figure of Jesus* (London, 1993; repr., 1995), 11–12.

8. Batey, "The Carpenter," 251.

9. Batey, "The Carpenter," 250.

10. Batey, *Forgotten City,* 80.

11. Batey, *Forgotten City,* 56.

12. Batey, *Forgotten City,* 78.

13. Batey, *Forgotten City,* 56. The evidence is a coin from the period of Caracalla (chap. 1, n. 34; Caracalla ruled the empire c. 211–16 C.E.).

14. Batey, *Forgotten City,* 140.

15. Batey, *Forgotten City,* 140; "Jesus and the Theatre."

16. Howard Kee, "Early Christianity in the Galilee: Reassessing the Evidence from the Gospels," in *The Galilee in Late Antiquity,* ed. Lee I. Levine (New York and Jerusalem, 1992), 15.

17. Kee, "Early Christianity," 15.

18. Burton Mack, *A Myth of Innocence* (Philadelphia, 1988), 66.

19. John Dominic Crossan, *The Historical Jesus: The Life of a Mediterranean Jewish Peasant* (San Francisco, 1991), 19, quoting with approval a seminar paper by Andrew Overman.

20. Thomas R. W. Longstaff, "Nazareth and Sepphoris: Insights into Christian Origins," *Anglican Theological Review,* Supplementary Series 11 (1990): 8–15.

21. F. Gerald Downing, *Jesus and the Threat of Freedom* (London, 1987); Downing, *Christ and the Cynics* (Sheffield, 1988); Mack, *Myth of Innocence.* Downing's view is that Jesus was a Cynic, whereas Mack maintains that Jesus was *like* a Cynic. See also Crossan, *Peasant,* 74–88, 340: Jesus established "Jewish and rural Cynicism rather than Greco-Roman and urban Cynicism."

22. Josephus, *War* 1.170.

23. See also Longstaff, "Nazareth and Sepphoris," 10.

24. Discussing the government of Sepphoris in Jesus' day, Kee cites Gabinius's administrative arrangements ("Early Christianity in Galilee," 15, n. 40). In a letter to the author he made it clear that he thinks that, in consequence, the government of Galilee in Jesus' lifetime was Roman.

25. E.g., Peitholaus; see Josephus, *War* 1.172.

26. See, e.g., Zeev Safrai, "The Roman Army in the Galilee," in *The Galilee in Late Antiquity,* ed. Levine, 103–14.

27. Ehud Netzer and Zeev Weiss, *Zippori* (Jerusalem, 1994), 16–19.

28. Josephus, *Antiquities* 20.219–22.

Sepphoris during the Byzantine Period

Zeev Weiss and Ehud Netzer

Significant structural changes took place in Sepphoris during the second half of the fourth century C.E.[1] Some of these changes were undoubtedly undertaken as a result of damage caused by the massive earthquake of 363 C.E., an event mentioned in a letter attributed to Cyril, a church father in Jerusalem at that time.[2] The Dionysos mosaic building—so named here for its magnificent mosaic carpet featuring scenes from the Greek god's life—and many other domiciles on the acropolis were destroyed in this catastrophe. Evidence of the same destruction, but on a smaller scale, was also found in lower Sepphoris, a well-planned expansion of the city limits on a plateau to the east of the acropolis. The city possibly also suffered some damage during the Gallus Revolt of 351 C.E., though Christian sources imply that this revolt brought about destruction in the city.[3] In any event, no remains of a fourth-century conflagration indicative of such an uprising have been revealed in the areas exposed either by the Hebrew University expedition or by the Joint Sepphoris Project.

The streets and colonnades that had been laid out east of the summit during the Roman period continued to function during the Byzantine period, but as a result of the 363 earthquake, which devastated other cities in the country as well, significant changes took place in the built-up areas of Sepphoris. Some buildings were renovated; elsewhere new buildings were erected, either on top of the ruins (as was the case in most parts of the Dionysos mosaic building) or in their place. In addition, apparently because of population growth during the Byzantine period, the built-up area of the city was enlarged. Evidence of this was found in the two *insulae* located to the north of the presumed *agora* (forum) and *macellum* (central market). New streets were built as direct extensions of the Roman street grid that was laid out more than two centuries before. The eastern *insulae* of the two was built on a relatively steep area and therefore necessitated the construction of high retaining walls with substantial fills behind them. The water system also attests to the expansion of the city as well as to its economical prosperity, as the large water reservoir to the east of the city was enlarged, apparently in order to meet the needs of the growing population.

Conversely, the remains exposed on the acropolis suggest a decline in the importance of that part of the city in this period. Only a small section of the Dionysos mosaic building—mainly its southern part with basement, which had contained a row of shops and workshops, including an oil press and a metal-working shop as well as a stable—was restored. Poorly planned buildings constructed out of stones in secondary use were erected above the rest of the ruined mansion. These new structures included one

fig. 31 A seated dove decorates the tall curved handle of this Byzantine-period bronze lamp from Sepphoris. See cat. no. 121.
Photo: Israel Antiquities Authority

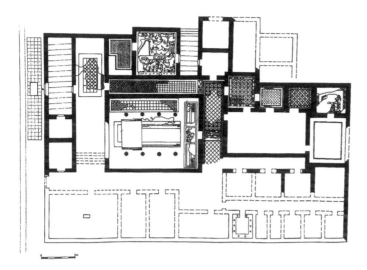

fig. 32 Plan of the fifth-century C.E. Nile festival building.
Courtesy: Hebrew University Expedition

or two ritual baths, attesting to Jewish residents. In the center of the acropolis, south of the Crusader citadel, are the remains of a storeroom building characterized by a large, central hall flanked by two adjacent rooms. A dozen large storage jars (*dolia*) were found *in situ* in this hall, which was paved with a white mosaic. The room to its west contained many smaller storage jars. Owing to the scant Byzantine remains on the western side of the acropolis, the full architectural setup here is unclear, but it appears that the standard of building was much lower than in the Roman period.

A somewhat different situation prevails on the hill's northern slope, to the northeast of the Roman theater. It appears that houses were built here, directly above domiciles of the Roman period, and that some of the elements of the earlier structures were incorporated into the new ones. One of these new houses contained a large room with a mosaic floor decorated with a geometric design featuring birds and pomegranates. It is difficult to determine the state of the theater during the Byzantine period. Presumably this large, tall building also was damaged, at least partially, in the earthquake of 363 C.E.

It appears, however, that the theater continued to be used in the late fourth and the early fifth century but was abandoned later in the Byzantine period, when most of its building stones were looted for other construction projects as well as for the production of lime. The latter possibility is suggested by the discovery, east of the stage, of a limekiln (used for reducing limestone to lime by burning) and, next to it, a group of large stones that had been removed from the theater.

In contrast to the relatively poor state of development of the acropolis in the Byzantine period, the well-planned civic center to the east of the summit, with the *cardo* (north-south) and the *decumanus* (east-west) commercial streets at its center, apparently flourished once the earthquake damage had been repaired, as did other areas of the city. The largest and most impressive building from the Early Byzantine period excavated by the Hebrew University expedition lies along the east side of the *cardo*. It was named the Nile festival building because the mosaic floor in one of its rooms depicts scenes of the Nile River festival celebrated in Egypt.[4] This edifice, with its several outstanding mosaic floors, was most probably built at the end of the fourth or at the beginning of the fifth century. Buildings from the Roman period, covering an area of about 55 x 50 meters, were demolished in order to clear a space for this structure.

Changes were also introduced in the eastern colonnade of the *cardo* along the western side of the Nile festival building, where the colonnade was converted into a sort of *narthex* (enclosed entrance) to the building. The colonnade's floor was repaved with mosaics featuring a geometric design. An inscription was revealed in this floor immediately in front of the building's main entrance. This inscription mentions the artists, Patricius and his father-in-law Procopius, who apparently created the building's colorful mosaic floors. Beyond this entrance was a small stone-paved courtyard.

The Nile festival building was divided into a number of wings. The most important one, which included the main entrance, was located in the northwestern part of the building. A large basilica-

fig. 33 Section of a panel from the Nile festival building featuring the figures of two hunters, one largely destroyed. See cat. no. 159. *Photo: Gaby Laron*

shaped hall, measuring 15 x 10 meters, occupied the center of this wing. Among the small portions of the hall's mosaic floor that have been preserved is a scene of hunting Amazons, located opposite what is possibly the entrance to the hall. To its north, in a room measuring 7 x 7 meters, lies the floor depicting the Nile festival. This room was entered via a small stone-paved courtyard on its eastern side, which served as another entrance to the building.

The Nile festival building was well planned. Its layout is notable for its system of corridors, which also were decorated with mosaic floors, primarily made up of geometric patterns. A panel depicting a centaur was exposed at the intersection of two of these corridors, next to the basilical hall. A nearby panel, located to the east of the basilical hall, in front

of its main entrance and directly opposite the Amazons' panel, shows two male hunters (cat. no. 159).

The building's northeast wing, having a sort of courtyard at its center, differed in character. All three rooms to the north of the courtyard have mosaic floors decorated with colorful geometric designs. East of the courtyard is a unit that consisted of a large room (7 x 5.5 meters) flanked by two average-size rooms (4.5 x 4 meters). The floor of the northern room features Amazons and horses. Only meager mosaic remains were found in the large room (a geometric design incorporating vines), and no mosaics survived in the southern room.

All that remains of the building's southern wing, built along the street to the south of the *decumanus*, are its foundations. Noteworthy here are the remains of a Roman-style lavatory with traces of water channels around its four walls.

The water systems in the Nile festival building included subterranean channels that provided a continuous flow of water. Within one of the central rooms, which has a particularly handsome geometric mosaic floor, is a basin that was fed directly by one of these channels. The room with the Nile festival floor and the basilical hall shared a common drainage system. These details suggest that ceremonies in which water was thrown over the participants, or on the floors, took place here. These ceremonies might have been related to the *Maiuma*, festivities in which the harvest and water played a key role.[5] Such celebrations were held during the Byzantine period at Birketein, north of Gerasa (modern Jerash), according to an inscription dated to the mid-sixth century.[6]

The central location of the Nile festival building, its size, its artistic richness, and its lack of any elements characteristic of residential use indicate that it probably served as a public building, perhaps a municipal basilica, which in Byzantine sources is mentioned as a place where regional meetings, lectures, and the like were held. "A basilica for the public benefit," in the words of Choricius, was erected in Gaza in the sixth century C.E.[7] Such an institution is known to have existed in other cities in the Land of Israel[8] and probably is mentioned in a

Greek inscription carved on a stone discovered at Sepphoris some years ago.[9]

The importance of the Nile festival building is reflected also in the changes that took place to its north. The buildings that had stood there were replaced by a square paved with rectangular flagstones. Remains of a small building with a profiled base—it probably served as a monument of some kind—were revealed to the northeast of this square. North of the square was a row of shops, fronted by a colonnade. These shops were later demolished and replaced by stone paving, thus extending the area of the square. The picture south of the square is unclear. Theoretically, a strip of garden might have separated the square from the Nile festival building, but in any event, there was access from the square to the building via the small courtyard next to the room with the Nilotic scenes.

Toward the end of the fifth or during the sixth century c.e., significant changes took place close to the intersection of the *cardo* and the *decumanus*. The foundations of two churches, which replaced earlier buildings, were exposed south of the *decumanus*. One of them was situated to the west of the *cardo*; the other, to its east. The location of these churches in the heart of Sepphoris, a city that had been populated mostly by Jews, indicates the growth and strengthening of its Christian community in the Byzantine period.

The church west of the *cardo* was about 17 x 23 meters in size. Only its foundations and a number of water cisterns built at the same time have survived. (Some of these cisterns might have provided water for religious ceremonies.) The atrium through which the church was entered could have been located in the unexcavated area on the west. An atrium measuring about 25 x 22 meters was exposed in front of the second church, east of the *cardo*. The courtyard of this church was paved with stone slabs and was surrounded by colonnades paved with mosaics. Only the width of this chuch, 18 meters, is known, and only the foundations have survived. To the south of this church is a group of rooms with a water cistern in their center. The cistern is from the Roman period but was incorporated into the new layout with only minor changes in the Byzantine period. In contrast

to the many other contemporary structures in the lower city, these churches are poorly preserved. Still, their presence in Sepphoris is of great significance, both because they reflect a growing Christian presence in a Jewish city and also because they provide important information concerning Byzantine architecture in Palestine. This urban feature of two churches situated opposite each other is rare in ancient Palestine.[10]

The changes introduced in the colonnades at the intersection of the *cardo* and the *decumanus* included not only a new mosaic paving but also a rearrangement of the columns and the roofs. The mosaics were of geometric design, some variegated, others in black and white. Three Greek inscriptions framed by medallions were incorporated in the new floors. These inscriptions mention a Father Eutropius, referred to as the *Episcopus*, during whose time the mosaics were laid. One inscription reads, for example, "Under our most saintly father Eutropius the Episcopus, the whole work of the mosaic was done by the provision of the most learned Marianus, the chief physician and father of the city, in the time of the fourteenth indiction." Although neither the exact dates of Eutropius's term of office nor when the colonnades were renovated is known, the inscriptions provide information about the administrative system of Sepphoris at the end of the Byzantine period, that is, the role of the municipal *Episcopus* and his activities for the welfare of the city's inhabitants.[11]

Some Roman-period structures continued in use, albeit with some renovations, throughout the Byzantine period. A good example is the Roman bathhouse west of the *cardo*. Others, such as the presumed *agora* (known as the basilical building), were partly abandoned; a bathhouse apparently was built during this period in the eastern part of that ruined building.[12] The development north of the *agora* during the Byzantine period included, as mentioned previously, two *insulae* separated by the street that formed the northward continuation of the *cardo*. This new extension was not paved with stone slabs but rather with plaster. To its west stood a luxurious domicile with a peristyle courtyard and mosaic floors. This building contained cellars for the storage of liquids, perhaps wine. Another structure, possibly a public building, stood to the east of this street. It appears that for reasons of topography the urban development did not extend north of these two *insulae*, yet the city continued to develop north-west of this area.

The nature of the residential facilities east of the summit is still not clear. The largest concentration of domiciles, some built already in the Roman period, was revealed southeast of the *cardo*, around a street intersection. One of them juts out into the adjacent streets. A building south of the Nile festival building is paved in a similar style, probably by the same artists.[13] Fragments of a second-story mosaic floor were found in the debris of a nearby building that was destroyed by fire at the end of the Byzantine period. Some of the houses in this sector contained agricultural installations, such as winepresses, storerooms, and the like.

The proximity of private and public buildings, both on the acropolis and in lower Sepphoris is rather surprising, as this phenomenon has not been encountered elsewhere in Palestine in cities of the Byzantine period. In both Roman and Byzantine Sepphoris large and ornate mansions were built close to simple homes, a feature noted throughout the city. Moreover, a clear and rigid division of the city into neighborhoods according to social, religious, or economic status cannot be discerned.

The Jewish community of Sepphoris, which retained its relative majority during the Byzantine period, built many synagogues. These structures were no doubt scattered throughout Sepphoris, but to date only two synagogues from the Byzantine period have been discovered; there is some evidence of a third, possibly from an earlier period. The limited archaeological evidence unearthed thus far is in contrast to the extensive literary evidence for synagogues at Sepphoris in the early centuries of the common era.[14]

fig. 34 A mosaic medallion from the eastern sidewalk of the *cardo* (main north-south street) with an inscription dating to the late Byzantine period that refers to the deeds of Bishop Eutropius and of Marianus, the chief physician.
Photo: Gabi Laron

One synagogue, known from the Aramaic and Greek dedicatory inscriptions found at the beginning of the twentieth century, was located in the western side of the upper city, near the remains of the Crusader church (see cat. no. 25).[15] Other fragments of dedicatory inscriptions, found on the summit by the Joint Sepphoris Project but not *in situ*, indicate the presence of another synagogue. A complete synagogue was excavated by the Hebrew University expedition northeast of the acropolis, not far from the city's center and adjacent to the street that ran parallel to the *cardo* on its western side.[16] This synagogue was an elongated building that faced away from Jerusalem; the entrance was in its southern wall. A narrow *narthex* separated the entrance from the main hall. The hall had only one aisle, on its northern side, thus differing from the majority of ancient synagogues, which had two aisles on either side of the nave, such as those at Beth Alpha, Maʿoz Ḥayyim, and Rehov.[17] On the basis of numismatic evidence, it appears that this synagogue was built during the first

half of the fifth century C.E. and that it was destroyed at the end of the Byzantine period.

The most significant remains of this synagogue are its mosaic floors with figurative motifs, geometric designs, and inscriptions.[18] It probably stood within a residential area and thus served members of the Jewish community living there. It is still too early to determine whether the location of the two synagogues on the periphery of the city symbolizes the restriction of the Jews to the outskirts of the city or, conversely, the spread of this community throughout the urban area even though the city's population in this period included people of other religions.

At its zenith, Byzantine Sepphoris comprised an area of more than 40 hectares and a population of approximately 15,000 to 20,000. Events at the end of the Byzantine period and in the Early Arab period brought an end to the city's growth and prosperity. Many of the Byzantine buildings uncovered at Sepphoris show clear signs of destruction by fire, a catastrophic event that could be associated with

fig. 35 A mosaic floor with geometric designs from the fifth-century C.E. Nile festival building. *Photo: Gabi Laron*

either the Persian occupation or the Arab conquest of the early seventh century, but it is also possible that these structures burned as the result of an earthquake, the exact date of which cannot yet be determined.

The number of inhabitants began to decrease in the Early Arab period, and the standard of living dropped, phenomena reflected in the urban layout. Many buildings were abandoned or used for purposes other than those for which they had been intended. The most striking such example is the Roman bathhouse west of the *cardo*, which apparently was converted into an industrial complex. Very little is known about the character of the city during the Early Arab period. Some of the main streets of lower Sepphoris were preserved, but their surfaces were elevated. Only a few buildings that were erected alongside these streets at that time have been uncovered. Those that have do not appear to form part of a distinct urban layout. Some of these structures are of a low standard, and it appears that large areas were not made available for development in this part of the city.

The architectural layout of Sepphoris, with its various public and private buildings, is very significant, but it is the city's numerous and colorful mosaics that rank Sepphoris among the important mosaic centers of the Roman and Byzantine East. To date, more than forty mosaic floors have been uncovered in both private dwellings and public buildings throughout the city. The most important mosaics feature rich and varied iconographic depictions similar to those found in other cities in the Middle East. Some of the geometric designs are of very high quality. Sepphoris boasts mosaic floors from the third and fifth centuries C.E., contrasting time frames that illustrate the stylistic development of this art. The unearthing of this unique assemblage of mosaic pavements, which vary in terms of iconography, composition, style, and chronology, has contributed greatly to our understanding of mosaic art in ancient Palestine and its development. The presence of these mosaics suggests that Sepphoris, like other cities throughout the Eastern and Western Roman Empires, had its own, local artisans.

The importance of these mosaics lies not only in their quantity but also in their iconographic and stylistic richness. Remarkable also is that they existed in a city populated mostly by Jews, thus providing a different perspective on Jewish urban society in Roman and Byzantine Palestine. This new perspective, together with valuable information from the talmudic literature, enables us to gain a more nuanced picture of Jewish society and its attitude toward the Hellenistic culture within which it lived. Future excavations will undoubtedly shed much more light on the size, character, and development of the "Ornament of all Galilee," as the capital of Herod Antipas was described by Flavius Josephus, as well as on Sepphoris in the days of Rabbi Judah Ha-Nasi (the Patriarch) and the codification of the Mishnah.

NOTES

1. The information contained herein is based mainly on excavations conducted during the years 1990–96 under the directorship of the authors on behalf of the Institute of Archaeology, the Hebrew University of Jerusalem. For previous publications see Zeev Weiss and Ehud Netzer, "Two Excavation Seasons at Sepphoris," *Qadmoniot* 95–96 (1992): 113–21 (in Hebrew); Netzer and Weiss, "Byzantine Mosaics at Sepphoris: New Finds," *Israel Museum Journal* 10 (1992): 75–80; Netzer and Weiss, "New Mosaic Art from Sepphoris," *Biblical Archaeology Review* 18, no. 6 (1992): 36–43; Weiss and Netzer, "Archaeological Finds from the Byzantine Period at Sepphoris," *Michmanim* 8 (1995): 75–85 (in Hebrew); Netzer and Weiss, *Zippori* (Jerusalem, 1994); and Netzer and Weiss, "New Evidence for Late-Roman and Byzantine Sepphoris," in *The Roman and Byzantine Near East: Some Recent Archaeological Research*, ed. John H. Humphrey, Journal of Roman Archaeology, Supplementary Series, 14 (Ann Arbor, 1995), 162–76. Also see our article on Sepphoris in the Roman period in this catalogue.

2. Sebastian P. Brock, "A Letter Attributed to Cyril of Jerusalem on the Rebuilding of the Temple," *Bulletin of the School of Oriental and African Studies* 40 (1977): 267–86.

3. For the Christian sources on the Gallus Revolt see Joseph Geiger, "The Gallus Revolt and the Proposal to Rebuild the Temple in the Time of Julianus," in *Eretz Israel from the Destruction of the Second Temple to the Muslim Conquest*, ed. Z. Baras et al. (Jerusalem, 1982), 202–17 (in Hebrew).

4. For a more detailed discussion of this festival and its associated mosaic floor, as well as other mosaics found in this structure, see our article on the Nile festival building in this catalogue.

5. Such festivities are mentioned in some Jewish sources; see Chanoch Kohut, *Aruch Completus*, vol. 3 (Vienna and New York, 1878–92), "Maiumas" and the references cited there.

6. C. Bradford Welles, "The Inscriptions," in *Gerasa, City of the Decapolis*, ed. Carl H. Kraeling (New Haven, 1938), no. 279.

7. *Choricius Gazaeus*, ed. R. Foerster and E. Richtsteig (Leipzig, 1929), 3, 55.

8. Baruch Lifshitz, "Inscriptions grecques de Césarée en Palestine," *Revue Biblique* 68 (1961): 122–23.

9. Michael Avi-Yonah, who published this inscription, identified the building mentioned in it as a church, but Leah di Segni's new reading of the Sepphoris inscription leads to a different conclusion; see Avi-Yonah, "A Sixth Century Inscription from Sepphoris," *Israel Exploration Journal* 11 (1961): 184–87, and di Segni, "The Involvement of Local, Municipal and Provincial Authorities in Urban Building in Late Antique Palestine and Arabia," in *The Roman and Byzantine Near East*, ed. John H. Humphrey, 325.

10. Some churches were built near each other, as can be seen at Gerasa or Pella, for example, but situating two buildings opposite each other on either side of the main thoroughfare, as found at Sepphoris, has few parallels in this region; see Carl H. Kraeling, ed., *Gerasa, City of the Decapolis*, 185–99, and Alan G. Walmsley, "Pella," in *Archaeology of Jordan—Field Reports*, vol. 2, ed. D. Homes Fredricq and J. B. Hennessy (Leuven, 1989), 423–36.

11. See Yaron Dan, *Urban Life in the Land of Israel at the End of Ancient Times* (Jerusalem, 1984), 93–102 (in Hebrew), and Charlotte Rouché, *Aphrodisias in Late Antiquity*, Journal of Roman Studies Monograph, 5 (Ann Arbor, 1989), 75–79.

12. For more on this building and its contents, see James F. Strange's article in this catalogue.

13. The earlier mosaic floors of this house are mentioned in our companion article on Sepphoris in the Roman period.

14. In its description of the funeral of Rabbi Judah Ha-Nasi, the Palestinian Talmud mentions that there were eighteen synagogues in the city, some of which are known by name; see Palestinian Talmud, *Kil'ayim* 9, 32 a-b, and Netzer and Weiss, *Zippori*, 55.

15. For the Aramaic inscription see Joseph Naveh,
On Mosaic and Stone (Jerusalem, 1978), 51–52 (in Hebrew).
For the Greek inscription see Lea Roth-Gerson, *The Greek
Inscriptions from the Synagogues in Eretz Israel* (Jerusalem,
1987), 105–10 (in Hebrew).

16. Zeev Weiss and Ehud Netzer, *Promise and Redemption:
A Synagogue Mosaic from Sepphoris* (Jerusalem, 1996).

17. On the synagogues of Palestine see Gideon Foerster,
"The Ancient Synagogues of Galilee," in *The Galilee in
Late Antiquity*, ed. Lee I. Levine (New York and
Jerusalem, 1992), 289–319, and Rachel Hachlili, *Ancient
Jewish Art and Archaeology in the Land of Israel* (Leiden,
1988), 141–60.

18. See our separate article on this mosaic, also in
this catalogue.

Sepphoris in the Arab Period

Seth Ward

Sepphoris was a major population center in Galilee during the Roman and Byzantine periods. The objects displayed in this exhibition illustrate its high level of material culture and prosperity during the early centuries of the Christian era. But this period of efflorescence did not extend past the first half of the seventh century c.e., during which Galilee experienced first an ongoing war between Persia and Byzantium and eventually the Muslim conquest. The site apparently was inhabited during later periods, and it continued to be visited by pilgrims and travelers; its strategic importance was recognized in the Crusader period and in the eighteenth century. But it never appears to have regained its former population size or standard of living. This survey of the history of Sepphoris in the Arab period is based primarily on literary sources. Much of the following discussion is based on extrapolation from limited material and should be considered largely conjectural.

Arabs and Pre-Islamic Sepphoris

Before Islam, several Arab tribes had a presence in the Holy Land; these included the Lakhm, Judhām,

and ᶜAmila tribes, who appear to have been interrelated, and the Ghassanids. The Judhāmites in the south and the Ghassanids in the north, east of the Jordan, were clients of the Byzantines; they formed a buffer between the desert and its nomadic warriors, whose marauding raids were a constant concern to the settled population. In early Islamic times, the ᶜAmila in particular are associated with Galilee.[1]

Also during this period there were strong economic and social ties between Mecca, Muhammad's hometown, and the lands of the eastern Mediterranean. Muhammad himself, in the late sixth and early seventh centuries, had led caravans to Syria and Palestine, and he may have spent extended periods among Jews and Christians there.[2] Umayya, a leading businessman of Mecca and the great-grandfather of three caliphs, lived in Palestine for ten years in the sixth century; his kinsman Hāshim, Muhammad's great-grandfather, also had ties to Palestine and died in Gaza.[3] Although not much can be gleaned from literary sources about specific products involved in trade between Arabia and Sepphoris, one item apparently was clothing. "Sepphorean cloaks" are mentioned in the context of a famous exchange between Muhammad and the Byzantine emperor, whom Muhammad had invited to adopt Islam.[4]

While in exile, the businessman Umayya is said to have been given a slave girl of Sepphorean Jewish heritage, whose son he freed and adopted. Various

fig. 36 Two Arab-period jugs discovered at Sepphoris. The buff-colored Khirbet Mefjar-type vessel dates to the 8th-9th centuries c.e. See cat. no. 89.
The jug with black-painted geometric designs (cat. no. 130) is from the medieval period or later (13th-17th centuries).
Photo: Mariana Salzburger for the Israel Antiquities Authority

Umayyad descendants were called "a Jew from the Jews of Sepphoris" or "an unbeliever [Arabic *ʿilj*] from the unbelievers of Sepphoris."[5] (An *ʿilj* may be defined as a "man who is sturdy, strong, non-Arab and an unbeliever."[6]) These comments are meant to disparage the purity of birth and belief of various members of this leading family, with descent from a Jewish slave girl providing the least desirable genealogical social status.[7] Although the whole taunt may have been a politically motivated product of anti-Umayyad sentiment, given the importance of genealogy among the Arabs it cannot be dismissed as totally without basis. Nevertheless, we should be careful about jumping to conclusions about the historical significance of these statements for recovering the history of Sepphoris. The original form of the taunt may well have been the one with *ʿilj*, not "Jew," and even an authentic reference to a Sepphorean Jewish slave woman does not necessarily tell us whether, in the sixth century, Jews were in the majority at Sepphoris or were no longer economically or socially dominant there. It is possible that she was taken captive in a raid or that her family maintained a Sepphorean identity but had left the town years or even generations earlier.

Despite the existence of a Christian community at Sepphoris on the eve of the Islamic conquest, the anti-Umayyad taunts refer to Sepphorean Jews and unbelievers but not to Christians. Similarly, Arabic material uses the Semitic "Ṣaffūriyya" in referring to the city rather than the Greek "Diocaesarea," as Sepphoris was primarily known to such early Christian writers as Eusebius.[8]

From the Islamic Conquest to the Crusades

The Islamic Conquest

In 614 C.E. the Persians wrested control of Galilee from the Byzantines. Many towns, including Sepphoris, opened their gates to the Persians without a fight.[9] Thirteen years later, when they were defeated decisively by the Byzantines in their Mesopotamian heartland, the Persians agreed to return all the land they had conquered. The Byzantine emperor Heraclius returned to Palestine triumphantly, marching through Tiberias to Jerusalem in 629. But his victory was short-lived, as Syria, Palestine, and Egypt would soon be conquered by the new Islamic state.

ʿUmar ibn al-Khaṭṭāb became caliph in 634. He appointed four generals to complete the conquest of Syria; one of them "conquered Acre [Akko], Tyre and Sepphoris" and Galilee's villages,[10] probably in 635. Tiberias was the only city in the area that capitulated peacefully.[11] Presumably the inclusion of Sepphoris in the short list of conquered cities rather than in a list of villages indicates that it was still considered a major site at the time of the Islamic conquest and underscores that it was conquered by force: Sepphoris thus did not throw its gates open to the Muslim conquerors as it had to the Persians in 614. This conquest may have involved the total destruction of the town and perhaps was the occasion for seventh-century fire damage apparent in many locations throughout the site.[12] There is no indication of protracted fighting or reconquests, however, or, indeed, any further details of conquest at Sepphoris or at any neighboring locale. The cause or exact date of the fire cannot be established with certainty, and it may have resulted from an earthquake, such as the one that rocked the area just two years before the conquest, or from some other natural or accidental cause, such as the Year of Ashes in 639 C.E., a period marked by extended drought, widespread fires, and especially a deadly plague throughout Palestine.[13]

Sepphoris in the Arab Period

In the centuries between the conquest and the Crusades, Sepphoris was not a major center and seems not to have had a significant Muslim community. It was part of the province of Jordan (*Jund al-Urdunn*), more or less identical to the Roman province of Palaestina Secunda, whose administrative center had been Tiberias. In this region, as in Syria and Palestine as a whole, the Muslims tended to settle in the largest pre-Islamic cities, such as Damascus and Tiberias, rather than in the towns or countryside, where the Muslim population grew slowly, more by conversion than immigration.[14] Under the Umayyads (661–750), who ruled from Damascus, many areas in the nearby Holy Land received special

Chiricahua Apache

Geronimo

fig. 37 **Panoramic view from the south of the sizable Arab village of Saffuriyeh prior to its destruction in Israel's War of Independence in 1948.**
Photo: Kelsey Museum Archives, Sepphoris Archive

attention, especially Jerusalem. But Galilee was far removed from the political and intellectual centers, especially after 750, and literary evidence specific to Sepphoris is scant.[15]

COINS

Sepphoris was one of several towns in which Islamic coinage was introduced in 697 during the reign of the caliph ʿAbd al-Malik.[16] According to Yaʿakov Meshorer, copper coins were minted in Sepphoris only for a short time.[17] Yet of some four hundred coins found in the 1931 University of Michigan excavation, only four were Islamic, all from the earliest period before ʿAbd al-Malik's Islamic coin reforms. Indeed, the most recent of the four was dated no later than 668 and is probably even earlier than that.[18]

ARCHAEOLOGICAL EVIDENCE

Although there is some archaeological evidence for continued occupation of the site during the Arab period, much of it is ambiguous or unpublished. To date, Zeev Weiss, director of the Hebrew University excavation project, has found artifacts but no structural remains from the Arab period; he nevertheless speculates that some of the stones missing from structures of the southeast part of the site were removed during this time. Moreover, he believes

more study is needed before determining with certainty the date and purpose of what seems to have been a retaining wall around the theater, the Byzantine city, and the acropolis. In his view, a date from the Arabic period cannot be ruled out. Both the University of South Florida and the Duke University excavations have recovered considerable ceramic and other evidence from the Arab period, but because it lies so close to the modern surface, most of it is poorly preserved. The South Florida team has excavated several workshops from this period in the northwest sector of their eastern excavation areas. It is possible that the southern slope was inhabited during this period, but soundings conducted there by the Joint Sepphoris Project of Hebrew University and Duke University produced very limited results due to the extensive debris of the modern Arab village of Saffuriyeh, which was destroyed in 1948.[19]

FAMILY TRADITIONS

As at other locations in Galilee, oral traditions allege a continuous occupation from Roman-Byzantine times, if not earlier, continuing into and throughout the Arab period. Tsvika Tsuk has found several families with detailed traditions regarding living uninterruptedly in Sepphoris almost until the present. In all cases, the families claim originally to have been Jewish. One family converted to Islam in the early tenth century; the descendants of another became

Christian under the Crusaders then Muslim after Saladin's conquest in 1187; two other families became Muslim, but current members do not remember when.[20] A similar family tradition of continuous occupation is suggested by the report of Rabbi Petachya of Regensburg of his visit to Sepphoris in the late twelfth century. There he met a local spice seller and physician named Nehoray, who showed him a written pedigree of descent from Rabbi Judah Ha-Nasi (known as the Patriarch or the Prince), who died in 217 c.e. Nehoray's shop was near the tomb, which he identified as that of Rabbi Judah; Petachya's account suggests this was the only Jewish family in town.[21]

References to Individuals from Sepphoris in Cairo Geniza Documents

The hundreds of thousands of documents that have been found in the Cairo Geniza, a repository for no-longer used writings in the attic of Cairo's Ben Ezra Synagogue, have yielded up a multitude of references to the towns and Jewish residents of Palestine during the Arab period but only a very few references to Jews from Sepphoris. A work on cemeteries and funerals was written by Yefet b. ᶜAmram b. Moses ha-Ḥazzan al-Jazfīnī from Sepphoris,[22] and we know of a copyist named "Shemaiah b. Abraham of blessed memory from the city of Sepphoris."[23] Both Yefet and Shemaiah are probably from the eleventh century. Another eleventh-century letter refers to "the son of the Sepphorean."[24] This period is the best attested in the Geniza, and it is certainly possible that other documents might still come to light.

Islamic Biographical and Geographical Dictionaries

The Islamic tradition is particularly rich in encyclopedic dictionaries, including biographical works; typically it is possible to locate biographies of major and minor figures in law and religious sciences, medicine, and other fields. Persons who lived in or were born in Sepphoris would be called al-Ṣaffūrī in Arabic, but a search of the biographical literature for this period turned up no references to anyone with this title.[25] The geographical literature was slightly more forth-

coming. Al-Yaᶜqūbī, writing at the end of the ninth century, gives the date of the conquest of Sepphoris and describes the population of this district as "a mixture of Arabs and non-Arabs."[26] Yāqūt's geographical dictionary (early thirteenth century) merely mentions the location and spelling of the town,[27] and al-Bakrī included it in what is essentially a gazetteer of little-known places.[28] Not surprisingly, Sepphoris is not included in the major geographical descriptions of the then-known world with its various major cities.[29] There is one kind of geographical literature, however, that features a more-detailed approach: itineraries and travels, especially among travelers describing tombs and holy sites.

Sepphoris in Sacred Geography

Sepphoris figured in the sacred geography and itineraries of Judaism, Christianity, and Islam. For Christians, the most important associations at Sepphoris are with Mary and her parents, Anne and Joachim, as discussed by Jaroslav Folda in his essay on the Crusader Church of Saint Anne in this catalogue. Muslims venerate Jesus as a prophet, and Mary figures in the Qur'ān (known in English as the Koran). In Islamic sources, her father is called ᶜImrān; her mother, Ḥanna.[30] The association of Jesus with Nazareth and the towns in its environs is well known to Muslims, but the holy places generally reported in Muslim travelogues relate more usually to Hebrew biblical figures, such as Moses and the tribes of Israel. Kafr Manda, near Sepphoris, is sometimes given as the location of the tomb of Ṣafūra (Zippora), the wife of Moses. Presumably this is in part because of the similarity of the names of the biblical figure and the village.[31]

Jewish travelers generally associated the site of Sepphoris with rabbinic-period individuals, especially Rabbenu Ha-Kadosh, "our Holy Rabbi," that is, Rabbi Judah, who was believed to have been buried at Sepphoris with his wife, his students, or his sons Shimon and Gamaliel. More correctly, the tomb at Sepphoris is identified as that of his grandson Yehuda Nesi'a, whose name also translates to "Judah the Prince." Some Jewish travelers, however, were aware that the elder Rabbi Judah's tomb was consid-

fig. 39 This Roman-period mausoleum to the west of Sepphoris, locally known as the Tomb of Jacob's Daughters, may have been a destination for Jewish pilgrims who journeyed to Sepphoris during the Arab period. They came to visit the tombs of famous local sages, including Rabbi Judah Ha-Nasi, who actually was buried at Beth-She°arim. This mausoleum is sometimes identified as the burial place of his grandson, Rabbi Yehuda Nesi'a.

fig. 38 Crowning the Sepphoris acropolis, the citadel, first erected in the Byzantine period, was reconstructed in the Crusader period as a watchtower. Rebuilt in 1745 by the bedouin Shaykh Ḏāhir al-°Umar, it was repaired again during the reign of the Ottoman sultan °Abd al-Ḥamīd (1846–1909) when the structure was reconstructed to serve as a schoolhouse for local Arab villagers.
Photo: Kelsey Museum Archives, Sepphoris Archive

erably distant from Sepphoris. As Eshtori ha-Parchi noted, the grave said to be that of Rabbenu Ha-Kadosh is only a half-hour walk from the village, whereas Beth-She°arim, the location of the elder Rabbi Judah's tomb according to the Talmud, is a two-hour walk away.[32] Among the other graves that have been located in or near Sepphoris by various travelers are those of Jonah the Prophet, Rabbi Hiyya the Babylonian, and the Daughters of Jacob.[33] A fifteenth-century Jewish traveler found tombs of many of Jacob's sons within a day or two walk of each other in the vicinity of Sepphoris, under Islamic control.[34] In the eleventh century, Sepphoris, which is not mentioned in the Bible, may have been identified with the biblical city Tirzah, according to the aforementioned eleventh-century Geniza document, but this identification is otherwise unknown.[35]

Crusader Period to the Present

Sepphoris was captured from the Muslims by the Crusaders in 1099. They called the site Le Sephorie and fortified its citadel, and in 1187 they gathered there to make war against the Muslim forces led by Saladin. An Arab historian wrote that "they arranged their troops and raised their crosses. They were about 50,000 and more."[36] Although the number is surely exaggerated, it was clearly the largest army ever raised by the Latin Kingdom of Jerusalem.[37] After Saladin defeated the Crusaders at the Horns of Hattin, "the people of Sepphoris fled and no one was found there," although they left behind "wealth and treasures."[38] Saladin himself visited the area after the battle, while the Crusaders fled to Acre (Akko).[39] Another Arab historian wrote about the Crusader defeat, "Ṣaffūriyya was empty [*ṣafirat*] of its inhabitants; no one who could whistle [*ṣāfir*, that is, a human], even though it had an ample supply of treasures."[40] Le Sephorie returned to Crusader hands in 1240 and was reconquered by Mamluk forces under the sultan an-Nasir Rukn-ad-Din Baybars in 1263.[41]

Despite the great treasure there as reported by Arab sources, except for Petachya's reference to Nehoray we hear of few individuals who actually lived in Sepphoris during the Crusader period.

Benjamin of Tudela, who reported on the Jewish communities he found throughout the world, visited Sepphoris about 1165 and did not recount finding a Jewish community there. Christian travelers also remarked on Sepphoris's small population: John of Würzburg (1170) described it as sparsely populated, and John Phocas (1185) wrote that Sepphoris "has almost no houses and displays no trace of its original prosperity."[42] We do learn, however, of a John Semes appointed by the Crusaders in Nazareth to be "Rais of Saphorie." Semes was probably a native-born Christian or Muslim landholder surnamed al-Shams in Arabic.[43]

After Crusader times, there seems to have been a steady growth in the Muslim community but few Christians or Jews. In the century following the Ottoman conquest of the area in 1516, at least a dozen individuals who were born in or lived in Sepphoris are known from Islamic biographical literature.[44] This may reflect the large increase in Islamic education in Syria and Palestine under the Mamluks and Ottomans. Despite the phenomenal growth in overall Jewish population in Galilee and in Palestine as a whole in this period, there is no indication that Jews lived in Sepphoris at this time. Although Sepphoris is mentioned in a number of Jewish legal opinions from the fifteenth into the eighteenth century, these references have been shown not to reflect the existence of a Jewish community there but rather the conventional use of well-known cities from the Mishnah and Talmud to refer to arbitrary place names.[45]

The citadel of Sepphoris was rebuilt in 1745 by Shaykh Ḍāhir al-ᶜUmar, a bedouin who controlled most of Galilee in the mid-eighteenth century.[46] The citadel was repaired again during the reign of the Ottoman sultan ᶜAbd al-Ḥamīd, probably shortly after 1889,[47] and served as a school until the 1948 war. At that time, the Arab village there (Saffuriyeh) had about 3,000 residents; it was destroyed during the war.

The sources surveyed here present a picture of Sepphoris as a small village after the Islamic conquest. A large city under the Byzantines, it may have escaped damage in 614 when it opened its gates to the Persians in the Byzantine-Persian wars. But many of its people may have fled or were killed at that time or in the 630s, when it was conquered by force and when plague and natural disasters hit the region; many locales in Galilee and elsewhere in the Land of Israel never regained the population and importance they had had in ancient times. Sepphoreans earned their living from crafts and trade, including textiles. For a short time under the Umayyads they minted copper coins. No doubt some were involved in providing services to travelers and especially to pilgrims, as the town was located along major routes, with sites of interest to Muslims, Christians, and Jews. At first, the Muslims were not a majority, but the Muslim population grew in size as the old families converted to Islam. Nevertheless, Sepphoris and its district did not lose its multireligious character until after the Crusader period. The Crusaders recognized Sepphoris as a site of some strategic and religious importance with a small fortified citadel and a church; it was one of sixteen *bourgs* in the Latin Kingdom and a major staging point for war in 1187. Yet the civilian population in the village clearly remained quite small. Its population seems to have increased in the early Ottoman period, and in the eighteenth century, Ḍāhir al-ᶜUmar accorded it some secondary strategic importance. Yet it never again attained the prominence it had held in late Roman and Byzantine times.

NOTES

1. For introductions to these tribes, see articles on each in the *Encyclopaedia of Islam* (Leiden, 1960–). Moshe Gil, *A History of Palestine 634–1099* (Cambridge, England, 1992), sections 16–26, discusses the buffer states and discounts "semitic" sentiment for the Arabs in pre-Islamic Palestine.

2. Muhammad was hired by Khadīja to lead a caravan to Syria and Palestine when he was twenty-five years old, in approximately 595. According to Theophanes, writing sometime after 813, Muhammad lived among both Jews and Christians while he was in Palestine looking for sacred writings. Muhammad's reliance on Jews and especially Christians may be part of Theophanes's anti-Muslim polemic, but the notion reflects the nature of pre-Islamic business contacts in the area. See Harry Turtledove, trans., *The Chronicle of Theophanes* (Philadelphia, 1982), 35.

3. On the Gaza links of Muhammad's grandfather, great-grandfather, and the latter's brother, see references in Gil, *Palestine*, section 18. Also see references in n. 4.

4. Aḥmad ibn Ḥanbal, *Musnad* (Cairo, 1948), 74:75. See Patricia Crone, *Meccan Trade and the Rise of Islam* (Princeton, 1987), 102.

5. See the brief discussion of this story by Gil, *Palestine*, section 2, n. 3, and in an article by Michael Lecker, "Links between Qurashīs and Jewish Women," *Jerusalem Studies in Arabic and Islam* 10 (1987): 19–20. I am grateful to Professor Lecker for bringing this article to my attention. In addition to the references given there, note a reference to Sepphorean pagans by the ninth-century historian al-Ṭabarī, *Tarikh al-rusul wal-mulūk* (Cairo, 1960–1977), 6:349/2:1075 (in Arabic), trans. Martin Hinds, *the Zenith of the Marwanid House*, vol. 23 (Albany, 1990), 22–23.

6. Hinds, *Zenith*, 25.

7. See Lecker, "Links," 18 on the pejorativeness of being Ibn al-Yahūdiyya. Similar remarks on the low social status of descendants of unfree Jewish women were made by Crone, *Meccan Trade*, 102, n. 70.

8. See Yehudah Neeman, *Sepphoris in the Days of the Second Temple, Mishnah and Talmud* (Jerusalem, 1993), 53–55 (in Hebrew). "Diocaesarea" was of course pagan in origin, dating from the days of Hadrian in the early second century c.e. On the history of the introduction of this term, and for an overview of this period of history at Sepphoris, see Stuart Miller's essay on Hellenistic and Roman Sepphoris in this catalogue.

9. For maps of the Persian-Byzantine wars, noting cities that opened their gates to the Persians, see Haim Beinart, ed., *Atlas of Medieval Jewish History* (New York, 1992), 18.

10. Al-Balādhurī, *Futūḥ al-Buldān* (Leiden, 1866), 115f. For additional sources on the conquest of this region, see Gil, *Palestine*, 57.

11. As is typical, there is some slight variation in the dates reported by Arab historians; most historians reconstruct the conquest of Galilee to 635. To reconcile the various sources, Fred McGraw Donner, in *The Early Islamic Conquests* (Princeton, 1981), suggests that Damascus and other locales changed hands several times, but he does not suggest this for Galilee. For other sources, see Gil, *Palestine*, section 56f., and Donner, 112ff.

12. Evidence of fire damage was pointed out to me by Zeev Weiss during a site visit.

13. Other sources date the Year of Ashes a year or two earlier. Donner, *Conquests*, 152 and 245; 322, n. 286 (mostly on plague). Gil, *Palestine*, section 74. Theophanes, *Chronicle*, 35, dates an earthquake to 632/633.

14. See Donner, *Conquests*, 245–48, on settlement policies in the region.

15. See Donner, *Conquests*, 247, on the disinterest of Iraqis in the details of conquests in Syria. Gil, *Palestine*, throughout, also mentions the paucity of the sources.

16. Both Ibn Taghrī Birdī, *al-Nujūm al-Zāhira fī mulūk Miṣr wal-Qāhira* (Cairo, 1929–56), 1:177, and Ibn al-Athīr, *al-Kāmil fī al-Taʾrīkh* (Cairo, 1886), 4:416f., report that one Samīr or Sumayr the Jew minted silver coins for ʿAbd al-Malik; he appears to have been associated with the court of the Umayyad governor in Iraq, Hajjāj b. Yūsuf. It is tempting to suggest but hard to determine if the designation of a mint at Sepphoris reflects the continuity of a Jewish community there.

17. Yaʿakov Meshorer, *The City Coins of Eretz-Israel and the Decapolis in the Roman Period* (Jerusalem, 1984).

18. Catherine S. Bunnel, "Catalogue of the Coins," in Leroy Waterman et al., *Preliminary Report of the University of Michigan Excavations at Sepphoris, Palestine, in 1931* (Ann Arbor, 1937), 77, coins 387–90.

19. Site visits; Eric M. Meyers, Carol L. Meyers, and Ehud Netzer, *Sepphoris* (Winona Lake, 1992), 9.

20. Tsvika Tsuk, *Tsippori ve-atareha* (Jerusalem, 1987), 117.

21. Elkan N. Adler, *Jewish Travelers in the Middle Ages*, repr. ed. (Dover, N.Y., 1987), 86.

22. See Jacob Mann, *The Jews in Egypt and Palestine and Palestine under the Fatimid Cailphs*, repr. ed. (New York, 1970), 2:357; see also comments of Gil, *Palestine,* para. 323, n. 89.

23. Gil, *Palestine,* para. 323, n. 89.

24. Gil, *Eretz Yisrael bi-tekufah ha-Muslemit ha-rishona, 634–1099* (Tel Aviv, 1983), document 190, a 14 (2:325ff.), dates this document to 1039.

25. I surveyed several indexed biographical dictionaries as well as the two most comprehensive dictionaries of *nisba* titles, ʿIzz al-Dīn Ibn al-Athīr's *al-Lubāb fī tahdhīb al-ansāb* (Beirut, 1972) and al-Samʿānī's *al-Ansāb* (Beirut, 1988).

26. Al-Yaʿqūbī, *Al-Buldān* (Beirut, 1988), 88–89; trans. Gaston Wiet, *Les Pays* (Cairo, 1937), 327–28 of Arabic.

27. Yāqūt, *Muʿjam al-Buldān*, ed. Ferdinand Wüstenfeld (Leipzig, 1866–73), under the word.

28. Abū ʿUbayd al-Bakrī, *Kitāb Muʿjam mā istaʿjam,* ed. Ferdinand Wüstenfeld (Göttingen and Paris, 1876–77), vol. 2, 609. This passage was cited in Simcha Assaf and Leo A. Mayer, *Sefer ha-yishuv,* vol. 2 (From the Arab Conquest to the Crusades) (Jerusalem, 1944), 53 (in Hebrew).

29. For example, it is not found in the works of Ibn Ḥawkal *(Sūrat al-Arḍ),* al-Muqaddasī, and al-Istakhrī, published, translated, and indexed by M. J. [Michael Jan] de Goeje, *Indices, Glossarium, et addenda et emendanda,* Bibliotheca Geographorum Arabicorum, 4 (Leiden, 1879).

30. On Mary in Islam, see A. J. Wensinck [Penelope Johnstone], "Maryam," in *Encyclopaedia of Islam,* vol. 2, and the Qurʾān: 3:31–42, 29:1–35, 23:52.

31. This suggestion was made, for example, by Janine Sourdel-Thomine, editor and translator of ʿAlī al-Harawī, *K. Al-Ishārāt ilā maʿrifat al-ziyārāt* (Damascus, 1953), 21, 96; translation (Damascus, 1957), 54, n. 4–5.

32. Tzvi Hirsch Edelman, ed., *Kaftor va-Feraḥ* (Berlin, 1852), 48b.

33. Jonah and Hiyya are identified by Benjamin of Tudela and, based on identifications by other travelers, may have been located near, rather than in, Sepphoris. On the Daughters of Jacob, see Nahman Avigad, *"Kever Bnot Yaakov* near Sepphoris," *Eretz Israel* 11 (1973): 41–44 (in Hebrew), and Eleazer L. Sukenik, "Some Remains of Sepphoris," *Tarbiz* 3 (1932): 107–9 (in Hebrew).

34. Isaac b. al-Farrā of Malaga (1441); see Abraham Yaʿari, *Masaot Eretz Yisrael shel Olim Yehudim* (Tel Aviv, 1946), 109f. Isaac found the graves of Reuven, Simeon, Levi, Judah, Dina, and Benjamin, "all guarded by non-Jews."

35. See n. 22.

36. Mujīr al-Dīn al-ʿUlaymī, *Al-Uns al-Jalīl* (Cairo, 1866), 284.

37. P. H. [Percy Howard] Newby, *Saladin in His Time* (Boston, 1983), 113ff., totals 13,200 knights, turcopoliers, and infantry. Steven Runcimann, *History of the Crusades,* vol. 2 (Cambridge, England, 1952), 439, reconstructs an earlier assemblage of Crusader forces at Sepphoris, in 1183.

38. Al-ʿUlaymī, *Al-Uns*, 287.

39. Al-ʿUlaymī, *Al-Uns*, 318, reports that Saladin *tarak al-athqāl bi-arḍ Ṣaffūriyya*: "he left buried treasures in the land of Sepphoris." *Athqāl* is sometimes used to refer to the human dead buried in the earth.

40. ʿImad al-Dīn al-Kātib al-Iṣfahānī, *al-Fatḥ al-qussī fī al-fatḥ al-qudsī;* see Carl Landberg, ed., *Conquête de la Syrie et de la Palestine* (Leiden, 1888), 33.

41. Meron Benveniste, *Crusaders in the Holy Land* (Jerusalem, 1970), 260ff.

42. John Wilkinson, *Jerusalem Pilgrimage 1099–1185* (London, 1981), 64, 319.

43. Benveniste, *Crusaders*, 260, and Joshua Prawer, *The Latin Kingdom of Jerusalem* (London, 1972), 368.

44. Described in Muṣṭafā Murād al-Dabbāgh, *Bilāduna Filasṭīn* (Kafr Qarʿ, 1988), 7:2, pp. 93ff.

45. Meir Benayahu, "Was There Jewish Settlement in Sepphoris after the Talmud?" *Melilah* 3–4 (1949/50): 103–9 (in Hebrew). Benayahu counters the suggestion of Baruch Toledano, "Jewish Settlement in Sepphoris 1525–1874," *Tarbiz* 17 (1946): 190–93 (in Hebrew).

46. For a study of the career of Ḍāhir al-ʿUmar (Ẓāhir al-ʿUmar al-Zaydānī), see Aḥmad Hasan Joudah, *Revolt in Palestine in the Eighteenth Century* (Princeton, 1987).

47. Tsuk, *Tsippori ve-atareha*, 32.

The Crusader Period

and the Church of Saint Anne at Sepphoris

Jaroslav Folda

The Crusader church of Saint Anne is located on the west side of the Sepphoris hill where the medieval village, known to the European Crusaders as Le Sephorie, was situated, on the main route between the port of Acre (Akko) and the town of Nazareth.[1] Sepphoris is perhaps best known from Crusader times as the well-watered campsite from which, on 2 July 1187, the Crusader army marched to meet catastrophic defeat two days later at the Horns of Hattin by the forces of the Ayyubid sultan Saladin.

Sepphoris was originally conquered by the Crusaders when Tancred, nephew of Bohemund of Antioch, established himself in the region of Galilee after the capture of Jerusalem in July 1099. The Latin Kingdom of Jerusalem was established in December 1100 with the coronation of Baldwin I as its first king. By the middle of the twelfth century its territory had grown to include land from Beirut to ᶜAqaba and from the Mediterranean coast to the east bank of the Jordan River and the Dead Sea. Although overshadowed as a town and a Christian holy site by its larger and more important neighbor,

Nazareth, Sepphoris appears to have been held by the Crusaders continuously until Saladin overran the Latin Kingdom in 1187, following the aforementioned battle of Hattin on 4 July. Sepphoris returned to Crusader hands by treaty, apparently as part of the corridor of access to Nazareth, negotiated by the German emperor, Frederick II, in 1229. According to the medieval chronicler Geoffroy de Beaulieu, in March 1251 King Louis IX of France visited the village—and no doubt the church—on his pilgrimage to Nazareth. The village, the springs, the church of Saint Anne, and the Crusader citadel at Sepphoris all fell in April 1263 to the powerful Mamluk sultan an-Nasir Rukn-ad-Din Baybars, who wreaked destruction on captured Christian churches as a matter of policy.

The medieval village claimed the mother of the Virgin Mary as its own; Latin pilgrims' accounts, for example that of Fretellus, written in 1137, or that of Theodorich, written circa 1173, tell us that: "Blessed Anna, the mother of the mother of Christ came from Sepphoris."[2] And according to some, such as John of Würzburg (c. 1165), Sepphoris was the birthplace of the Virgin Mary by her mother, Saint Anne, wife of Joachim. Tradition starting with the sixth century also held that the Virgin Mary had lived there as a child.[3] The Piacenza pilgrim (c. 570) refers to relics of the Virgin Mary he saw in Sepphoris (Byzantine Diocaesarea): ". . . we venerated what they said was the flagon and the bread-basket of St.

fig. 40   General view of the east end of the Church of Saint Anne at Sepphoris. Visible are the triple arches of the central apse and its choir bay, the shallow south apse, and the entrance to the north room, which was walled up in modern times. The floor of the central apse consists of a rough outcropping of bedrock. A modern second story rises above the twelfth-century arches.
Photo: Sepphoris Regional Project

fig. 41   Aerial view of the Church of Saint Anne at Sepphoris.
Photo: Joint Sepphoris Project

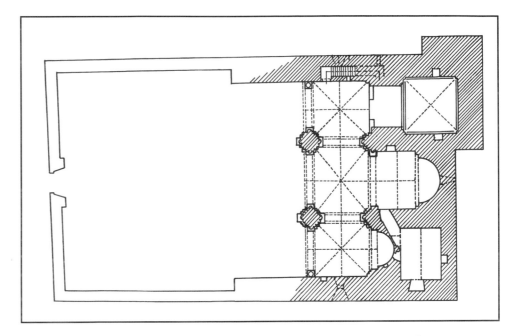

fig. 42   Plan of the Church of Saint Anne at Sepphoris.
Courtesy: R. Denys Pringle and Peter E. Leach

Mary."[4] From these relics the belief apparently arose that Mary had lived at Sepphoris as a girl, a tradition known in the twelfth century and accepted by some but doubted by others.

After the Crusader period, the Church of Saint Anne again became a focus of attention when the Franciscans began organizing pilgrimage visits to Sepphoris from Nazareth about 1600. In 1639 Francesco Quaresmius specified that the church, built of ashlar masonry (*quadratis lapidus*), was situated on the site where the house (*domus*) of Joachim had stood.[5] However, because the specific identification of the house of Joachim and Anna with the Church of Saint Anne at Sepphoris first appears in these seventeenth-century sources, the association between the two may be a postmedieval development derived from circumstantial evidence.

The Crusader Church of Saint Anne originally contained a wide central nave (the main longitudinal space for the congregation) with two side aisles. The nave and aisles were four or five bays in length, a bay being the spatial unit defined by four pier supports. The complex eastern end, which survives to the height of the apses and vaulted rooms, consists of two apsidal terminations semicircular in plan and vaulted with a half dome: a large central apse and a smaller apse on the south side. Behind the south apse, in the southeast corner of the church, is a rectangular room. On the northeast side of the church is a square vaulted room without an apse.[6]

The central apse is the focal point of the eastern end: it is announced by the highest, largest arch, has a rectangular choir space for the clergy in front of it, approximately 4 meters deep with exposed bedrock at the floor level one meter high in its rear half, and a small, very deeply splayed round-arched window midway up the center of its semicircular wall. By contrast, the smaller apse to the south side is very shallow, apparently to allow space in the fabric of the building for a hidden room of some 4 x 3 meters behind it. There is no apse on the north side but a high-vaulted room approximately 5 meters square. The squared-off exterior of the eastern end has rectangular projections in the northeast corner, where the wall was thickened to support a tower. A modern second story was apparently built onto the eastern end by the Franciscans some time after 1870, when they acquired the property with the church, which still belongs to the Franciscan Custody of the Holy Land. However, the orphanage of the Sisters of Saint Anne, founded near the church in 1924, holds the keys.[7]

Other than the apses and vaulted rooms, very little of the original church remains. The bases of two composite piers in the nave exist along with the bases and two fragmentary column shafts on the side walls that define the first bay of the nave and side aisles. Small portions of the original walls, ashlar-faced with rubble fill, enclose the first bay to the height of the apsidal arches. Small, deeply splayed round-arched windows pierce these walls on both the north and south sides above the stringcourse molding.

West of the first bay, the church precinct is defined by a lower modern wall, probably built in 1879 on the foundation courses of the original church exterior wall but without reproducing its original thickness.[8] A single western entrance near the place where remains of the original western wall were located defines the approximate length of the nave and gives access to the church enclosure, where a number of fallen column segments, capitals, and bases have been arranged to separate the nave from the aisles. Some of these fragments must have been used in the engaged columns of the aisles or as parts of other nave piers, but among them there are also some pieces that may not have belonged to the church originally and probably were brought from elsewhere in the village.

If the modern enclosure corresponds to the original plan of the building, the basic dimensions of the Crusader church would be approximately 37 meters in length and around 22 meters in width, with aisle bays roughly 5 meters square. Thus the church was medium sized by Crusader standards but *very* large for a parish church in a village the size of Sepphoris. The original walls are about 2.25 meters thick on the north and south sides; the composite pier bases, 2 meters square. The main apse rises some 10 meters to the top of its slightly pointed arch.

The surviving parts of the church are built of small ashlar (even-faced rectangular stone) masonry with material that must have come from a local source, although the location of the quarry is not known. As is often the case in Crusader building,

there is some evidence of reused material, but much of the stone, in contrast to that in the citadel at Sepphoris, was newly quarried and exhibits the typical Crusader characteristic of diagonally striated dressing derived from the tool, either an ax or less often a chisel, used to cut the stone. The masonry however, lacks the masonry marks often found on Crusader work. This may indicate that local Arab or Templar stonemasons rather than recently arrived westerners were employed.[9] (Templars were members of a monastic military order founded in Palestine to protect pilgrims to the holy places.) In contrast, the architectural design seems closely related to other well-known Crusader churches, although no single parallel offers every special feature found in the church at Sepphoris.

Because the site of the church has yet to be fully excavated, questions of dating and of the possibility of earlier Byzantine-period churches or Roman-period synagogues cannot be answered. However, excavations conducted early in the twentieth century by the Franciscan archaeologist Prosper Viaud uncovered mosaics with Aramaic inscriptions under the original north wall of the Crusader building, indicating that the church was built partly over an early synagogue.[10] These mosaics were apparently covered or destroyed by the construction of the Crusader church, and there are no other identifiable reused materials from the synagogue.

The rectangular plan of the Church of Saint Anne at Sepphoris is comparable to the church at Abu Ghosh (west of Jerusalem) built for the Hospitallers, the monastic order of Saint John of the Hospital of Jerusalem, established to care for pilgrims to the Holy Land; its size and proportions are similar to those of the Church of Saint Anne in Jerusalem; and its architectural articulation is similar to the Crusader churches at Tortosa (Tartus in Syria) and Ramla (near Lydda). Some of its other characteristics are quite unique or at best indirectly parallel to certain aspects of the Church of Notre Dame at Tortosa. One unusual feature is that although the eastern end of the church at Sepphoris has the standard three arches facing the nave and aisles, there are only two apses as such. The greatly thickened walls on the north side with a squarish, originally groin-

fig. 43 The north wall of the Church of Saint Anne as seen from the nave. Although a modern door has been cut into the north wall, the deeply splayed window of the first bay is preserved.

vaulted (arched masonry consisting of intersecting barrel vaults) room seem to indicate that a tower was intended above this room, which may have served as a sacristy or place for the clergy to vest and prepare for the liturgy even though it does not communicate directly with the central apse. Such towers were often used for bells, as at the Holy Sepulchre (c. 1149) in Jerusalem, at the Church of the Nativity (c. 1160s) in Bethlehem, and possibly at the church of Notre Dame Tortosa (after c. 1150). Towers were useful also as lookouts on fortified buildings.

A second curious feature of the church at Sepphoris is the small room located behind the apse on the southeastern side. Today there is a medium-

sized rectangular window for that room in the wall of the south apse, a window that presumably was added in modern times. In the Crusader period this room apparently communicated directly only with the central choir through an opening just behind the engaged columns on the south side. This small opening—one has to bend down to get through it— is paired with a niche on the opposite wall of the choir. Neither the entry nor the niche are easily visible from the nave, and the entry is high above the level of the floor of the apse at that point.[11] These features suggest that it was not to be used for regular ceremonial access and thus probably was not intended as a sacristy. Given its somewhat hidden character, in that its entrance could be masked as one of a pair of niches in the choir, and its small size, it is not unreasonable to suspect that this room served as a treasury for precious relics or valuables.

The third unusual feature of the eastern end is found in the main apse and choir itself. Just behind the points where the niche on the north side and the entry on the south side are located, the present "floor" of the choir rises approximately one meter with the presence of roughly dressed bedrock and extends into the apse behind. The retention of exposed bedrock within a Crusader church can indicate a holy site of special importance, as with the Holy Sepulchre and the hill of Calvary in Jerusalem or the grottoes of the Annunciation in Nazareth and the Nativity in Bethlehem. At Sepphoris the rock perhaps was intended to mark the traditional site of the house (*domus*) of Joachim and Anna, where the Virgin Mary was believed to have been born and raised. A similar claim was made for the grotto under the Church of Saint Anne in Jerusalem. Such multiple attributions for the same event occasionally arose as the Crusaders attempted to locate where in the Holy Land the events of the life of Christ and his mother had taken place. There is no evidence other than the existence of the rock for the identification of this spot with Mary's childhood home. Thus this identification is highly speculative. However, if we entertain the respective merits of the two sites as the place of Mary's birth, what would have distinguished Sepphoris from Jerusalem was the former's direct accessibility: the visiting pilgrim could see the rock

fig. 44 The "floor" of roughly dressed bedrock in the choir and central apse of the church may have been intended to mark the traditional site of the house of Joachim and Anna, where the Virgin Mary was believed to have been born and raised.
Photo: Lindsey Bute

immediately behind the high altar. Furthermore, the proximity of Sepphoris to Nazareth, where Mary lived with Joseph, also would have added authenticity to the identification of this place with the house of Joachim, Anna, and the child Mary. Indeed, the rebuilding of the Church of the Annunciation in Nazareth in the 1170s, with its grotto of the house of the Virgin, may well have been contemporary with the construction of the Church of Saint Anne in Sepphoris and thus may have stimulated the identification of the latter as a holy site.

Despite the lack of written sources to document the history of the church, we can feel fairly certain that it was dedicated to Saint Anne in the Crusader period. Sometime after Tancred conquered Galilee for the Crusaders, the holy sites of Nazareth and Sepphoris were recognized, and in due course new

churches were constructed. At Nazareth a Crusader church was erected immediately after 1099 and later was enlarged, probably after 1170. The church at Sepphoris also was constructed probably in the later years of the twelfth century. Because it was a large parish church (apparently dedicated to the holy site alone without the additional function of being the seat of a Latin bishop), a date after the earthquake in Galilee in 1170 would be a reasonable possibility for its erection. Certainly the inclination of European scholars to date the church in line with earlier developments in the West, as per comparisons with churches in Burgundy (France) or in Apulia (Italy), must be resisted in favor of an assessment based on the Crusader context of the second half of the twelfth century. The richly decorative style of mature Crusader Levantine-Romanesque churches with which Saint Anne's at Sepphoris can be compared provides the most substantial visual evidence for this proposition.

At the time of the construction of the Sepphoris church, the architect and the patron, who may possibly have been a Templar, no doubt knew of the church of Saint Anne in Jerusalem; similarities in the size and the proportions of the two churches, therefore, can hardly be accidental. Because it apparently was important that the church at Sepphoris be distinct in some way, a few of the main features of the Jerusalem church, such as the dome over the crossing, the transepts, and the underground grotto, were omitted.[12] In keeping with the tradition that Sepphoris was the birthplace of both Anna and Mary, and because of the proximity of the church to Nazareth, the rock in the choir and apse probably marked in some way the site, within the church, of the earlier house of Joachim and Anna.

When Sepphoris fell to Saladin in 1187, although Christian access to the site was cut off, the church was not damaged. Later, after the successful negotiations of Frederick II in 1229 and Richard of Cornwall in 1241, pilgrims could once again visit Sepphoris on their way to and from Nazareth. In the mid-1260s Sepphoris was again lost to the Crusaders when Baybars conquered Galilee. Nazareth was taken, and its Church of the Annunciation was largely destroyed; presumably at this time the Church of Saint Anne also was destroyed. Later pilgrims and travelers consistently mention the eastern end as the sole element to survive.[13] Thus the fragment of the church that is visible today, with the exception of the second story and walled enclosure added by the Franciscans, likely is the church that Baybars left in ruins circa 1263.

NOTES

1. I would like to express my warm thanks to R. Denys Pringle (Edinburgh) for making many valuable suggestions and for generously sharing his rich material on the Crusader church. Pringle's corpus of Crusader churches in progress, *The Churches of the Crusader Kingdom of Jerusalem*, of which vol. 1 has appeared (Cambridge, England, 1993), will include an entry (no. 196) on the Church of Saint Anne at Sepphoris in vol. 2, which is forthcoming. I am, of course, responsible for the views presented in this discussion. See also my earlier discussions of this church: *The Art of the Crusaders in the Holy Land: 1098–1187* (Cambridge, England, 1995), 320–21, and "The Church of Saint Anne," *Biblical Archaeologist* 54 (1991): 88–96.

2. Rorgo Fretellus, *Descripcio cuiusdam de locis sanctis*, in *Rorgo Fretellus de Nazareth*, ed. P. C. Boeren (Amsterdam, Oxford, New York, 1980), p. 25, chap. 37: "Ex Sephori beata Anna mater matris Ihesu." See also *The Work on Geography*, and Theoderic, in John Wilkinson, *Jerusalem Pilgrimage: 1099–1185* (London, 1988), 193, 313.

3. John of Würzburg, *Descriptio Terrae Sanctae*, in *Peregrinationes Tres: Saewulf, Iohannes Wirziburgensis, Theodericus*, ed. R. B. C. Huygens, Corpus Christianorum, Continuatio Mediaevalis, 139 (Turnhout, 1994), 80–81.

4. For the Piacenza pilgrim see John Wilkinson, *Jerusalem Pilgrims before the Crusades* (Warminster, 1977), 79, 155. See also the comments on references to the various pilgrims' accounts referring to the association of Sepphoris with the family of Joachim and Anna in Wilkinson, *Jerusalem Pilgrimage*, 61, 245 n. 1, lines 111–12, 313, and 319.

5. Francesco Quaresmius, *Historica Theologica et Moralis Terrae Sanctae Elucidatio*, vol. 2 (Antwerp, 1639; ed. C. Tarvisio and republished in Venice, 1881), 852.

6. The *Survey of Western Palestine* reproduces a tiny sketch plan that suggests that the southeast rectangular room may have been rebuilt since Conder and Kitchener inspected it in the 1870s. See C. R. Conder and H. H. Kitchener, *The Survey of Western Palestine*, vol. 1, *Galilee* (London, 1881), 335. The plan followed here is that of R. Denys Pringle and Peter E. Leach, who see the southeastern corner of the church as original to the first story.

7. Bellarmino Bagatti, *Antichi Villaggi Cristiani di Galilea* (Jerusalem, 1971), 118–19. A photograph taken in 1873 by the Palestine Exploration Fund shows the eastern end with no second story and the nave occupied by village houses, so the rebuilding must have been done after that.

8. Bagatti, *Antichi Villaggi Cristiani di Galilea*; note, however, that Edward Robinson, *Later Biblical Researches in Palestine*, 2d ed. (Boston, 1857), 111–12, refers to wall building already in 1852.

9. R. D. Pringle, "Some Approaches to the Study of Crusader Masonry Marks in Palestine," *Levant* 13 (1981): 173–99, and Sabino de Sandoli, *Corpus Inscriptionum Crucesignatorum Terrae Sanctae* (Jerusalem, 1974), xliv–xlvii and *passim*. Pringle points out (176–77) that such marks, judging from the evidence where they appear elsewhere, could have been used by non-Western, non-Frankish masons, such as Greeks, Armenians, and Arabs, but it is also possible that a team of local masons from Sepphoris or nearby worked on this church and used no marks at all, or at least none that is visible. The lack of masonry marks appears to reflect a situation in which they were not needed, whoever the masons were. It is possible, for example, that Saint Anne's at Sepphoris was a parish church sponsored by the Templars, and perhaps the masons belonged to that order. I am indebted also to my colleague Caroline Bruzelius of the American Academy in Rome for discussing masonry marks with me.

10. Prosper Viaud, *Nazareth et ses deux Églises de l'Annonciation et du Saint Joseph d'apres les fouilles récentes* (Paris, 1910), 179–84, with a study of the mosaics by Charles Clermont-Ganneau, 185–91.

11. The current level of the "floor" of the nave is not the original twelfth-century level but somewhat lower; when Viaud excavated here he apparently dug through the medieval floor to get down to the wall footings.

12. Given that we know nothing certain about the configuration of the church to the west of the extant cruciform piers, it is possible that the Church of Saint Anne at Sepphoris had a dome and/or inscribed transepts, as at Saint Anne's in Jerusalem, or a dome like that of the church at Jacob's Well east of Nablus, or inscribed transepts like those at Sebaste northwest of Nablus. On the other hand, until we are shown otherwise, it is reasonable to assume that the church at Sepphoris was designed to be distinct from that of Saint Anne in Jerusalem in certain ways in order to help establish its identity. Therefore, it probably was four or five bays long with no dome or transepts.

13. See Robinson, *Later Biblical Researches*, 111–12. The Church of Saint Anne at Sepphoris was not the only church to survive Mamluk or natural destruction with only the apse end remaining. The most famous extant example near Sepphoris is the Cathedral of Tyre; see Camille Enlart, *Les Monuments des Croises*, vol. 2 (Paris, 1926), pl. 149, fig. 472.

Some Mosaics and Buildings
of Sepphoris

The Dionysos Mosaic

Carol L. Meyers, Eric M. Meyers, Ehud Netzer, and Zeev Weiss

The largest and most splendid of the rooms in the palatial Roman building discovered adjacent to the theater is its large reception hall, or *triclinium.*[1] The grandeur of this room derives from its spaciousness and its airy views of the peristyle (colonnaded) courtyard to the south but especially from the stunning mosaic, about 9.0 meters by 7.0 meters in size, covering its floor. Other rooms in the building contain tessellated floors—some with no design, others with brightly colored floral or geometric patterns—but the *triclinium* mosaic with its vivid mythological and natural scenes relating to the popular god Dionysos offers exceptional beauty. Laid early in the third century C.E., it remained virtually intact, except for a repair or renovation at its southern end, until the building was destroyed in the fourth century, probably as a result of the earthquake of 363 C.E.

The arrangement of the floor is typical of Roman period *triclinia*: an undecorated (except for a thin black border) white section forms a U-shape around a decorated T-shaped section formed of varying sized tesserae (tiles) of twenty-three different colors. The decorated section itself consists of three parts: the Dionysos panels, the acanthus leaf medallions, and the processional panels.

---

fig. 45 **A nude youth with bow-and-arrow and a "portrait" of a beautiful woman, the so-called Mona Lisa of Galilee, from the acanthus scroll border of the Dionysos mosaic.**
Photo: Gabi Laron

The Dionysos Panels

The central part of the colored mosaic is a large rectangle subdivided into fifteen panels depicting the life of the Greek god Dionysos.[2] As the last god to become an Olympian, Dionysos (or Bacchus, as the Romans knew him) was a popular deity among both Greeks and Romans. His mythology is complex, but perhaps its most outstanding feature is his linkage with the grapevine and wine, making him a god of revelry, feasting, drunkenness, and ecstasy. Closely related to his association with the grapevine is his role as a god of fecundity and fertility for both animals and vegetation.

Eleven of the central panels, and half of a twelfth, have escaped serious damage. Their good state of preservation, along with a Greek inscription in each, allows the scenes to be well understood. The panels depict various episodes in the life of Dionysos and also rituals or ceremonies that celebrated this god in Greco-Roman religion. The central panel, the largest of the fifteen, contains a scene well known from other Dionysos mosaics. It depicts the gods Herakles (Latin name Hercules) and Dionysos, whose names constitute the inscription, engaged in a Drinking Contest, or Symposium, an appropriate representation in a room used for banquets. Two other panels, both labeled ΜΕΘΗ (Drunkenness), depict the results of the Drinking Contest. Both Dionysos and Herakles are inebriated; the former is

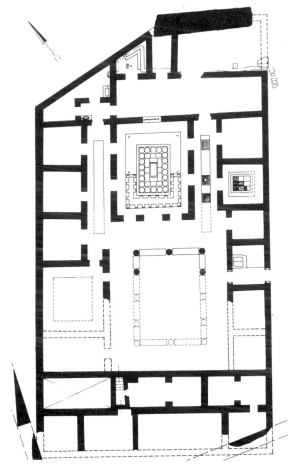

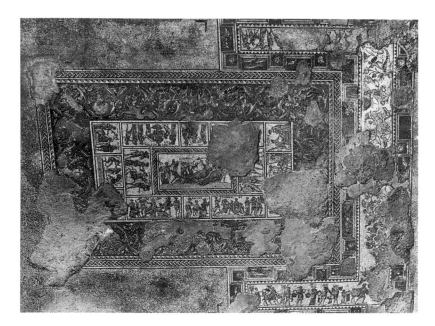

fig. 47 An overview of the mosaic floor of the *triclinium*. The central rectangle is divided into fifteen individual panels with Dionysiac scenes and surrounded by a border of acanthus leaf medallions. The acanthus border is framed in turn by a U-shaped border of processional panels and a Nilotic scene on the southern end. *Photo: Gabi Laron*

fig. 46 Plan of the Dionysos mosaic building showing the location of the *triclinium* (reception hall) mosaic, near the top center of the plan. *Courtesy: Hebrew University Expedition*

still in control of himself, but the latter is sprawled on the ground while being partially supported by a *maenad* (female devotee) and a satyr.

Another group of panels preserves vignettes of the god's life story. His childhood, for example, is represented in a scene labeled ΔΙΟΝΥCΟΥ ΛΟΥΤΡΑ (Bathing of Dionysos), in which the nymphs of Mount Nyssa, who raised Dionysos after his mother, Semele, was killed by the jealous Hera (whose husband, Zeus, was Dionysos's father), give the infant god his bath. Another, showing him as a young boy seated on a goat, supported by one woman and led by another, probably represents part of the Education of Dionysos. His young adulthood is marked by a panel labeled ΠΟΜΠΗ (Procession) and showing him in his chariot, returning triumphantly from a trip to India. His wedding to

fig. 48 A damaged panel showing the triumphal procession (ΠΟΜΠΗ) of Dionysos returning from his conquest of India. The god, riding in a chariot, holds his *thrysos* (sacred staff) in his right hand. One of the satyrs (male followers of Dionysos) accompanying him plays a double flute.
Photo: Gabi Laron

fig. 49 Panel portraying the drunkenness (MEΘH) of Herakles after his defeat in a drinking contest with Dionysos. The bearded hero is assisted by a *maenad* (female devotee) and a male follower of Dionysos. His club rests on the table at the left.
Photo: Gabi Laron

Ariadne appears in a large panel bearing the inscription YMENAIOC (Marriage): the seated bride and groom are surrounded by four attendants, and a small *eros* figure is crowning the god with a wreath.

A number of other panels also apparently relate to the cult of Dionysos. One labeled ΠΟΙΜΝΑΙ (Shepherds) shows a seated figure milking a goat and flanked by two figures watching the milking—a *maenad* holding the *thrysos* or the sacred staff of Dionysos and a male figure wearing the tunic and boots that initiates to the god's cult sometimes wore. Another shows four figures, one a centaur, in procession and is labeled ΔωΡΟΦΟΡΟΙ (Gift-bearers). One other lively scene shows three satyrs surrounded by grapevines and busily involved in an activity labeled ΛHNOBATE (Treading the Grapes). Another panel depicts two *maenads*, one of them playing the *aulos* (double flute), and a satyr and is labeled KωMOC (Joy).

Tho Acanthus Leaf Medallions

Surrounding the Dionysos panels is an elaborate rectangular frame containing twenty-two medallions formed by intertwining acanthus leaves. Unlike the central rectangle, which has white tesserae as its background, the charming polychrome flora and fauna of the frame are set against a black background. Hunting scenes depicting a variety of wild animals chased by naked *erotes*, or cupids, are found within the medallions. Various species of brightly colored birds occupy the spaces between them.

This full and animated composition, set off by a double geometric border, serves to highlight the two female busts that appear, one in each of the central medallions on the short sides of the acanthus frame. The figure on the south side is severely damaged. But the northern one is the spectacular image that, when first uncovered, heralded the importance of the mosaic floor as a whole. It is a portrait of a beautiful woman, adorned with earrings and a laurel wreath. Because of the small naked figure poised with bow-and-arrow over her right shoulder, possibly representing *eros* (cupid), it has been conjectured that she is Aphrodite, goddess of love. That these armed figures appear throughout the medallions, however, make it more likely that they are simply hunters. Her identity is thus unknown. She has been dubbed the Mona Lisa of Galilee because, like the woman in Leonardo da Vinci's famous painting, her mysterious eyes seem to follow the viewer and her lips hint at a smile. The superb painterly qualities of this portrait and the timeless beauty of the woman surely place it among the masterpieces of ancient art.

fig. 50   The west border panel with a processional scene featuring eleven gift-bearing figures (six visible here), one of whom rides a donkey. The offerings, including baskets of fruit, floral garlands, ducks, and roosters, reinforce the association of Dionysos with fertility. *Photo: Gabi Laron*

Processional Panels

One long panel in the shape of the letter U surrounds the southern end of the central rectangle and its frame of acanthus volutes. Probably it featured one continuous procession when the mosaic was first laid. Parts of the procession were damaged at some point and then repaired. As a result, an entirely different scene now occupies the southern portion, and patches and undecorated areas appear on the eastern side. The western side is thus the best-preserved part of this third part of the Dionysos mosaic, all of

which is framed by a geometric border containing small panels with human heads (masks?) and groups of fish and birds.

Altogether nineteen human and animal figures occupy the eastern and western processional panels. Most of the humans—men, women, and children—are carrying items that would appear to be offerings: baskets laden with fruit, flower garlands, ducks, roosters. One woman plays the *aulos* (double flute). These people are apparently participating in a grand parade, resembling other artistic renderings of the cult of Dionysos, in honor of the god. Participants typically carry offerings from the products of the land as well as ritual or votive objects.

The replacement scene on the south is strikingly different in technique and context, although its white background links it with the east and west processional scenes as well as with the fifteen central panels. It features a Nilotic scene: the Nile River and a series of humans and animals, including a crocodile, set against the river's rich vegetation. The nude male figures are hunting the fauna of the Nile. This Egyptian scene, which contrasts starkly with the other elements of the Dionysos mosaic, strangely adumbrates the elaborate Nile scene in a mosaic laid at Sepphoris several centuries later.[3]

NOTES

1. For further discussion and description of the mosaic and its context see the following by Eric M. Meyers, Ehud Netzer, and Carol L. Meyers: "Artistry in Stone: The Mosaics of Ancient Sepphoris," *Biblical Archaeologist* 50 (1987): 223–31; "A Mansion in the Sepphoris Acropolis and Its Splendid Mosaic," *Qadmoniot* 21 (1988): 87–92 (in Hebrew); and *Sepphoris* (Winona Lake, 1992). For more about the building itself, see Zeev Weiss and Ehud Netzer's article on Sepphoris in the Roman period in this catalogue.

2. Sometimes spelled Dionysus. For additional attention to Dionysos as a theme in Late Roman mosaics, see Christine Kondoleon, *Domestic and Divine: Roman Mosaics in the House of Dionysos* (Ithaca, 1994), and Rena Talgam and Zeev Weiss, "'The Life of Dionysos' in the Mosaic Floor of Sepphoris," *Qadmoniot* 21 (1988): 93–99 (in Hebrew), and "The Dionysos Mosaic Floor of Sepphoris," in *VI Coloquio Internacional Sobre Mosaico Antiguo-Palencia-Mérida 1990* (Palencia, 1994), 231–37.

3. See the essay on the mosaics of the Nile festival building by Zeev Weiss and Ehud Netzer in this catalogue.

The Eastern Basilical Building

James F. Strange

Since 1987 the University of South Florida Excavations at Sepphoris has excavated a grand building on the east side of the site.[1] The building, about 40 x 60 meters in extent, occupied a single city block, with the main entrance and its four porches opening onto the *cardo* (the north-south commercial street) to the southeast. Unfortunately, some of the history and use of the building at its east end has been obscured by the remains of a bath that was built there in the Byzantine period. Nevertheless, it is clear that the basilical building occupied about 35 x 40 meters of the city block and that its porches occupied 25 x 40 meters of the same block.

The building was founded early in the first century C.E., perhaps as early as the turn of the century. The foundation of the south wall was actually a refounding on a preexisting wall. In this case the lowest course of foundation stones was cut to receive new stones with defined margins, "Herodian" stones. This same type of foundation, with stones dressed in the Herodian style, is visible at the east end of the building in the main facade, which borders on the sidewalk of the *cardo*. The presence of stones dressed in this fashion from early in the first century suggests that construction of the building may have begun under Herod Antipas, son of Herod the Great, who,

at his death in 4 B.C.E., bequeathed Galilee and Perea to Antipas. The completed structure went out of use and was entirely destroyed about the middle of the fourth century C.E. as a result of the Gallus Revolt against Rome in 351, the earthquake of 363, or both events.

The general plan of the building is basilical with porches. (A basilica is an oblong building typically containing both a broad central aisle, or nave, flanked by colonnaded side aisles and, at the end, a semicircular projection known as an apse. In Roman times basilicas were used for courts of justice or as places of public assembly.) In this instance, a row of columns on either side of the nave supported the stone beams upon which rested the clerestory (a horizontal row of windows in the upper wall) and the lofty roof. These columns rested on Attic bases without pedestals and had Ionic capitals. Glass from the clerestory windows was found scattered everywhere, especially at the western end of the building. Toward the end of the building's existence elaborate mosaic floors were laid in the central nave. Bright white mosaic floors, which augmented the available light from the clerestory windows, were laid elsewhere in the building. The white mosaics of the aisles featured black bands that seemed to direct foot traffic. These double bands led down the side aisles (on the north and south) and across an aisle near the west end of the building that extended from one side of the central area to the other.

fig. 51   Two details of the fresco panels from the eastern basilical building. The panels feature geometric designs, floral patterns, and birds.
Photos: Gabi Laron; Lucille A. Roussin

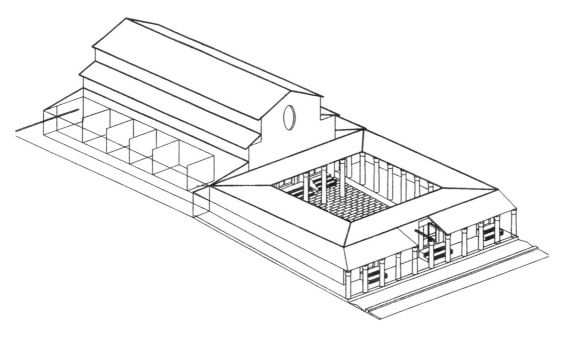

fig. 52 Reconstruction of the eastern basilical building, showing the main entrance and its four porches opening onto the *cardo* (main north-south street).
Courtesy: University of South Florida Expedition

A row of small rooms, shops, or offices lined the southern and northern sides of the building. Of those rooms that have been excavated so far, all but one contain elaborate mosaic floors in geometric patterns—a stepped, plastered pool rather than a geometric mosaic floor was discovered in one of the rooms—and mosaics in some of the rooms feature detailed representations of birds. These rooms did not open directly onto the street, as is the rule with shops attached to a basilica; they were accessible only from within the building. A long corridor, which may have been a service corridor for these rooms, separated them on the south from the south street.

Inconsistent with the building's basilical plan, there was no apse on the west wall,[2] which was founded deeply into the slope of the hill. The west end of the building did contain a special area, however; it was delimited on the south and north by the small rooms or shops, on the east by the columns

and white mosaic of the cross aisle, and on the west by the west wall of the building. This special area, which spanned the 24 meters across the western end of the basilical interior, did not serve as a tribunal (the raised seat of a judge), as it was not elevated above eye level. The actual space within the columns and the west wall is a virtual square, measuring about 11 meters north-south and 11.75 meters east-west. In the center of this space is an extraordinary mosaic depicting birds and fishes.[3] In the original use of the space, heavily plastered pools were situated to the north and south of the central mosaic. The pool on the south was equipped with two elaborate drains near the top of the pavement that surrounded it. Each pool was surrounded by six Attic columns with Ionic capitals in two rows of three each. The combination of pools, mosaic, frescoed walls, and columniation centered on the long axis of the building suggests that this may have been a special reception hall or a suite for entertaining, perhaps even an *oecus* (a reception room sometimes used also as a dining room) or dining hall.[4] When the building was renovated at the end of the third century or at the beginning of the fourth, the northern pool was filled in and a white mosaic with a black trellis pattern was installed—changes perhaps occasioned by a new administration with a new aesthetic.

Most of the walls (and some columns) within the building are covered with four layers of plaster. Layers one and three are white, but layers two and four feature spectacular fresco panels of green, red, orange, blue, and black or floral patterns, foliage, and birds. These panels resemble the plastered and painted walls of aristocratic residences of the third century C.E. The last painted layer, which is predominantly red, is similar to the painted rectangular panels on public buildings of the fourth century C.E. Together with the colored mosaic floors, these vivid frescoes must have lent a sumptuous aesthetic character to the building.

Between the columns of the central area east of the birds and fishes mosaic is another mosaic, this one principally a geometric pattern. One panel of

glass were simply swept into the drain. This is a valuable clue in trying to determine what took place inside the building, as discussed below.

Many long iron nails, probably from the roof beams that fell to the floor as a result of the destructions of the fourth century, were found on the floors everywhere inside of the building. Many bronze nails, about 3 to 7 centimeters long, also were found; these nails probably were from wooden furniture and

fig. 53 Details of geometric and floral designs from the birds and fishes mosaic in the eastern basilical building. *Photos: Gabi Laron*

this mosaic, oriented on the long axis of the building, shows a cityscape and a Greek inscription that reads "Good Luck."

The floor of the porch just inside the eastern facade of the building was a full two meters lower than that of the mosaic at the western end of the building. The floor of this area was also a mosaic, but only a fragment of a once-elaborate geometric pattern survives. The remains of cisterns with ceilings formed of Roman vaults were uncovered beneath this porch. Two of the cisterns were still in use in the medieval period, for the Fatimid Arabs built houses at this end of the ruined building.

Also discovered beneath the floors of the building were well-built drains, one of which can be traced for more than forty meters from a point near the west end of the north aisle to the eastern wall at the *cardo*. These drains still conduct water during the winter rains, and some of the most impressive individual finds, including fragments of thousands of glass vessels, have come from these otherwise concealed channels. Evidently breakage took place somewhere west of the north aisle, and the pieces of

shelving. Several hundred small, fourth-century, bronze coins were found lying flat on the floor, mostly near the west end of the building, to the east of the birds and fishes mosaic. Hundreds of fragments of glass vessels and sherds of ceramic storage jars and local amphorae (two-handled storage jars) were found directly on the floors as well. Two nearly intact amphorae of a type well known from the eastern Mediterranean were recovered in the second-story collapse, which was found to contain the remnants of mosaic floors, suggesting that the rooms above the reception hall were as elaborately decorated as the rooms beneath.

The question of what the building was used for continues to vex the excavators. The special area at the west end of the building may have been a reception hall, as has been mentioned. That so many coins were found on the floor to the east of this area suggests some kind of economic activity. The quantity of short nails is an indication that frames for stalls or other kinds of wooden furniture stood on the floor here and there. The presence of so many storage jar fragments may point to the storage or selling of some commodity, which, given the quantity of glass frag-

fig. 54 **Some of the many geometric mosaic carpets found in the eastern basilical building.**
Photo: Lucille A. Roussin

ments, could have been a liquid (oil-based perfume or wine or both). One more clue about the use of this building may be the representation in the western mosaic of a bird with its feet tied, a unique depiction in eastern pavement decoration and one that tends to be associated with reception or dining halls. If economic activity was conducted in such a sumptuous surrounding, it may well be that the building served as a market for luxury goods. The rabbis refer to an upper market and lower market at Sepphoris, and this building may have been the lower market. Still, the presence of the *oecus,* or at least of a reception hall, means that this suggestion regarding the building's economic function must remain tentative. It is also possible that the building was a public basilica in which local residents could rent space for receptions, economic ventures, offices, or other uses. The most important historical point is that in the Roman period at Sepphoris a splendid building existed on the main *cardo* of the city and served an up-scale clientele.

- if market, why no opening to outside ?

120

NOTES

1. The University of South Florida team is directed by James F. Strange with associate directors Dennis E. Groh and Thomas R. W. Longstaff, and field director C. Thomas McCollough.

2. The basilica at Pompeii had no apse either. See D. S. [Donald Struan] Robertson, *Greek and Roman Architecture*, 2d ed. (Cambridge, England, 1969), 268f. and fig. 113, and Lawrence Richardson, *Pompeii: An Architectural History* (Baltimore, 1988), 95–99. The Severan basilica at Leptis Magna in North Africa featured an internal apse at either, narrow end. See Ranuccio Bianchi Bandinelli et al., *The Buried City: Excavations at Leptis Magna* (New York, 1966), 92–94.

3. See Lucille A. Roussin's discussion of this mosaic in this catalogue.

4. Note the *oecus* in the Casa del Labirinto and in the Casa del Vibio at Pompeii in Richardson, *Pompeii*, 165 and 319. Vitruvius (*De Architectura* 6.3.7–11), the first-century-B.C.E. Roman architect and engineer, used *triclinium* and *oecus* interchangeably and was aware that the "Egyptian" type of *oecus* resembles a basilica, because it has an upper story with windows between the upper columns; see Vitruvius, *On Architecture*, in two volumes, trans. Frank Granger, Loeb Classical Library (Cambridge, Mass., and London, 1962), vol. 2, books 6–10. The presence of a true *oecus* or dining hall in such a grand building would suggest that this building is a villa, but there is no evidence of a kitchen or hearth.

The Birds and Fishes Mosaic

Lucille A. Roussin

The basilical building at Sepphoris contains one of the largest series of mosaic pavements in a single building yet uncovered in Israel. Almost all of the rooms opening off the inner aisle were paved with polychrome mosaics, which display a variety of compositions: a luxurious acanthus scroll, a landscape portraying the banks of the Nile, and a variety of geometric designs.[1] These mosaics are particularly interesting because they exhibit both a high level of artistry and a wide range of stylistic influences from the major centers of mosaic production around the Mediterranean.

The art of mosaic is the art of decorating architectural surfaces—ceilings, walls, or floors—with designs constructed of small, regularly cut cubes of colored stone or glass. These small stones, called tesserae, are usually of local limestone and marble. Gold, green, and blue glass tesserae are sometimes used to highlight areas of the design. In antiquity, tesserae were available in a wide range of colors, and several shades of one color were used to achieve the subtle modeling effects.[2]

Among the most unusual of the pavements at Sepphoris is the large mosaic, measuring 8.5 x 6 meters, along the west side of the basilical building. The work is of a very high quality, involving very small and carefully laid tesserae. The basic geometric design of the field consists of interlaced circles forming curvilinear squares; along the edges of the field, where the design meets the border, the circles become semicircles, with quarter circles in the four corners. The elaborate border consists of a row of the ribbon twist design, a row of looped guilloche (interlacing curved lines), another strand of ribbon twist, and a two-strand braid, which continues into the field forming the tangent circles of the field design. Near the center of the pavement was a 1.5-meter square panel that is not extant but probably contained a figural scene or an inscription.

A variety of motifs is depicted within the small, framed square panels inscribed in each of the circles of the field. Birds constitute the most common of the preserved motifs. Although most of the birds appear to be generic in shape, three are distinctive. A semicircle along the north border and another semicircle along the south border are decorated with plump partridges that hold long-stemmed flowers in their beaks. One of the best-executed designs of the mosaic is that of a large bird, perhaps a partridge, made out of tesserae only 3 millimeters square. The body of the bird is beautifully executed in shades of ocher highlighted with green glass tesserae; unfortunately the head has not been preserved. Sea creatures make up the next most-popular motif. Among the most beautifully executed are a dolphin and a red mullet along the north side of the mosaic.

fig. 55   Hare eating grapes from the birds and fishes mosaic of the eastern basilical building at Sepphoris.
Photo: Gabi Laron

fig. 56　Overview of the birds and fishes mosaic from the eastern basilical building. *Photo: Gabi Laron*

Three of the panels within interlaced circles of the field are decorated with motifs unparalleled in late antique mosaic decoration of the Eastern Roman Empire. A golden syrinx, better known as the pipes of the Roman satyr Pan, is represented in one of the panels, along with a golden flute. Along the west side of the mosaic is a shallow basket full of purple fruits with green leaves. The work is of a very high quality, the designs carefully laid with tiny tesserae—some of green and blue glass—only 1 millimeter square. The depiction of a bird with its feet tied also is a unique motif in eastern pavement decoration.

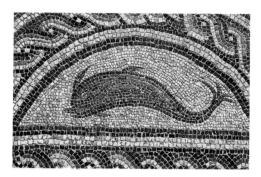

fig. 57　Dolphin. *Photo: Gabi Laron*

The basket of fruit and the bird apparently ready to be cooked are keys to the iconographical origins of the design, which should be read as a *xenia*. Most loosely defined as a still life picture within a painting or mosaic, the term *xenia* is derived from a passage in the writings of Roman architect Vitruvius in which

he explains the Greek custom of offering a gift of hospitality (*xenium*) to visitors.[3] The flowers and pomegranates that decorate some of the panels are part of the traditional *xenia* motif, but the live animal imagery—the running hare and the animate fish and birds—are problematic. Strictly speaking, only when represented as dead or as being readied for consumption do animals and birds qualify as *xenia*, but there is a tendency in late antique pavement decoration to

fig. 58　Pomegranates. *Photo: Gabi Laron*

combine them with other animal imagery.[4] This particular *xenia* imagery may provide an indication of the function of this room within the building, as *xenia* pavements most often decorate either dining rooms (*triclinia*) or the large reception room, sometimes dining room (*oecus*), both of which are traditionally situated off the peristyle (colonnaded court).[5]

Carefully executed repairs in this pavement indicate that the building was in use for a long time. The braid borders of the circles were so carefully repaired that the repairs are sometimes hard to detect, but in the process some of the plant and animal motifs were replaced with geometric designs similar to the checkerboard patterns along the north and south sides of the mosaic. Along the north side of the mosaic the observer can compare the grace of the original *Hederae* (symbolic ivy leaves) with the stiff leaf forms of the later repairs, and along the edge of the east side, where one of the semicircles was carefully repaired using only small, white tesserae, the hard-edged later rosette can be seen in comparison with the more graceful form used in the original pavement.

This mosaic may provide interesting evidence of strong connections with North African—especially Tunisian—mosaic workshops, which were among the most prolific and creative in late antiquity. For one thing, the overall composition of this mosaic has no parallels in mosaic pavement decoration in the eastern provinces; it is, however, of a type common in North African mosaic decoration, and it has an exact parallel in a mosaic dated to the first half of the third century C.E. in the Maison aux Communs at Thuburbo Majus, Tunisia.[6] For another, the square framed panel in the center of the Sepphoris mosaic is more characteristic of the small figural panels set into overall geometric designs in North African pavement

fig. 59 Partridge with a long-stemmed flower in his beak from the birds and fishes mosaic. *Photo: Gabi Laron*

design than of any of the large, illusionistic framed picture panels set into geometric floor mosaics in the East (see especially those at Antioch).[7] Also significant is the motif of the hare nibbling grapes, a motif often used in the decoration of mosaic threshold panels in Tunisian villas, such as that found in the House of the Dolphins at El Jem. In addition, the *xenia* motifs, like the overall design of the Sepphoris mosaic, are particularly popular in Tunisian mosaic decoration, and they point to western origins of the designs—and perhaps even of the artisans.

The style and quality of the mosaics in the basilical building point to a date in the third quarter of the third century C.E. The range of stylistic influences discernible in the mosaics—from Antioch and Apamea in Syria to the prolific workshops of North Africa—attest to the prosperity of Sepphoris and to its importance as a center of commerce during the late antique period.

NOTES

1. Lucille A. Roussin, "A New Mosaic from Sepphoris in the Galilee," in *VI Coloquio Internacional Sobre Mosaico Antiguo,* Oct. 1990 (1993), 221–30.

2. In Late Roman mosaic decoration, the average number of colors in the mosaicist's palette was thirty. See J. Lassus, *Réflections sur la Technique de la Mosaïque*, Les Conférences-Visites du Musée Stephane Gsell, 1955–56 (Algiers, 1956), 17. For the Palestinian pavements, the average palette consisted of ten to twelve colors.

3. *De Architectura* 6.7.4; see Vitruvius, *On Architecture,* in two volumes, trans. Frank Granger, Loeb Classical Library (Cambridge, Mass., and London, 1962), vol. 2, books 6–10.

4. Christine Kondoleon and Lucille A. Roussin, Review of *Recherches franco-tunisiennes sur la Mosaïque de l'Afrique antique. I: Xenia* (Collection de l'École Française de Rome, 125 [1990]), *Bullétin de l'Association pour l'Étude de la Mosaïque Antique* 14 (1993): 262–63; Wassila Ben Osman, "Association du thèmes des xenia avec d'autres thèmes dans certaines mosaïques de Tunisie," in *Xenia,* 74.

5. Aïcha Ben Abed-Ben Khader, "Mosaïques à xenia et architecture en Afrique," in *Xenia,* 79–84.

6. Aïcha Ben Abed-Ben Khader, *Thuburbo Majus. Les mosaïques dans la region ouest,* Corpus des Mosaïques de Tunisie, vol. 2, fasc. 3 (Tunis, 1987); the mosaic is that of Passage 20, illustrated on p. 113. I must stress that I am not positing a direct connection between Thuburbo Majus and Sepphoris.

7. Doro Levi, *Antioch Mosaic Pavements* (Princeton, 1947); J. Balty, *Mosaïques antiques de Syrie* (Brussels, 1977).

The Mosaics of the Nile Festival Building

Zeev Weiss and Ehud Netzer

But why The Nile ??

The Nile festival building containing a spectacular mosaic floor is the largest and one of the most impressive structures excavated thus far at Sepphoris.[1] Located east of the *cardo* (the north-south commercial street) opposite the bath house, the building is dated to the early Byzantine period. Its central location within the city layout, its artistic richness, its size and numerous rooms lead us to conclude that it was a public building, perhaps a municipal basilica that served the local community. An eight-line inscription within a plain geometrical design that was laid on the sidewalk in front of the western entrance to the building includes the names of two artists, Procopius and his son-in-law Patricius, presumably the artisans who created the mosaics inside building.

Originally the entire building was paved with colorful mosaics. Some have been uncovered in a fine state of preservation, mostly in the northern part of the building. The level of preservation varies, from mosaics found almost intact (Nile festival room) to those from which only a few pieces have been found *in situ*. Mosaic floors in two of the excavated rooms (Nile festival room and the easternmost room) were paved entirely with figurative scenes; other excavated

mosaics have geometrical patterns; some, a combination of both. Several rooms found in various parts of the building had geometrical mosaics, some of which are preserved in their entirety. The designs are numerous and varied in both form and color. One room in the western side of the building, for example, had a long mosaic carpet with a design combining squares and rhombuses, each encompassed within a different geometrical design. Two other rooms had floral designs as well: small flowers set throughout the entire carpet surrounded by a geometrical design.

Several figurative panels were found to be incorporated within carpets with geometrical designs; such panels probably were meant to indicate a change in direction for the regulation of traffic in the building or to emphasize the entrance to an important space. For example, a panel depicting a centaur leaping on his two hind legs with his forelegs thrust forward was found next to where the two main corridors met, outside the northeastern corner of the basilical hall.[2] His raised arms hold above his head either a shield or bowl inscribed with the Greek words for "God helps." Another panel, only partially preserved, portrays a pair of naked hunters standing next to a tree and a wild boar walking at their feet (cat. no. 159).[3] The placement of this panel, next to the assumed opening into the basilical hall, indicates

fig. 60 **A detail from one of the mosaics of the Nile festival building at Sepphoris.** *Photo: Gabi Laron*

fig. 61 An overview of the Nilotic mosaic in the Nile festival building.
Photo: Zeev Radovan

an entrance. An almost completely preserved panel was revealed on the other side of the entrance, inside the hall. This panel depicts two figures; one is an Amazon, and both are mounted on horses. They are hunting a panther and a lion and are accompanied by a dog, who chases the animals.[4] A structure resembling a city gate or a fortress is depicted behind them.

Other rooms were decorated entirely with figurative designs, one of which is partly preserved and another of which is complete. Traces of similar floors have been found in two other areas, such as the basilical hall; unfortunately the hall and its mosaics were destroyed in antiquity.

A mosaic floor depicting Amazons has been partially preserved in the easternmost room of the building. The border of the floor is a frame made up of geometrical shapes and pomegranates. The scenes inside the main carpet, which is partially destroyed, are divided into two horizontal strips. Two horses standing on either side of a tree are depicted at the two edges of the upper strip. A canopy hangs from the tree between them. Two women, most likely Amazons (of whom only traces have been found),

were seated looking at each other underneath the canopy. A row of dancing Amazons, of which only three and traces of a fourth have been found, originally covered the entire lower strip. They are clothed in short dresses and Phrygian hats. The Amazon on the right holds a spear in her left hand. The exact reference to the scene depicted in this carpet is not yet clear, but it presents some festival or celebration held in honor of the two seated Amazons in the upper strip.

The Nile mosaic is the largest (7.6 x 6.2 m.) and most beautiful of the mosaics in this building. Its primary depictions are of elements connected with celebrations related to the annual inundation of Nile, which was thought to bring abundance to the world. The mosaic's double border consists of a band of stepped pyramids and a band of guilloche (two-strand twist). A row of birds spans the width of the room at the top of the carpet. In the center of this top row is a wreath held on either side by the beaks of two birds; inside it is a Greek inscription that reads "Have Success."

The Nile River, which streams out of the mouth of a hippopotamus or an ox, runs across the center of

128

fig. 62   This female figure in the Nilotic mosaic personifies Egypt as a land of abundance. She leans on a basket of fruit and holds an overflowing cornucopia in her left hand.
Photo: Gabi Laron

fig. 63   Nilometers were used to measure the flood level of the Nile, which in turn determined the annual tax rate. One nude man stands on the back of another to inscribe "IZ" (for 17 cubits) with a hammer and chisel on the Nilometer represented in the Nilotic mosaic. *Photo: Gabi Laron*

the floor. This main branch of the river sets off the upper portion of the floor as a smaller stream winds its way through the hunting scenes depicted in the lower portion. Adorning the lower section are lively illustrations associated with the river's fauna and flora. Among these scenes are fish floating in the bend of the river, a fisherman holding his catch, a woven basket functioning as a fish net, a stork eating a snake, and a bird perched on a lotus flower.

A Nilometer, positioned on top of a rectangular structure with an arched entrance facing the river, is depicted above the Nile. The Nilometer was used to measure the water level of the flooded river, thereby determining the annual tax rate.[5] Nilometers were posted at many sites along the river, usually near temples in a round or square pit dug near the river bank.[6] The mosaic artist at Sepphoris, who wanted to emphasize the level of the water that brought prosperity and fertility to the land, rendered the Nilometer as a rounded mast or tower engraved with successive marks and numbers to indicate the various levels reached by the flood waters. A youth must stand on the back of a kneeling figure in order to inscribe, with a hammer and chisel, the number IZ (for 17 cubits) at the top of the Nilometer.[7]

The large figures of a reclining man and woman appear in the upper two corners of the carpet. The figure on the left is Egypt personified as a woman, as indicated by the Greek inscription above it: AIGY[PTOS]. A cloak drapes her back and legs; her

upper body is uncovered. She reclines against a basket full of fruit and with her left hand holds up a cornucopia overflowing with fruit. The male personification of the Nile River appears across from her in the righthand corner. He sits on the animal out of whose mouth the Nile flows. The male figure extends his arms toward two nude figures who approach him bearing gifts. One figure holds a round wreath and a bird; the other extends a measuring rod and a wreath. Below them, a third nude figure supports the foot of the Nile god with one hand and with the other presents him with a wreath.[8]

The portion below the Nile River features images of the festivities held to celebrate a beneficially high flood level. On the right is a column with an Attic base and a Corinthian capital. Standing atop the column is a statue, made of black tesserae (tiles), of a man holding a spear in one hand and a torch in the other. Next to the torch is the number IZ, which, as previously noted, also appears at the highest level of the Nilometer. Two horsemen, the leader bearing a torch (bouquet of flowers?), proceed

fig. 64 A tall column with an Attic base and a Corinthian capital supports a statue of a man holding a spear in one hand and a torch in the other. The column is one of several monuments represented in the mosaic; they apparently adorned the city of Alexandria in antiquity. *Photo: Gabi Laron*

toward the left from the center as a boy wearing a tunic watches from behind. An יז appears next to this scene as well. The horses gallop toward Alexandria (labeled in Greek letters), represented by a city gate flanked by two round towers; next to the city is another, taller, round tower with a flame coming out of its top, probably a depiction of the Pharos (lighthouse) of Alexandria, one of the seven wonders of the ancient world.[9] The depiction of Alexandria and the Pharos next to it suggests that the column and the black tesserae statue above it also represent a monument that stood in the city.

The area to the right of and below the column extending over the bottom of the carpet features numerous hunting scenes in which various large animals are shown attacking and devouring their prey: a lion eating an ox, a bear eating a wild boar, a panther seizing a gazelle. Some of the victims are pictured in pairs; as one is being eaten, the other stands by, watching.

Nilotic scenes as well as hunting scenes are well known in Byzantine art, but the integration of the two themes within one frame, as in this Sepphoris carpet, is rare in Roman-Byzantine mosaic art.[10] The carpet's rich and varied combination indicates that the artist took a free approach in designing the floor and creating its many elements. The overall sensa-

tion is one of movement, but because the scenes proceed sequentially, the observer is able to separate the various themes. Humorous touches add a further distinguishing aspect.

The Nile festival mosaic as well as the others found at Sepphoris are important in understanding the development of mosaic art in this region. The Dionysos mosaic was produced according to the emblem tradition, whereby each image was conceived as an independent frame. This technique dates back to the Hellenistic period and characterizes Roman mosaic art until the fourth century C.E., after which mosaic work in the East underwent a significant change. In mosaics dating from the fifth century, the floor surface is no longer divided into separate panels but rather is rendered as a single unit,[11] with scenes covering the entire floor and images facing in every direction. The Nile mosaic as well as the one featuring the dancing Amazons differ, in both theme and composition, from that devoted to Dionysos. They belong to a large group of mosaics discovered in other cities in the East, such as Antioch or Apamea. The arrangement of the mosaic as a single carpet comprising various images, and particularly the hunting scenes, link the mosaics of the house of the Nile festival with those of others in eastern Mediterranean cities of the Byzantine era.

NOTES

1. For the architectural details of the building as well as for its functions, see our essay in this catalogue on the archaeological finds at Sepphoris during the Byzantine period.

2. The posture of the centaur resembles that in the *dōrophoroi* panel of the Dionysos mosaic (see the essay on that mosaic in this catalogue) of the early third century C.E. as well as in the *Keshet* sign of the zodiac from the synagogue, which is dated to the early fifth century C.E. These correspondences, and other evidence, suggest that the city had its own mosaic industry. The artisans used existing models and were inspired also by earlier mosaics in the city.

3. A parallel to this scene appears in the central panel in the south wing of the transept of the Saint Demetrius church at Nikopolis; see Ernst Kitzinger, "Studies on Late Antique and Early Byzantine Floor Mosaic, 1. Mosaics at Nikopolis," *Dumbarton Oaks Papers* 6 (1951): 83–122.

4. Similar themes appear in mosaic pavements at Apamea, for example; see Cecile Dulière, *La mosaïque des amazones* (Brussels, 1968), 1–15. This subject also appears on a Coptic tapestry from Egypt dated to the fifth century C.E.; see Annemarie Stauffer, *Textiles of Late Antiquity* (New York, 1995), 10, 22. One can find it also on silver plates dated to the sixth century C.E. in the Dumbarton Oaks Collection; see Marvin C. Ross, *Catalogue of the Byzantine and Early Mediaeval Antiquities in the Dumbarton Oaks Collection: Metalwork, Ceramics, Glass Painting*, vol. 2 (Washington, 1962), pls. 2, 9.

5. Naphtali Lewis, *Life in Egypt under Roman Rule* (New York and Oxford, 1983), 105–17.

6. See, for example, the case of the Serapis compound not far from Alexandria in Alan Rowe, *Discovery of the Famous Temple and Enclosure of Serapis at Alexandria* (Cairo, 1946), 31–32.

7. Illustrations of Nilometers have been found in two places in Israel: the house of Leontis at Beth-Shean and in the Church of the Multiplication of the Loaves and Fishes near the Sea of Galilee. The former is a rather schematic description, whereas the latter resembles the Nilometer from Sepphoris; see Nehemiah Tzori, "The House of Kyrios Leontis at Beth-Shean," *Eretz Israel* 11 (1973): 229–47 (in Hebrew), and Alfons M. Schneider, *The Church of the Multiplication of the Loaves and Fishes* (London, 1937), 52–80. A precise iconographic parallel to the Nilometer with the two youths next to it appears on a silver bowl in the collection of the Hermitage Museum in Saint Petersburg; see Hayford Peirce and Royall Tyler, *L'Art Byzantin*, vol. 2 (Paris, 1934), 82, pl. 44a.

8. A similar parallel to this scene appears on an ivory vessel in the Museum of Wiesbaden; see Kurt Weitzmann, ed., *The Age of Spirituality* (New York, 1979), 191–92.

9. Pliny, *Natural History* 36.83; see D. E. Eichholz, trans., *Pliny: Natural History*, in ten volumes, Loeb Classical Library (Cambridge, Mass., and London, 1962), vol. 10, books 36–37; also see Susan Handler, "Architecture on the Roman Coins of Alexandria," *American Journal of Archaeology* 75 (1971): 58–61.

10. Nilotic scenes appear in mosaics as early as the first century B.C.E.; see, for example, the mosaic from Palestrina in Paul G. P. Meyboom, *The Nile Mosaic of Palestrina* (Leiden and New York, 1995). For Nilotic scenes from Palestine see n. 7 above and Michael Avi-Yonah, "The Haditha Mosaic Pavement," *Israel Exploration Journal* 22 (1972): 118–22. For examples of hunting scenes in mosaics, see Irving Lavin, "The Hunting Mosaics of Antioch and Their Sources," *Dumbarton Oaks Papers* 17 (1963): 181–286, and Christine Kondoleon, *Domestic and Divine: Roman Mosaics in the House of Dionysos* (Ithaca, 1994), 271–314.

11. Lavin, "The Hunting Mosaics of Antioch," 185–203.

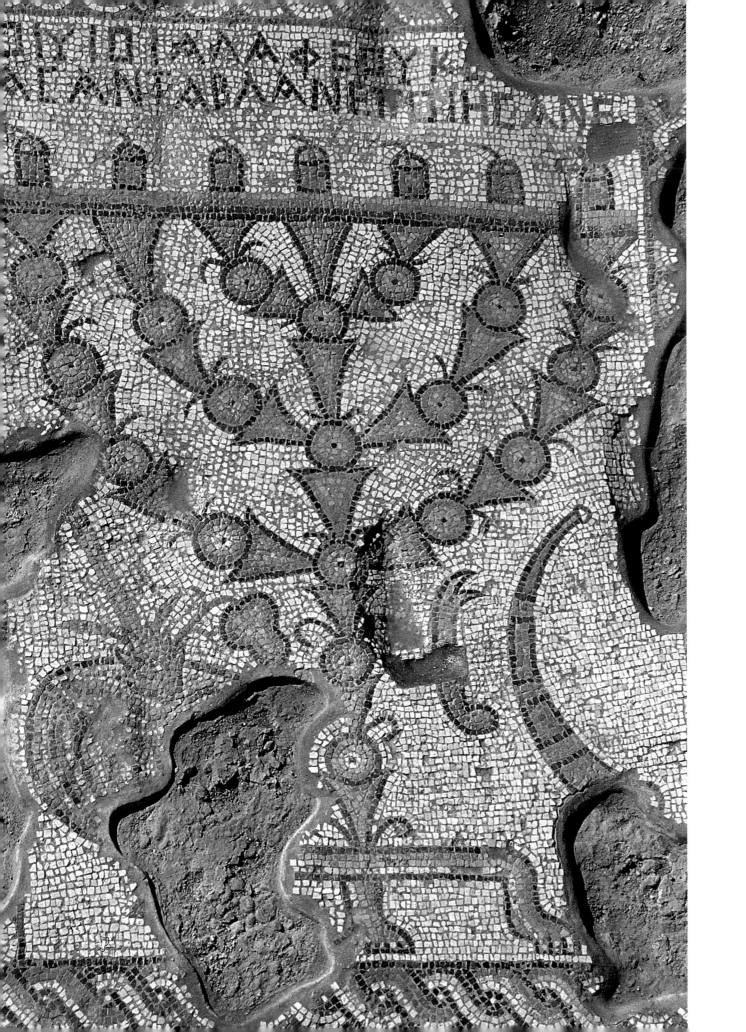

The Synagogue Mosaic

—see S. Fine for another interpretation.

Zeev Weiss and Ehud Netzer

A magnificent mosaic floor was exposed in the main hall of the Byzantine-period synagogue.[1] It has the form of a single elongated carpet featuring figurative depictions. In addition, a long, narrow carpet decorated with geometric designs, in which were incorporated dedicatory inscriptions in Aramaic, was found in the single aisle that existed next to the hall, on the north. Other smaller carpets were located between the columns separating the hall from the aisle; they too contained designs and dedicatory inscriptions.

The elongated mosaic carpet in the main hall, 13.5 x 4.5 meters in size, is divided into seven strips of unequal widths; some of them are subdivided further into two or three panels. The largest strip contains a zodiac; four strips are above it, and only two are below. All in all the carpet has fourteen panels of various sizes; they are separated from one another by strips of colored guilloche (two-strand twist) and contain various motifs that are well known in Jewish art.

Many of the panels are partly damaged, and two of them were almost totally destroyed. Nevertheless, it is possible to identify most of the themes that once appeared in the damaged parts and even to reconstruct some of the missing areas. Each of the scenes making up the main carpet is oriented westward, toward the *bema* (elevated platform in the synagogue) and along the orientation of the nave's longitudinal axis. Some of the human figures or animals depicted in the panels stand on strips of ground, but in most cases the entire background is made up of white tesserae (tiles). The dedicatory inscriptions, mostly in Greek, that are incorporated into the panels bear little or no relationship to the scenes with which they appear.

The description of the mosaic floor will proceed strip by strip, starting from the synagogue's *bema* on the west and ending with the entrance to the hall on the east. The first strip, adjacent to the *bema*, contains three panels. In the central panel is a round wreath of stylized leaves with a Greek dedicatory inscription at its center. A male lion with its head facing the center is depicted in each of the side panels. The left front paw of both lions grips the head of a bullock (young bull). The upper part of the strip has been destroyed completely as the result of the looting of the *bema* sidewall. It should be mentioned that the words "blessed be he" are discernible on the surviving part of the central inscription.

The second strip also contains three panels. The middle one depicts the facade of a building that is only partly preserved; on either side of it are three Ionic columns that support a Syrian gable (the base is arched) with a conch at its center. The outer angles of the gable are decorated with acroteria

---

fig. 65 **One of the two lighted** *menorah*s **(lampstands) from the synagogue mosaic at Sepphoris. The lampstand is a schematic presentation of the Tabernacle** *menorah* **with its calyxes and petals as described in Exodus 25:31–36 and 37:17–22.**
Photo: Gabi Laron

Ark
Temple
Synagogue
Torah shrine

fig. 66 Plan of the mosaic floor of the complete synagogue excavated to the northeast of the acropolis. The mosaic originally covered the entire floor of the building. Although the mosaics from the *narthex* (vestibule) have been destroyed, and those of the aisle are badly damaged, the nave mosaic is essentially well preserved.

Courtesy: Hebrew University Expedition

having a floral design. Below the gable is an entrance closed by two doors decorated in relief in simulation of wooden doors. Below the building is a single incense shovel, in contrast to the pair of shovels in the synagogue mosaics at Hammath Tiberias and Beth Alpha.[2] Such architectural facades are common in Jewish art, but their significance remains problematic. Do they depict a Holy Ark, similar to those that once stood in the synagogues of antiquity?[3] Or does the building symbolize the Tabernacle or the Temple that was once the focus of national religious life?[4] Or might they represent both the Holy Ark and the Temple/Tabernacle?[5]

A *menorah* (seven-branched lampstand) and other Jewish symbols are depicted in each of the panels next to the facade. The *menorah* has three legs designed as the paws of a lion. The central stem and the six branches issuing from it are made up of alternating spherical units and triangular goblets with two buds sprouting between them. At the top of the *menorah* is a horizontal bar on which rest seven cups from which flames emerge, all of them directed toward the left. On the left of the *menorah* in both panels are depicted the Four Species (*Arba'a Minim*): the *lulav* (palm branch), *hadas* (myrtle), and *'arava* (willow), which are tied together, are located within a round vessel; next to them is the *etrog* (citron). A *shofar* (ram's horn) decorated with three colored rings is visible to the right of the *menorah*. Between the *menorah* and the *shofar*, fire tongs were added in the two panels, but only the one in the right-hand panel is preserved completely. This detail, rare in ancient Jewish art, appears frequently next to the *menorah* in Jewish manuscripts from the thirteenth and fourteenth centuries c.e.[6] Both the fire tongs and the incense shovel were used by the priests when maintaining the *menorah*, everyday activity performed both in the Tabernacle and Temple (Lev. 24:1–4).

The third strip of the mosaic is not divided into panels and contains a scene with three components that should be viewed from right to left. A round water basin stands on an Ionic column. Two heads (of bullocks?) are affixed to the left side of the basin, and streams of water flow from their mouths into an

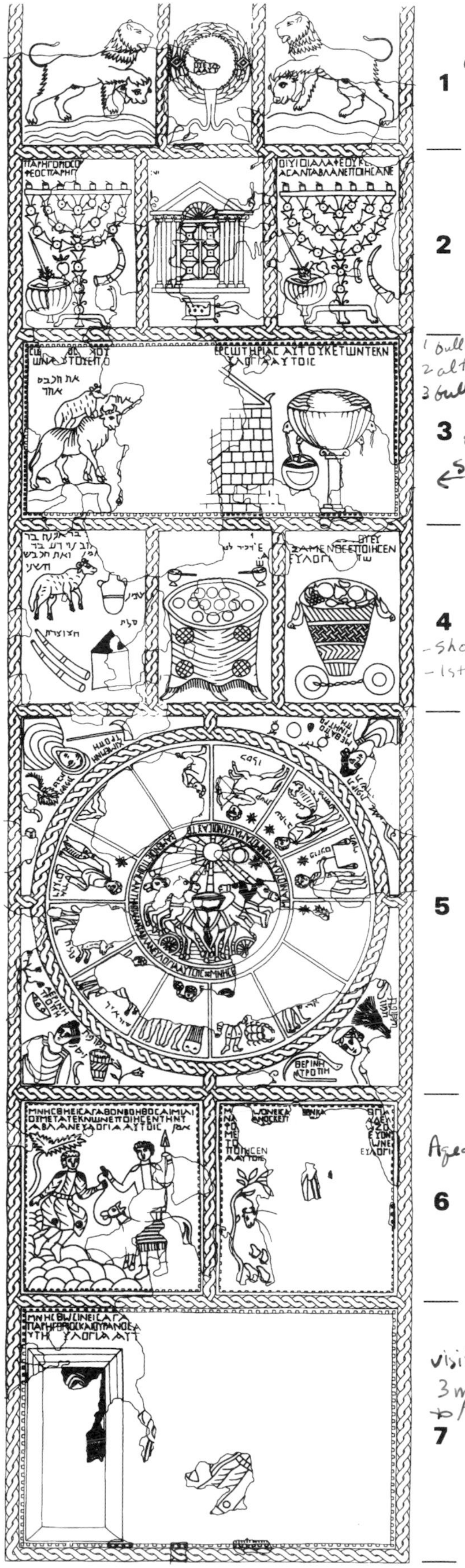

adjacent round bowl. In the center of the panel is a large altar, only half of which has been preserved. It is built of hewn stones and apparently stands on a stepped base. Two of its corners are decorated with horns, and the destroyed part should be similarly reconstructed; in other words, it is a four-horned altar of the type described in the Book of Exodus and apparently well known from archaeological discoveries. The top of the altar features various shades of red, suggesting the fire that burned on it every day. Aaron, the high priest, stands next to the altar, as attested by the inscription to the left of the remains of a human figure dressed in a robe. On the left of the panel are depicted a bullock with a lamb above him, and next to the lamb is an inscription with an excerpt from the Bible: "The one lamb" (Num. 28:4; compare with Exod. 29:39).

The continuation of the scene is located in the panel on the left in the fourth strip of the mosaic, where the perpetual sacrifice (or, more contextually, the daily sacrifice), mandated for both the Tabernacle and the Temple, is depicted: a lamb, fine flour, and oil. Above the lamb is an inscription reading "and the other lamb" (Exod. 29:41). The Hebrew word *shemen* (oil) to the right of a black storage jar that has two handles and is decorated with a white band indicates its contents. Below the jar is a vessel containing fine flour, according to the word *solet* (fine flour) to its right. To its left is a pair of trumpets accompanied by the word *hatzotzrot.* Trumpets were played during the perpetual sacrifice.

It seems that these two panels serve together as a narrative description of Exodus 29, a chapter that deals with the story of the consecration of Aaron and his sons for service in the Tabernacle and that ends with the passage relating to the perpetual sacrifice.[7] The three main foci in this chapter are depicted in these two panels. The water basin on the right side of the large panel symbolizes the first stage of the purification ceremony (Exod. 29:4). The sacrifice of the bullock opposite the door of the Tabernacle is depicted in the middle of the panel. Aaron the high priest stands next to the altar for perpetual sacrifice

fig. 67 Diagram of the synagogue's elongated nave mosaic, which measures about 13.5 x 4.5 meters. ***Courtesy: Hebrew University Expedition***

located in the court of the Tabernacle. The bullock, the first sacrifice as a burnt offering during the consecration ceremony, stands next to Aaron (Exod. 29:10–11). The perpetual sacrifice mentioned in the third and last part of Exodus 29 (38–45) is shown at the left edge of the third strip, with continuation in the panel below it. Here, as in the Bible, the perpetual sacrifice symbolizes the Divine Presence in the chosen place.

The other two panels in the fourth strip of the mosaic depict additional aspects of the Tabernacle ritual, but they are not a continuation of the scene adjacent to them. The shewbread table is depicted in the middle panel. (The shrewbread, or in modern English translations, the bread of the Presence, was baked fresh weekly and laid out on a special table in the Tabernacle and Temple; the bread that was replaced was to be eaten only by priests from the lineage of Aaron.) This special table was round with three legs and was covered by a tablecloth decorated with rounded emblems and braided fringes. The twelve loaves of unleavened bread that were placed on the table appear as round objects. Two pellets of frankincense (a special feature of this bread offering) are depicted on either side of the table in the space above it. A wickerwork basket of first fruits, including grapes, a pomegranate, a fig, and others, appears in the panel on the right; the poor would bring their first fruits to the Temple in such baskets.[8] The rim of the basket is decorated with a pair of birds with their heads hanging downward. A pair of cymbals joined together by a chain is located below the basket of first fruits.

The zodiac is depicted in the fifth strip. The design includes two concentric circles, both encompassed within a square. Zodiacs, as a central theme of ornamentation, can be found in several ancient synagogues, such as those at Hammath Tiberias, Beth Alpha, and Na‘aran.[9] The inner circle of the Sepphoris zodiac depicts a chariot of Helios, the sun god, drawn by four horses. The blue, wavelike lines

fig. 68 The zodiac from the synagogue mosaic at Sepphoris. The two concentric circles of the zodiac are set within a square measuring 3.3 x 3.3 meters. *Photo: Gabi Laron*

fig. 69 This shewbread table (or table of the bread of the Presence), in contrast to the biblical description (Exod. 37:10–16) and other pictorial representations, is round and has three legs. Some of the twelve round loaves of bread on the table have been destroyed. Above the table are two censers for incense. *Photo: Gabi Laron*

that fill the lower part of this circle resemble a source of water, possibly the sea, from which the chariot emerges. The sun, moon, and one star appear above the chariot on a blue background. In this rendering of the zodiac, the sun replaces the expected image of Helios, which notably is missing in the Sepphoris zodiac. The sun has been placed in the center, its rays extending in all directions. The lowest ray projects downward, toward the chariot, a detail creating the illusion that the sun is located within the chariot. A Greek dedicatory inscription is located in a band around this circle.

The outer circle depicts the twelve signs, which are to be viewed in a counterclockwise direction. Some of the elements included in the twelve signs of the Sepphoris zodiac are unique to this floor. All the figures are portrayed with their feet outward and their heads toward the center of the circle. A young male figure and also a star accompany each of the signs. Most of the figures are clothed in robes covering the upper part of their bodies, although some are almost naked, and one is probably wearing a tunic. The names of the signs as well as those of the respective months appear in Hebrew. Notable among the signs are Libra, shown as a man looking to his right and holding a balance in his left hand; Scorpio, a scorpion with six legs, two anterior pincers, and a long tail that curves upward; and Sagittarius, depicted in the form of a centaur leaping to the right and gripping a bow and arrow with both hands. Although some of the signs have been destroyed in one way or another, they can still be identified.

Personifications of the four seasons, represented by frontal views of female busts, appear in the corners of the framing square. Several artifacts representing the agricultural activities symbolic of each season appear beside these busts. Inscriptions in both Hebrew and Greek also appear in these corners. The placement of the seasons corresponds to the matching months. Spring (*tekufat Nisan*), for example, wears a sleeveless dress in shades of yellow. Her curly hair is gathered on top of her head and is held in place by a pin decorated with flowers. Also depicted in this corner are a small sickle, a basket, and a round basin with flowers in it and a flowering lily and a

branch of other flowers. Winter (*tekufat Tevet*) wears a grayish cloak that fully covers her head, and her figure expresses somberness. Next to her are an ax with a long handle, a small sickle, fruit, and a tree, one of whose branches has been cut off and thrown to the ground, the significance of which is not clear.

The zodiac, which was common in pagan art, was a popular motif for synagogue floor mosaics for a long period. However, the combination of the seasons, the twelve signs, and Helios appears only in synagogue art.[10] Despite stylistic changes over a period of time, the subject and basic composition did not change. In this respect, the Sepphoris synagogue mosaic represents a significant exception. Although its basic layout remains true to the traditional format, the additional iconographic details—and even more so the missing ones—make this zodiac unique. The design of the seasons, the signs, and the chariot differs stylistically from that of other synagogue zodiacs. The number of symbols representing each season is greater than in other floors, and the insertion of the Greek names of the seasons is found only in the Sepphoris zodiac. The array of details that creates each sign differs from the common format, and the Greek dedicatory inscription around the inner circle makes its first appearance in the Sepphoris floor. Finally, the absence of the sun god Helios (*Sol invictus,* traditionally portrayed as a charioteer riding in his chariot) is the most significant feature of this zodiac, and it raises many questions.

The sixth strip of the mosaic contains two panels. One of them was found to be largely destroyed, but the little that has survived explicitly indicates what was once present. These two panels depict the story of Genesis 22, the sacrifice of Isaac.[11] On the left panel appear two youths whom Abraham has left, together with an ass, at the foot of the mountain. The ass, which has a colored packsaddle on its back, stands in the foreground of the scene; behind him is one of the youths. The other youth is seated on the left beneath a tree whose branches spread above him. In one hand he holds the reins of the ass. The youths wear long-sleeved, short tunics and black shoes. The story continues in the badly damaged right panel. Discernible on the left margin of this panel is a tree, with few branches, onto which a ram (only its head has been preserved) is tied with a reddish colored rope. Below it are visible two pairs of shoes, removed by Abraham and Isaac when they reached the site of the sacrifice, a detail that does not appear in other known depictions of this episode. Another part of the mosaic is preserved at the center of the scene, where the blade of a hafted knife can be identified as well as, to its right, the remains of a cloak. The depiction of the ram tethered to a tree as a direct continuation of the panel showing the two youths at the foot of the mountain leaves no doubt about the theme of this panel. As can be inferred from the numerous depictions of this story in Byzantine art, Abraham apparently stood in the foreground of the panel, gripping the knife in his left hand.[12] Isaac probably was located on the right, in front of the altar. The ram on the left side of the panel completes the well-known portrayal of the biblical narrative.

The seventh and last strip of the mosaic, adjacent to the doorway of the hall and thus seen first by anyone entering the synagogue, is poorly preserved. Nevertheless, it can be determined that it shows the visit of the three men to Abraham, an event that precedes the biblical story of the sacrifice of Isaac. Only a few parts of this panel have survived, but on the basis of scene at San Vitale in Ravenna, Italy, one can reconstruct the image that once appeared here.[13] The three men were probably in the foreground; next to them, Abraham, acting as host, while Sarah stood in the tent depicted on the margin of the panel. This depiction, next to that of the sacrifice of Isaac, is a combination that appears also at San Vitale. The combination of the story of the sacrifice of Isaac as a sequel to the scene of the visit of the three men to Abraham by the oaks of Mamre makes its first appearance in Jewish art in the Sepphoris synagogue. The two scenes create a complete iconographic unit, with one clear message: the promise to the children of Abraham. God promised Abraham that not only would his son Isaac be worthy of succeeding him but that God would bless all of Abraham's offspring—so many offspring that they would not be able to be

counted. God also promised to protect the descendants of Abraham and to shield them from danger in the future.

The variety of depictions in this mosaic, and their iconographic richness, are outstanding in Jewish art. The main theme is that God is the center of creation. God has chosen His people, the people of Israel; and in the future, because of the promise to Abraham on Mount Moriah, God will rebuild the Temple and redeem the descendants of Abraham. The prime aim of this concept, which appears also in Jewish prayers, in rabbis' sermons, and in *piyyutim* (poetry), was the artistic transmission of a clear message to the community about the rebuilding of the Temple and future redemption.[14] The depictions in the Sepphoris synagogue mosaic are perhaps also an artistic expression of the Judeo-Christian dialogue regarding the identification of the chosen people, the future Temple, and the messiah during whose time redemption will occur.[15] Hints of this dialogue can be found both in rabbinic literature and in the works of the early church fathers.[16]

Some of the narrative scenes depicted in the central carpet of the mosaic have not been found, to date, in any other synagogues of ancient Palestine. They bear some resemblance to the frescoes found more than sixty years ago in the synagogue at Dura-Europos (modern Salahiyah on the Euphrates in eastern Syria), a similarity not limited to the organization of the panels or to the choice of some of the themes. Findings at both sites indicate that Jews were accustomed to decorating their synagogues with narrative art expressing biblical stories. The various scenes in the fifth-century-C.E. Sepphoris mosaic are a connecting link between the art of Dura-Europos and that of Byzantine illuminated manuscripts, as well as medieval Jewish manuscripts, in which some parallels to this floor can be found.

Marginal handwritten notes:
- No shoes. Compare Moses?
- Combine 3 visitors with Agedah. Compare literature (piyyutim, sermons, pisha).
- Weiss interp: promise to Abr. to protect offspring. other interp?
- oh?
- * But really a combination of narrative ritual + calendrical.

NOTES

1. For details on the architecture of the synagogue, see an essay on the archaeology of Sepphoris during the Byzantine period in this catalogue.

2. Moshe Dothan, *Hammat Tiberias* (Jerusalem, 1983), pl. 27; Eleazar L. Sukenik, *The Ancient Synagogue of Beth Alpha* (Jerualem, 1932), pl. 8.

3. Joseph C. Sloane, "The Torah Shrine in the Ashburnahm Pentateuch," *Jewish Quarterly Review* 25 (1934): 1–12; Dothan, *Hammat Tiberias*, 33–39; Eric M. Meyers and Carol L. Meyers, "The Ark in Art: A Ceramic Rendering of the Torah Shrine from Nabratein," *Eretz Israel* 16 (1982): 176–85

4. Elisheva Revel-Neher, "L'Alliance et la Promesse: Le symbolisme d'Eretz Israël dans l'iconography juive du moyen âge," *Jewish Art* 12–13 (1986–87): 135–46.

5. Cecil Roth, "Jewish Antecedents of Christian Art," *Journal of the Warburg and Courtauld Institutes* 16 (1953): 22–24.

6. Carl O. Nordström, "The Temple Miniatures in the Peter Comestor Manuscript at Madrid," in *No Graven Images,* ed. Joseph Gutmann (New York, 1971), 39–74. A pair of fire tongs appears in Samaritan art between the branches of the *menorah* in the mosaic of the Samaritan synagogue at El-Hirbeh; see Izchak Magen, "Samaritan Synagogues," *Qadmoniot* 25 (1993): 70–72 (in Hebrew).

7. A depiction of the consecration of Aaron for service in the tabernacle also appears at Dura-Europos, but a careful comparison of the two scenes reveals several differences between them; see Carl H. Kraeling, *The Synagogue—The Excavations at Dura Europos,* final report, vol. 8, pt. 1 (New Haven, 1956), 125–31.

8. Mishnah, *Bikkurim* 3:8.

9. Rachel Hachlili, "The Zodiac in Ancient Jewish Art: Representation and Significance," *Bulletin of the American Schools of Oriental Research* 228 (1977); Gideon Foerster, "Representations of the Zodiac in Ancient Synagogues and Their Iconographic Sources," *Eretz Israel* 18 (1988): 380–91 (in Hebrew).

10. Foerster, "Representations of the Zodiac," 382.

11. The story of the attempted sacrifice of Isaac also appears in the synagogue mosaic at Beth Alpha; see Sukenik, *The Ancient Synagogue,* 40–42.

12. Isabel Speyart van Woerden, "The Iconography of the Sacrifice of Abraham," *Vigiliae Christianae* 15 (1961): 214–55; Joseph Gutmann, "The Sacrifice of Isaac: Variations on a Theme in Early Jewish Art and Christian Art," in *Thaisos von Mauson,* ed. D. Ahrens (Köln, 1984), 115–22.

13. Otto Demus, *Byzantine Mosaic Decoration* (London, 1948), fig. 41.

14. For talmudic references see Zeev Weiss and Ehud Netzer, *Promise and Redemption: A Synagogue Mosaic from Sepphoris* (Jerusalem, 1996), esp. 34–39.

15. Kurt Weitzmann and Herbert L. Kessler, *The Frescoes of the Dura Synagogue and Christian Art* (Washington, 1990), 178–83.

16. See, for example, Marc G. Hirshman, *The Bible and Its Exegesis—Between the Rabbinic Sages and the Church Fathers* (Tel Aviv, 1992), 74–92 (in Hebrew).

Sepphoris Today

Zippori National Park

Ehud Netzer and Binyamin Shalev

The Zippori National Park, which was officially opened to the public on 15 October 1992, attracts thousands of visitors annually—about 140,000 in 1995—because of renewed archaeological interest in Zippori (known in English as Sepphoris). Extensive archaeological exploration at the site began in the summer of 1985, at which time two archaeological expeditions were working there: the University of South Florida team, headed by James F. Strange, and the Joint Sepphoris Project of Duke University and the Hebrew University of Jerusalem, directed by Eric M. Meyers, Ehud Netzer, and Carol L. Meyers.[1] The proposal to turn the site into an "archaeological park" was initiated at the very outset of the Joint Sepphoris Project's activity.

To a certain extent Sepphoris drew visitors even before these excavations began. The public had been attracted by the beauty of the surrounding natural woods and of the Jewish National Fund forests, consisting primarily of pine trees, which were planted after 1948 at the site itself as well as on some of the surrounding hills. Equally enticing is the mild climate of central Galilee, coupled with its ready accessibility via major highways. The remains of a Roman-period mausoleum and a Crusader church to the west of the site and an intriguing water system to its east were major attractions, although the favorite spot for most visitors was the Crusader/Ottoman citadel at the top of the hill. These attractions inspired Ehud Netzer, with the encouragement of the Meyerses, to recognize its potential as an archaeological park along the lines of parks he was personally involved with, such as Masada and Herodium.[2]

The Jewish National Fund, after hearing the proposal for a national park at Sepphoris, was the first public authority to act on the idea. Preliminary plans were drawn up, and in the winter of 1985–86 workers employed by the Jewish National Fund cleared much of the Roman theater. Meanwhile, the government of Israel proclaimed Sepphoris a national park encompassing an area of 4,000 acres covered mostly by natural woods and Jewish National Fund forests. The National Parks Authority then commissioned Gideon Sarig, a landscape architect, and Larry Belkin, a graduate of the North Carolina State University School of Design, who had helped to develop several ancient sites, to plan the archaeological park.

Excavations during the 1985 and 1986 seasons revealed well-preserved remains of dwelling houses, a narrow paved road, and an abundance of cisterns on the western side of the hill. The discovery in the 1987 season of the magnificent mansion with the Dionysos mosaic, which features the beautiful woman who has since come to be known as the Mona Lisa of Galilee, was a major breakthrough in the development of the site. The mosaic floor excited the archaeological community and received international coverage in the media. Although the mosaic was moved to Jerusalem in 1988 to be exhibited in the Israel Museum (through the generosity of the Gottesman family from New Jersey), it was meant to be returned to the site once proper conditions for display were established. Larry Belkin was commissioned to plan a building at the site to house the mosaic floor. In the summer of 1992, with the help of a generous donation from the Jesselson family of New York, the building was completed and the mosaic floor was returned to its original location.

Also at that time, the Israel National Parks Authority, together with the Jewish National Fund, completed basic services at the site, including a new access road, utilities, and a small kiosk for snacks and souvenirs. The local Galilee Foundation joined in efforts to develop the site physically and to establish Zippori National Park as an educational and historical as well as archaeological site. As excavations at Sepphoris continued, additional extraordinary mosaic floors were uncovered, including the Nile festival mosaic, which was exposed in 1991 by the Hebrew University expedition headed by Ehud Netzer and Zeev Weiss. Because of these finds, the Ministry of Tourism included the site in a series of archaeological development projects, such as those at Beth-Shean and Caesarea, which employed immigrants from the former Soviet Union.

The Zippori Project, a multiyear program with the long-range goal of developing Sepphoris from an archaeological dig into a major tourist site, was formally established by the Ministry of Tourism, together with the Israel National Parks Authority, the Jewish National Fund, and the Galilee Foundation, in April 1992. Binyamin Shalev, who lives at Hosha'ya, one mile to the north of the site, became director of the project, a position he continues to hold, assisted by Tsvika Linder and Anat Moran. During 1993 and 1994 more than one hundred new immigrants, most of whom had settled in Upper Nazareth and other sites in the vicinity of Sepphoris, were employed at the park. They were occupied initially in the excavations of the Institute

of Archaeology of the Hebrew University of Jerusalem and later in preservation, restoration, and development operations. Because many of the projects require special treatment of ancient building materials, several training programs were established to instruct workers in the restoration and preservation of antiquities. Training was conducted by the Israel Antiquities Authority through a special program sponsored by the United Jewish Appeal. Preservation of the mosaics was undertaken by professional restorers from Jerusalem and Rome.

The development program of the Zippori National Park has included the complete restoration of the Crusader/Ottoman citadel into a modern information center; the preservation and development of the Roman reservoir, which was excavated under the direction of Tsvika Tsuk from Tel Aviv University; partial restoration of the Roman theater; the erection of a roofing system over the Nile festival building, a Byzantine public building that contains a dozen mosaic floors; the construction of roofing systems over other ancient buildings with mosaic floors, including a Roman market and a Byzantine-period synagogue; the preservation of mosaics; the restoration and preservation of the ancient roads and paths; general preservation and restoration of antiquities, including a number of well-preserved ritual baths; continued archaeological excavations under the auspices of the Archaeological Institute of the Hebrew University, Duke University, the University of South Florida, and other institutions; the development of a permanent infrastructure for the park; the development of recreational areas; and landscaping and site development.

In addition to the physical development of the site, a series of educational and cultural programs enhance the visitor's appreciation of Zippori National Park. For example, the Guide Center, which conducts tours in five languages, provides educational services for visitors to the park. In addition, Zippori Explorer, an interactive multimedia program that highlights the Byzantine-period mosaics from the Nile festival building and the ancient water system, is located in the Information Center at the citadel. Visitors to the park can also

144

fig. 71 Here members of the Hebrew University team are
excavating in the lower eastern area of the site.
Photo: Ehud Netzer

purchase a do-it-yourself mosaic kit, which helps them participate in as well as enjoy the ancient art of mosaic making.

The performing arts also are featured at Zippori National Park. "Zippori Live," an authentic reproduction of the ancient city of Sepphoris from the year 200 C.E., is staged by some twenty-five, specially trained actors/interpreters who demonstrate scenes from daily life at Sepphoris as described in talmudic texts and rabbinic literature. In addition to the different areas of the park where the actors perform, the marketplace is brought to life through a series of craft workshops that re-create the ancient methods and techniques of that period. Many evening concerts and festivals are held in several recreational areas of the park as well. The comfortable weather during the summer season makes Sepphoris a natural spot for these activities.

During the course of the year 2000, the Ministry of Tourism together with the city of Nazareth (located five kilometers south of Sepphoris) will sponsor *Nazareth 2000* to commemorate the two-thousandth anniversary of the birth of Jesus. The celebration will draw thousands of additional tourists to the area, and plans are underway to establish new entrances to the site and a permanent visitor center in order to create more direct access to Zippori National Park from Nazareth.

All of these projects are based on the archaeological remains that have been excavated to date. Many more exciting buildings and objects undoubtedly will be unearthed as excavations continue. Further exposure of the streets and buildings on the western summit and to the east of the hill ultimately will permit visitors to walk into the ancient city as they do at similar sites, such as Ephesus on the Aegean coast of Turkey and Pompeii in southern Italy. The restoration of the theater will add another dimension to the site, enabling it to function as a "living community center" during most days of the year.

Between 1992 and 1995 approximately $8 million was invested in the development of Zippori National Park. Most of these have been public funds, although the Galilee Foundation has successfully raised funds for special projects from private individuals and foundations. Given its rich archaeological potential, and assisted by continued development, Sepphoris is certain to become one of the most-visited sites in Israel, where it will once again live up to its ancient designation as the "Ornament of all Galilee."

NOTES

1. Two years before James F. Strange had implemented a partial survey of the site as well as a few soundings near the citadel.

2. Ehud Netzer, who has an architectural as well as an archaeological background, already had experience in developing archaeological and historical sites, having played a critical role at these sites as well as in the Old Jewish Quarter of Jerusalem and in that city's Yemin Moshe Quarter. At Lower Herodium, for example, Netzer initiated the restoration of the formal gardens of Herod the Great in the Roman style. The project, which has been hampered by political events in the area, has yet to be completed.

Conclusion

Eric M. Meyers

Although this exhibition focuses on the site of Sepphoris, several of the essays contained herein and many of the artifacts on display point to the larger context and broader chronological range in which the city, and its setting in Galilee, can be duly appreciated. First and foremost, however, this exhibition is a vivid representation of the importance and grandeur of the site itself. From at least the Late Hellenistic period onward (c. 100 B.C.E.), inhabitants of the strategically located Sepphoris hill invested their time and energy in shaping the hilly landscape into a site of unparalleled beauty. By the first century C.E. the rocky terrain had been altered to accommodate new settlers and a new urban plan; and the site's naturally defensible location led the first-century Jewish historian Flavius Josephus to call it the "Ornament of all Galilee," alluding to extensive renovations that had been made to the city as well as to its impregnability.

During the early centuries of settlement the fundamental character of the site had gradually changed: initially a locale in the Iron Age hinterland, and later, in the Persian period, an important peg in the strategic planning of Achaemenid imperial administration of the province of Beyond the River, by the Early Roman period the site had become a Jewish

"oriental" city of the Eastern Roman Empire. There was to be only one other Jewish city in Galilee, Tiberias, and both cities continued to be dominant influences in Jewish culture throughout late antiquity. What is perhaps surprising about Sepphoris is the extent to which its predominantly Jewish population accommodated the cosmopolitan Roman lifestyle and aesthetic. The construction of the theater, the lower city, the water system, and the palatial Dionysos mosaic building, all over the course of the first two centuries C.E., reflects the cultural mindset of a confident community despite the tensions created by past Jewish involvement in the two wars against Rome. Not only does the emergence of so elaborate an urban center at the very heart of Jewish life strike us as significant; in view of the dominant role that Galilean towns and villages played in developing the character of Palestinian Jewry, the ascendancy of Sepphoris to a position of great influence is itself worthy of attention.

The complex relationship between city and town in Galilee throughout late antiquity is one of the underlying issues that this catalogue raises and that this exhibition illustrates. There is far greater continuity between city and town than might normally be presumed, especially in Lower Galilee. Rabbi Judah Ha-Nasi's decision to relocate in Sepphoris was certainly not a coincidence—nor could it have been made solely on the basis of the attraction of the "salubrious" air and breezes of Sepphoris. By that

fig. 72 **Members of the Sepphoris Regional Project (Duke University) working in the residential area on the western summit of the Sepphoris hill.**
Photo: Eric M. Meyers

time, the end of the second century C.E., surely the attraction of working in a major urban environment where great sages had been teaching and where accomplished artists and artisans were engaged was a major factor in his decision to undertake the final preparation of the Mishnah there.

The degree to which such a distinguished cadre of rabbis and scholars and local citizens participated in the full range of Greco-Roman or Hellenistic culture has been viewed as surprising by some, despite the fact that familiarity with both Greek language and design had been in evidence in Palestine for centuries. Yet the presence of so many *miqva'ot* (ritual baths) from the earliest Roman strata to the latest Byzantine layers indicates that the local Jewish population saw no conflict between the traditional Jewish way of life and some aspects of the nascent Hellenistic, gentile way of life. The most exquisite utilization of pagan motifs in the service of traditional Jewish modes of thinking and belief is the magnificent Byzantine-period synagogue mosaic with zodiac excavated in the northeastern sector of Sepphoris. Indeed, the vigor and vibrancy of the Byzantine-period Jewish community is one of the most significant findings from the recent excavations at Sepphoris.

The visible emergence of Christianity as a major form of religious expression in the Holy Land after the conversion of Roman emperor Constantine in 312 C.E. also finds expression at Sepphoris in the churches and artifacts of Christian life uncovered there. The location of the public buildings of the earliest Christians at Sepphoris suggests their full integration into the urban life of the city, which in the Byzantine era was centered in the lower city in the eastern areas. However, numerous Christian artifacts have also been uncovered on the acropolis, indicating that Jews and Christians lived and worked side by side on the upper city as well. To this pluralistic mix of peoples must be added a group of pagans who thrived in Sepphoris throughout late antiquity, though their remains in many ways are the most elusive of all. The physical characteristics of the city closely resemble the pagan cities of the Roman East,

yet the finds from the excavations show the Jewish and Christian traditions to have been most firmly implanted there.

Like so many of the cities of the Eastern Roman Empire, Sepphoris flourished throughout the Roman and Byzantine periods. For all the observable discontinuity between these periods—especially in ceramics, artistic style, and other aspects of everyday life—there is also enormous continuity. While the conversion of Constantine unleashed new cultural forces that would enable Christianity to take root firmly in the East, and while the so-called Revolt of Gallus (351 C.E.) may have caused a political furor, it was the massive earthquake of 363 C.E. that leveled much of the cities of the East, including Sepphoris. The conviction of the local residents to continue to pursue their lives at Sepphoris is apparent at every turn in the enormous rebuilding and reconfiguration of space that occurred soon thereafter. In some areas the rebuilt city did not compare favorably with its Roman-period precursor, but its glory was recovered soon enough.

The archaeology of Sepphoris clearly shows the flourishing of Judaism in an urban environment from the first century until the dawn of the medieval period—at precisely the time when many Jews chose to settle in the Diaspora and when paganism was a prominent feature of many pagan cites and mixed environments of ancient Palestine. Christianity also began to develop in new and important ways at this time. Both the Jewish and Christian communities apparently found the syncretistic setting of Hellenistic culture a fertile setting and a vibrant catalyst for constructive symbiosis, as evinced by so much of the material culture from Sepphoris in Galilee.

Although there are traces of the epochal changes associated with the rise of Islam, which affected all Near Eastern history in the seventh and eighth centuries, it was not until the initiation of the Crusades several centuries later that the development of Sepphoris as a city came to an abrupt halt. And yet, out of this ending arose another beginning, as the

Christian pilgrim traditions already attached to the site took on a dramatic new form in the erection of the elegant Church of Saint Anne.

The numerous artifacts from other areas in Galilee that are included in this catalogue are meant to fill out the missing links in our visual presentation. Some of these gaps have arisen solely as a result of happenstance—an object could not be loaned, another was not available, and so on. In addition, it should also be said that all excavations are incomplete: five major expeditions have worked at Sepphoris, yet our knowledge of the site is still fragmentary. Only by looking to the larger context of Sepphoris in Galilee and in northern Palestine in the late antique era can we hope to achieve a greater understanding of what life at the site truly was like. Nonetheless, in gaining a sense of its beauty and its history, we cannot help but gain a new sense of the significance of our common heritage there.

Catalogue of the Exhibition

Before the Roman Period

1. Figurine of a Nude Female

Tel ʿEin Zippori; Sepphoris Regional Project
Late Bronze II, c. 1400–1200 B.C.E.
Lead
H: 6.5 cm.; W: 1.5 cm.
Israel Antiquities Authority 96-2223

This small lead figurine of a nude female holding her breasts is a solid piece that was probably formed in a stone or clay mold. Because of its flat back and its extremely flat silhouette—it measures only .7 cm. at its thickest point, the nose—it can be classified as a flat-cast figurine (rather than a round-cast one, which would be modeled on all sides). The simple form is virtually intact, although its right foot is slightly damaged and the right side of the head is missing the hint of the bobbed (or Hathor?) hairdo visible on the left side. The piece lacks the pegged or bulbous mushroom-shaped base to which such figurines often were attached.

The woman's head is bare, as is her body. In addition to the rather simply defined facial features, the body is marked by three tiny round protrusions: two at chest level form the figurine's breasts; one at hip level marks the distinct navel, larger than either breast. One further kind of body marking appears at the pudendum (vulva), where a triangular shape is suggested by a series of dots: a row of four below the navel, three below that line of dots, and one forming the point of the triangle. The legs extend downward from that point, in a rather rigid, lock-kneed pose; and the elbows are pressed into the waist, with the forearms extended upward, the fingers of each hand cupping a breast.

The figurine bears no hint of a headdress or of an elaborate coiffure; her only adornments are traces of ankle bracelets—one thin ring at the bottom of each leg—and either two thin bracelets or a somewhat wider cuff bracelet at each wrist. In addition, although the figurine's head had nearly broken off from the body when it was discovered, with attendant damage to the neck, a series of dots, representing a simple strand of beads, appears to be at the bottom of the short neck. The overall impression is that of a slim yet sturdy female whose shoulders are 25 percent wider than her hips.

Small metal figurines depicting the human body have been found throughout the ancient Near East, and a fairly large number of them have been exhibited in museums and published in books and catalogues. One catalogue of pieces from Syria-Palestine alone contains more than 1,700 items (Negbi, 1976). If one includes terracotta figurines in the same conceptual set, the number of small sculptural depictions of the human form reaches into the thousands. Although monumental sculpture seems to have been relatively rare in the Levant, the human impulse to represent one's body in some plastic medium finds rich expression in the variety of figurines discovered there.

The question of the identity of these figurines cannot always be answered. Many undoubtedly are images of female or male deities, particularly if they bear—as large numbers of them do—elaborate headgear, distinctive apparel, and/or insignia or implements of divinities known from other art forms. Similarly, if the figurines have been discovered in public sanctuaries or temples—as the preponderance of them have—the likelihood is high that they signify deities. However, figures such as this one, which is relatively unadorned, lacks insignia or headpiece, and apparently comes from a nonritual context, are more accurately classified as amulets or votive figurines, that is, used for magic or incantatory purposes in domestic religious settings. Thus, representations of nude females holding their breasts may have been used by women hoping to achieve successful lactation.

The date of this piece is probably Late Bronze II, for it comes from a fill that has mainly LBII materials but also some earlier (Middle Bronze) and later (tenth-century) sherds. As such, it fits the chronological profile in which Palestinian metal figurines from datable contexts, although having prototypes that go back to the third millennium, tend to come from Late Bronze and Iron I deposits.

The large quantity of ancient Near Eastern male and female figurines has been classified in various ways—according to gender, pose, material, adornment, and date. This ᶜEin Zippori example defies classification according to existing types. It is made of lead, whereas the majority of cast specimens are copper and bronze (with silver and gold used for hammered figures). Its tiny size makes it one of the smallest such objects; more typically figurines are 10 to 30 cm. or larger in height. Its posture and markings are more akin to those of ceramic figurines and metal pendants than to any one type of metal figurine or pendant. And its discovery in a small, nonurban site is virtually unparalleled.

The unique presence of this figurine is one piece of evidence, among others, that the Late Bronze (or early Iron Age?) settlement of ᶜEin Zippori included elite elements able to afford a tiny but somewhat costly object of representational art and of religio-magical value.—*CLM*

REFERENCES

McGovern, Patrick E. *Late Bronze Palestinian Pendants: Innovation in a Cosmopolition Age.* Journal for the Study of the Old Testament/American Schools of Oriental Research Monograph Series, 1. Sheffield, 1985.

Negbi, Ora. *Canaanite Gods in Metal: An Archaeological Study of Ancient Syro-Palestinian Figurines.* Publication of the Institute of Archaeology, 5. Tel Aviv, 1976.

Pritchard, James B. *Palestinian Figures in Relation to Certain Goddesses Known through Literature.* American Oriental Series, 24. New Haven, 1943; repr. 1967.

THE COLLARED-RIM JAR

The collared-rim jar is a large storejar, or pithos, typically a meter or more tall, with a folded rim and a short neck. It is most noticeably distinguished by, as its name implies, a thickening of the vessel wall at the juncture of the shoulder and neck yielding a molded ridge or "collar." Examples of this distinctive ceramic form are attested from a rather wide geographical range, but their numbers are greatest in the central hill country, from the Judean hills in the south to the Jezreel Valley in the north, where they represent a large portion of the total Iron I ceramic assemblage (Finkelstein, 1988: 272f). Fewer examples are known from the Jezreel Valley, Lower Galilee, and the coastal plains (Esse, 1992: 105); additional examples have been reported from several Transjordanian sites (Ibrahim, 1978: 122; Esse, 1992: 104f). (For a discussion of its presence at Tel ᶜEin Zippori, see Carol Meyers's article on the earliest settlements at Sepphoris in this catalogue.) Chronologically, the collared-rim jar is principally attested in early Iron I contexts, though its production, or at least use, may extend into the later part of that period and even into the early part of Iron II. The earliest known example comes from a Late Bronze II destruction at Aphek dated to the second half of the thirteenth century B.C.E. (Beck and Kochavi, 1985: 34, 40).

Because the central hill country in the Iron I period represents the geographical and temporal location of Israelite beginnings in the Land of Israel, according to biblical tradition, the collared-rim jar historically came to be viewed as indicative of the presence of early Israelites at a given site. This link between ceramic form and ethnic identity was first made by William F. Albright, who investigated a number of early Iron I sites in the hill country and contrasted their material culture with that of the earlier Late Bronze II Canaanite centers of the lowlands (Albright, 1937: 25). Along with plastered cisterns, terracing, and the pillared or "four-room house," the collared-rim jar came to be seen as distinctively Israelite.

fig. 73 Fragment of a Collared-Rim Jar

Tel ᶜEin Zippori; Sepphoris Regional Project
Iron Age I, c. 1200–1000 B.C.E.
Pottery
D (at rim): 15 cm.
Sepphoris Regional Project II.103
Not in Exhibition

In the light of more recent data, sociological as well as archaeological, collared-rim jars, among other so-called "indicators," are now viewed less as marks of ethnic affiliation and more as integral technological elements in the subsistence struggles of the highland agriculturalists. The contrast that was drawn between Israelite and Canaanite, reflected in part by the presence or absence of the collared-rim jar in a particular ceramic assemblage, might now be more prudently explained as a contrast between small rural sites in the highlands and large urban sites in the lowlands (London, 1989: 50ff). Markedly different geographical and social environments have their own distinct requirements in the realms of agricultural production, food storage, and product availability. These particular requirements may translate into differences in the ceramic repertoires, which in turn reflect different functional needs of populations of the two environments.—JSJ

REFERENCES

Albright, William F. "Further Light on the History of Israel from Lachish and Megiddo." *Bulletin of the American Schools of Oriental Research* 68 (1937): 22–26.

Beck, Pirhiya and Moshe Kochavi. "A Dated Assemblage of the Late 13th Century BCE from the Egyptian Residency at Aphek." *Tel Aviv* 12 (1985): 29–42.

Esse, Douglas L. "The Collared Rim Store Jar: Scholarly Ideology and Ceramic Typology." *Scandinavian Journal of the Old Testament* 2 (1991): 99–115.

Finkelstein, Israel. *The Archaeology of the Israelite Settlement.* Jerusalem, 1988.

Ibrahim, Moawiyah M. "The Collared-Rim Jar of the Early Iron Age." In *Archaeology in the Levant*, ed. R. Moorey and P. Parr. Westminster, 1978: 116–26.

London, Gloria A. "A Comparison of Two Contemporaneous Lifestyles of the Late Second Millennium B.C." *Bulletin of the American Schools of Oriental Research* 273 (1989): 37–55.

2. Galilean Pithos

Tel Dan; excavated by Avraham Biran for the Israel Antiquities Authority
Iron Age I, c. 1200–1000 B.C.E.
Pottery
H: 0.67 m.
Israel Antiquities Authority 67-1494

This Galilean pithos or storejar is similar in shape and size to the typical Iron Age I collared-rim storejar, of which it is a northern regional variant.

3. & 4. Impressed Storejar Handles

Tel ᶜEin Zippori; Sepphoris Regional Project
Iron Age I–II, c. late 11th–early 10th centuries
  B.C.E.
Pottery
L: 7 cm. and 6 cm.
Israel Antiquities Authority 95-4029 and
  95-4030

Thirty storejar handles bearing deliberate impressions and dating to the late eleventh–early tenth centuries B.C.E. were recovered during the 1993–96 excavation seasons at Tel ᶜEin Zippori. The marks, made during the fabrication process, were impressed into the still-wet clay of the upper portion of the handle.

Stamps of this kind can be divided typologically into two principal categories with a number of variant subtypes. The most common type bears a single round or slightly oblong impression, whereas the second type bears two impressions along a horizontal axis. Most of these impressions seem to have been made with a finger, though others were perhaps made with a rounded instrument. No trace of any negative seal image could be discerned. A very few examples of singly impressed handles seem to have been created with a hollow reed, which yielded an impressed ring. A few others apparently were punctured by a stick or other such instrument, which rendered a smaller, round, "punctate" impression.

Stamped handles are in no way unique to Tel ᶜEin Zippori; they have been discovered in Iron I–II contexts at numerous other sites in the Central Highlands, Jezreel Valley, and Akko Plains (Shiloh, Tell el-Ful, Giloh, Tell en-Naṣbeh, Bethel, ᶜIzbet Ṣarṭah, Tell Keisan, and Taᶜanach, among other sites), yet most of the examples found at these other sites are punctate markings and exhibit a greater variability both in the number of markings and in their spatial arrangement. More-over, many of these other sites have yielded marked vessels other than store jars, whereas only storejars at Tel ᶜEin Zippori are marked.

Some scholars maintain that such markings are potters' marks (e.g., Wood, 1990: 45f.); others suggest that they may simply be decorative in function (see Finkelstein, 1988: 287). Another possibility is that these marked handles are reflections of local administrative practices (Finkelstein, 1988: 287). This may be the case at Tel ᶜEin Zippori, where the size and the architectural features of Building Complex A and its associated material remains suggest administrative rather than domestic activity. A more precise interpretation of these handles is not possible until a more thorough study of their typology and their archaeological context is conducted.—*JSJ*

REFERENCES

Briend, Jacques. *Tell Keisan (1971-1976).* Orbis Biblicus et Orientalis, Series Archaeologica, 1. Paris, 1980.

Finkelstein, Israel. *The Archaeology of the Israelite Settlement.* Jerusalem, 1988.

Wood, Bryant G. *The Sociology of Pottery in Ancient Palestine.* Journal for the Study of the Old Testament Supplement Series, 103. Sheffield, 1990.

Zertal, Adam. "An Iron Age Cultic Site on Mount Ebal: Excavation Seasons 1982–1987." *Tel Aviv* 13–14 (1986–1987): 105–65.

5. Cup-and-Bowl Vessel

*Samaria, Palestine; discovered in Munshara
    Tomb C*
Iron Age II, 9th century B.C.E.
Ceramic
*H: 9.8–10 cm.; cup D (at rim): 10.2 cm.;
    bowl D (at rim): 19.1 cm.*
*W. F. Albright Institute of Archaeological
    Research 37193*

This example of an enigmatic type of ceramic vessel was found in an Iron Age tomb in Samaria, within the territory of what then would have been the northern kingdom of Israel. It is a double form, consisting of an inner cup, with molded rim, attached at its base to a shallow bowl with a rounded base. The entire vessel is wheel-made. Its interior consists of a coarse grayish-buff ware, and it is covered with a thick red slip.

These forms have a long history in Palestine, with the earliest examples coming from as early as the Early Bronze II-III (third millennium B.C.E.) and the latest ones from the end of Iron II (sixth century B.C.E.) Yet the preponderance of examples are from the Late Bronze, Iron I, and early Iron II periods. This example thus dates toward the end of its chronological range. Because it comes from a site in the northern part of the country, it fits the distribution pattern of these vessels, which appear mainly at northern sites. Although they have been found at dozens of sites, they are not found in the same quantities as are vessels intended for daily household activities.

That the function of the cup-and-bowl form has not been conclusively established is evident in the variety of names, some fanciful and anachronistic, used to describe them, for example, candlesticks, gravy boats, cup-and-saucers, vases for fresh flowers, torch holders, lamps. Some examples have been discovered in cultic settings, others in domestic or mortuary ones. The occasional traces of burning, along with Aegean parallels apparently intended for incense, make it possible that at least some were incense burners. Such vessels would be expected in a variety of contexts; and, given the expense of incense, they would have been luxury items rather than common domestic wares. Fragments of three cup-and-bowl vessels have been found in a tenth-century context at Tel ʿEin Zippori; their presence lends credence to the possibility that the early Iron II settlement included a building complex that had a specialized function (see the essay on Sepphoris and Lower Galilee in this catalogue).—*CLM*

6. Fragmentary Cup-and-Bowl Vessel

Not Illustrated
Tel ʿEin Zippori; Sepphoris Regional Project
Iron Age II, 9th century B.C.E.
Ceramic
D: 10 cm.
Israel Antiquities Authority 95-4028

———————————

This is one of three cup-and-bowl vessels found at Tel ʿEin Zippori. Their presence at the site may indicate a population able to import expensive aromatics not available locally.—CLM

REFERENCES

Meyers, Carol L. "Fumes, Flames, or Fluids? Reframing the Cup-and-Bowl Question." In *Boundaries on the Near Eastern World: A Tribute to Cyrus H. Gordon—Fourscore and Eight*, ed. Meir Lubetski, Claire Gottlieb, and Sharon Keller. Sheffield, forthcoming.

Tappy, Ronald. "Cup-and Saucers." In *The Archaeology of Israelite Samaria*. vol. I. Harvard Semitic Studies, 44. Atlanta, 1992.

7. Figurine of a Female with Hand-Drum

Palestine; exact provenance unknown
Iron Age II, c. 8th–7th centuries B.C.E.
Pottery
H: 21.8 cm.
Harvard Semitic Museum 5755

———————————

This figurine is typical of a wide variety of terracotta votive figurines known from the Iron II and later periods in ancient Israel and the Cypro-Archaic I (750–600 B.C.E.) and later periods in Cyprus. As a group, these artifacts portray men and women engaged in various activities, including the creation of music. The greatest quantities of these terracottas have been discovered in Cyprus. However, their method of manufacture probably originated in Syria-Palestine, and a representative sample of the objects has been recovered from Palestinian sites, especially northern ones with connections to the Phoenician coast.

This example was constructed by the attachment of a hand-modeled head to a wheel-made base, which is hollow and forms the skirt of the female figure. The ware is buff-colored and is decorated with black and red paint, including vertical stripes on the skirt to create an apron-like effect. The modeled part of the object consists of a woman's head, neck, and arms, with the curved arms holding a disc-shaped object. Because it is held at an angle with the woman's hand pressed against its flat side, the object can be identified as a portable frame-drum, or hand-drum. (Similar round objects, depicted as held parallel to the chest, usually are interpreted as cakes or loaves of bread.)

The figure appears to be somewhat crudely modeled in that the fingers are not individually delineated. That feature, however, is probably related to the fact that the

females are depicted playing an assortment of musical instruments, including flutes, cymbals, lyres, and hand-drums. The hand-drum, however, seems to be associated almost exclusively with females, as in this example and many similar ones. That association may reflect a distinct female musical tradition in which women accompanied, composed, and/or led the rhythmic songs that were performed, along with dance, at festive occasions.—*CLM*

REFERENCES

Meyers, Carol. "A Terra-cotta at the Harvard Semitic Museum and Disc-holding Female Figures Reconsidered." *Israel Exploration Journal* 37 (1987): 116–22, pl. 7A.

Meyers, Carol. "The Drum-Dance-Song Ensemble: Women's Performance in Biblical Israel." In *Rediscovering the Muses: Women's Musical Traditions*, ed. Kimberly Marshall. Boston, 1993: 49–67.

Vandenabeele, Frieda. "Phoenician Influence on the Cypro-Archaic Terra-cotta Production and Cypriot Influence Abroad." In *ACTS of the International Symposium "Cyprus between the Orient and the Occident,"* ed. Vassos Karageorghis. Nicosia, 1986: 351–60.

woman is meant to be playing a hand-held drum; her fingers would thus be tightly pressed together as she strikes the instrument's stretched membrane. The woman's face is rather finely rendered. The nose and mouth are outlined with narrow black lines; the almond-shaped eyes have distinct pupils and curved brows. Perhaps the only touch of extravagance in the other-wise simple portrayal is the treatment of the hair. Although smooth at the crown, with straight and even bangs, the hair falls in full and flaring locks at either side of the woman's face. The almost puffy spread of the thick strands covers her shoulders and ends at the crook of her bent arms.

In the repertoire of terracottas from ancient Israel and Cyprus, both males and

8. Rhyton

Sepphoris; chance find, followed by excavations by Emmanuel Eisenberg for the Israel Antiquities Authority
Persian period, 4th century B.C.E.
Terracotta
H: 29.5 cm.
Israel Antiquities Authority 79-356

The long horn of this terracotta rhyton terminates in the body of a winged hybrid creature. The partly restored horn was wheel-made, whereas the *protome* (representation of the head and neck of an animal), which combines the head of a lion, the body of a horse, and the wingspread of a bird (eagle?) was produced in a double mold. The lion's head is plastically modeled; it has an open mouth, fierce, bulging eyes, and a thick lower mane; these features, combined with the pointed horse's ears and mane and the addition of horns (now broken) on the lion's head create a remarkable griffin-like effect. Various ornamental elements and other details are emphasized by the red-painted decoration over black glaze; for example, the grooved outlines of the feathers of the wings are delineated by the paint. The creature, presented as reclining, rests on its forelegs; between them is a small hole, out of which wine was poured.

The horn-rhyton with an animal *protome* is believed to have originated in Achaemenid Persia. Precious metals, such as gold and silver, were initially used in its production; later imitations were made in faience, alabaster, and clay. The griffin motif, first encountered in Mesopotamia in the third millennium B.C.E., became a characteristic symbol of the Achaemenians, the ruling house of ancient Persia (Iran). That this particular vessel was made out of less costly material suggests that the horn-rhyton was popular as well among less wealthy segments of society. This type of drinking vessel was also produced in Greece, where Achaemenid prototypes, probably brought back from the Persian Wars after 480 B.C.E., were imitated.

The rhyton from Sepphoris, which was found by chance, probably was an import; it has western as well as eastern features and was produced in the Attic style. The vessel's fourth-century-B.C.E. date is supported by the numerous black-glazed Attic sherds found with it.—*MD-M*

REFERENCES

Eisenberg, Emmanuel. "A Greek Rhyton from Sepphoris." *Qadmoniot* 18 (1985): 31–33 (in Hebrew).

Hoffman, H. "The Persian Origin of Attic Rhyton." *Antike Kunst* 4 (1961): pl. 12.

Stern, Ephraim. "Achaemenid Clay Rhyta from Palestine." *Israel Exploration Journal* 32 (1982): 36–43.

PERSIAN-PERIOD INCENSE BURNERS

Large numbers of small, cube-shaped incense burners or altars, mostly dating to the Persian period (sixth-fourth centuries B.C.E.) have been found in Palestine. These burners are usually square and either squat or tall. Most are made of limestone, stand on four legs, and have a shallow basin at the top, which often bears traces of soot. Some of the burners are plain, whereas many others bear figurative and plant motifs as well as geometric designs. A few are decorated with reliefs or with attached animal sculptures. Because they have been found in sanctuaries, dwellings, and tombs, their function remains a matter of dispute; it is unclear whether they served ritual or secular purposes, or both.

Similar burners have been found in South Arabia, Mesopotamia, and Cyprus. Some of the Arabian burners bear inscriptions containing words for aromatic substances. Likewise, an incense burner from Lachish is inscribed with the word *lebonah* (frankincense).

William F. Albright (1976) mentioned the use in modern South Arabia of burners of the same general shape and size, and with the names of spices inscribed on their sides, suggesting that they served a secular purpose, as cosmetic burners. Quoting a book by S.W. Baker published in 1868, Albright described how seminomadic women of Sudan scented their bodies and clothes by placing hot coals in a hole in the floor of their tents, covering the coals with fragrant herbs and spices, and then crouching naked over the fumes, with their robes draped loosely over their backs, so that their skin and clothing would absorb the scent. The small burners may have been used in the home also for the purpose of fumigation. This brings to mind the practice mentioned in the Mishnah and Talmud of burning incense at the end of a meal (Berakhot 6:6) to create a pleasant atmosphere and to fill the room with a good scent. One should not, however, exclude the possibility that the cuboid incense burners were but a portable version of the larger cubic incense altars of the Iron Age.—MD-M

9. Incense Burner

Beth-Shean; excavated by Nehemiah Tsori for the Israel Antiquities Authority
Persian period, 6th–4th centuries B.C.E.
Limestone
H: 9 cm.; W: 6 cm.; D: 6 cm.
Israel Antiquities Authority 79-11

This tall, square incense burner was carefully shaped. It stands on four, carved out legs, which form an arch at the bottom of each side. Each arch is set within a high, recessed rectangular niche carved into each of the sides. The resulting protruding border gives the impression of an architectural facade, seemingly with columns along the sides and a lintel on top. Two of the incense burner's sides are complete, and two are damaged. The basin at the top is shallowly carved.

The decoration consists of a combination of incised lines and puncture-style chiseling in figurative and geometric motifs. Each side is ornamented with a similar geometric frame, in which a different figurative scene is set. The part of the protruding frame that is above the niche bears two horizontal bands of triangles separated by a double line. Each triangle is filled with a lattice pattern. Several vertical lines are incised on either side of this design, above the sides of the protruding frame, which are themselves decorated with a zigzag pattern that extends over the corners. Within the niche at the top, the pattern of triangles is repeated. Beneath it the figurative motifs appear, varying on each side. One of the complete sides depicts two animals of different sizes, apparently deer, one standing behind the other; the second also bears two animals, perhaps horses or donkeys, one apparently mounted by a rider. The scenes appearing on the broken sides are incomplete. One contains the back of an animal; the other, the image of a palm tree. The top of the burner, around the basin, is decorated with a pattern of triangles.

The style of this incense burner, particularly the use of figurative motifs set within geometric frames, is reminiscent of a group of Persian-period incense burners at Gezer and Tell Jemmeh.—*MD-M*

10. Incense Burner

Not Illustrated
Sepphoris; Joint Sepphoris Project
Persian period, 6th–4th centuries B.C.E.
Limestone
H: 11 cm.; W: 16.2 cm.
Israel Antiquities Authority 95-3884

This incense burner discovered at Sepphoris is remarkably large in comparison to others of the type, though only a portion of it has survived—one complete side and part of another. In all probability the original was a rectangular chest that stood on four carved out legs, which formed an arch at the bottom of each of the four sides. The basin was carved about one-third of the way down from the top. Traces of soot are still visible along the inside rim.

The sides of the burner were carelessly incised with a combination of figurative and geometric motifs. The decoration on the one complete side consists of an arch, created by two incised lines, which frames the opening between the legs. The arch is surmounted by a triangle, and both are flanked by what appear to be the images of two upright snakes facing one another. Two trees, one on the far left and one on the far right, complete the rather uneven symmetry of the scene. The damaged side is ornamented with geometric patterns, including a decorated rhombus and a circle encompassing a star motif. The top ridge of the burner is incised with a band of triangles bordered by double lines.

This incense burner, with its crude execution and combination of geometric and plant motifs, recalls other incense burners that have come to light at Gezer and Lachish. —*MD-M*

REFERENCES

Albright, William F. "The Beautician Reveals Secrets of Queen Esther's Cosmetic Aids." *Biblical Archaeology Review* 1–2 (1976): 4–6.

Shea, M. O. "The Small Cuboid Incense Burners of the Ancient Near East." *Levant* 15 (1983): 76–109.

Stern, Ephraim. "Incense Altars." In *The Material Culture of the Land of the Bible in the Persian Period*, 538–332 BC. Jerusalem, 1982: 182–95.

11. Vase Fragment

*Sepphoris; chance find by the University of
    Michigan Expedition*
Achaemenid, c. 465–330 B.C.E.
Fine-grained white stone
H: 5.5 cm.; W: 4.9 cm.; Thickness: 1.6 cm.
Kelsey Museum of Archaeology 90109

This fragment comes from the upper body
of a stone vessel. Parts of two lines of
cuneiform writing are incised in the outer
surface, reading from left to right (Stolper,
1980). The upper line has the beginning of
the royal name Artaxerxes in Achaemenid
Elamite signs; the lower line has the beginning of the name in Babylonian signs.
Most Achaemenid royal inscriptions, even
short texts on portable items, were multi-
lingual, with the text in the language of the
rulers, Old Persian, placed first. Intact
examples show that the inscription of the
original vessel from which this fragment
came was no exception. The original had
the text in Old Persian cuneiform above
the Elamite and running parallel to it.
Furthermore, like a few Achaemenid
objects made in Egypt, it also had an
Egyptian hieroglyphic version of the text
in a single vertical column running down
the body of the vessel perpendicular to
the middle of the cuneiform texts. All four
versions read: "Artaxerxes, King" (in
Egyptian, perhaps "Great King").

Old Persian
$[a\text{-}r\text{-}t\text{-}x\text{-}š\text{-}ç\text{-}a : x\text{-}š\text{-}a\text{-}y\text{-}θ\text{-}i\text{-}y]$

Elamite
$^{DIŠ}ir\text{-}tak\text{-}i[k\text{-}šá\text{-}iš\text{-}šá \ ^mEŠŠANΛ]$

Babylonian
$^{m}ar\text{-}ta \ a[k\text{-}šá\text{-}as\text{-}su \ LUGAL]$

Egyptian
$[Ȝrthšš \ pr\text{-}ˁȝ \ (pȝ \ ˁȝ)]$

The comparable intact examples are all of similar shape, proportions, and material but of somewhat different sizes. They have ovoid bodies, widening from shoulder to base, with short necks, wide out-turned rims, unperforated lugs below the shoulders, and plain bases; they are between 32 cm. high by 19 cm. maximum width and 20 cm. high by 13.5 cm. maximum width; they are made of a varieties of calcite described as alabaster or aragonite. A black paste filling is preserved in some of the incised characters of one example.

Because similar objects have quadrilingual inscriptions with the name of Xerxes, similarly arranged, these calcite vessels are attributed to Artaxerxes I (465–425 B.C.E.), son of Xerxes, while another vessel with a nearly identical inscription, but of different shape and made of granite, is attributed to Artaxerxes III (359–338 B.C.E.).

Excavated examples of such vessels or excavated fragments from them are scarcer than purchased examples without reliable provenances. Still, the objects seem to have been widely distributed throughout and even beyond the territories of the Persian empire. Fragments with inscriptions of Darius I (521–486 B.C.E.) in Egyptian hieroglyphics only were excavated at Susa, the site of one of the royal residences in Iran; and an intact vessel of Darius was said to have been found in Syria in 1931, the same year in which the Sepphoris fragment was found. Fragments with quadrilingual inscriptions of Xerxes I (486–465 B.C.E.) were excavated at Susa and in the temple quarter at Uruk in southern Babylonia, whereas intact examples were bought in Egypt, in Baghdad,

and in Aleppo. One intact Xerxes vessel was excavated at the Mausoleum at Halicarnassus, on the Aegean coast of Anatolia (Asia Minor), where one of the intact examples with a quadrilingual inscription of Artaxerxes I was also found. Another intact Artaxerxes vessel was discovered accidentally near Orsk (formerly Orenburg) in southern Russia, in a subsequently excavated Sarmatian burial mound attributed to the fourth or early third century B.C.E., not much later than the stone vessel itself. Another fragment from an Artaxerxes vessel was excavated at Susa, and still other intact and fragmentary examples were bought in Baghdad and in Egypt, and one was bought in Aleppo from a man who said that it came from Syrian Hierapolis.

Because of their shape, these vessels are sometimes characterized as containers for cosmetics or unguents, but their presence in the temple precinct of Uruk, the mausoleum, and the Orsk burial suggests that they were distributed beyond the Achaemenid courts as sumptuary goods— votive objects or precious curios.—*MWS*

REFERENCES

Burchardt, Max. "Datierte Denkmäler der Berliner Sammlung aus der Achämenidenzeit." *Zeitschrift für Ägyptische Sprache und Altertumskunde* 49 (1911): 74–77.

Kent, Roland G. *Old Persian*. American Oriental Series, 33. New Haven, 1935: 115 sub AVs.

Mayrhofer, Manfred. *Supplement zur Sammlung der altpersischen Inschriften*. Österreichische Akademie der Wissenschaften, philosophisch-historische Klasse Sitzungsberichte, 338 = Veröffentlichungen der Iranischen Kommission, 7. Vienna, 1978: 28–29.

Posener, G. *La première domination perse en Égypte*. Bibliothèque d'Étude, 11. Cairo, 1936: 137–51.

Schmidt, Erich F. *Persepolis*. II: *Contents of the Treasury and Other Discoveries*. Oriental Institute Publications, 69. Chicago, 1953: 84–87.

Stolper, Matthew W. Review of *Supplement zur Sammlung der altpersischen Inschriften*, by Manfred Mayrhofer. *Archiv für Orientforschung* 27 (1980): 176.

THE MIZPEH YAMIM HOARD

These four bronze objects were found together in 1986 during an archaeological survey at a site on the peak of Mount Mizpeh Yamim, at the southern edge of Upper Galilee. Later excavations (1988–89) have determined that the objects were found next to a temple and suggest that the site as a whole was a sanctified temple precinct. The earliest occupation was from Iron Age II (1000–586 B.C.E.), but the temple and other buildings were erected in the Persian period (586–332 B.C.E.). In the main room of the temple, three pillars supported the roof; offerings (mainly juglets) were found on benches situated around the walls; and at the west end was a stepped-altar, probably for a statue of the deity. Many bones, probably the remains of sacrifices, were found to the west of the temple. During the Hellenistic period (332–37 B.C.E.) the site became an open cult center and the altar was adapted to serve for sacrifices. Also during this period the site was deserted, probably as a result of violent destruction. The Phoenician inscription on the situla suggests that the Persian-period temple was Phoenician and that the deity worshipped was Astarte. The bronzes were found close to the altar and probably were deposited as votive offerings during the final stages of occupation. The Apis bull as well as a slate figurine of the Egyptian gods Osiris, Isis, and Horus were both broken and the parts widely scattered, suggesting that they were smashed as an act of desecration, perhaps by Hasmonean conquerers of the site.—*RF*

12. Egyptian *Situla* with Phoenician Inscription

*Mizpeh Yamim; excavations on behalf of
  Haifa University by Rafael Frankel
Persian period, c. 586–332 B.C.E.
Bronze
L: 16.7 cm.
Israel Antiquities Authority 87-1443*

This is a typical *situla*, an Egyptian libation vessel used in funerary rites. The Egyptian motifs are in four registers. The top register depicts a solar bark dragged by four jackals and greeted by four baboons. The second register depicts a worshipper, probably a priest, making offerings to a series of seven deities. The third register consists of

named after Osiris-Apis (the dead Apis), known by the Greeks and Romans as Sarapis/Serapis. His cult was popular among Greeks and Egyptians alike.

This example, although quite simple, is similar to the classic Memphite form both in stance and attributes. It strides with left legs leading, and the brush of the tail joins the right leg. On the forehead is an inscribed triangle; between the horns, a disc and *uraeus* (symbolic serpent); on the neck, a simple collar; and on the back, a winged scarab beetle, a blanket with slanting crisscross decoration, and a hint of a vulture with wings spread. The bull was discovered without its back left leg and base (see photo), but the leg was found elsewhere in the excavation and has been restored to its original position.—*RF*

Figurines in the form of recumbent ruminants were used in the region as weights, but these usually had a cavity in which to place lead in order to adjust the weight. The Mizpeh Yamim ram has no such cavity and is of solid bronze. However, because figurines identical to it are known to be weights—except that they are smaller in size, as part of a set containing several successive sizes—it is probable that this recumbent ram figurine served as a weight as well.—*RF*

kneeling figures representing the "souls of Pe and the souls of Nekten." The final register is the floral (lotus) decoration of the tip of the *situla*.

In addition there is a Phoenician inscription, apparently added at a later stage, stating that the *situla* was dedicated to the goddess Astarte by a man named Akhbo(r?), the son of Bod Eshmun, in thanks for her having answered his prayer. The inscription is engraved horizontally on the strip between the rim and the first register and vertically between the beginning and the end of the second register. —*RF*

15. Prancing Lion Cub

Mizpeh Yamim; excavations on behalf of
Haifa University by Rafael Frankel
Persian period, c. 586–332 B.C.E.
Bronze
H: 4.7 cm.; L: 8.6 cm.
Israel Antiquities Authority 87-1441

---

13. Apis Bull

Mizpeh Yamim; excavations on behalf of
Haifa University by Rafael Frankel
Persian period, c. 586–332 B.C.E.
Bronze
H: 7.5 cm.; L: 7.8 cm.
Israel Antiquities Authority 87-1440

The Apis bull was an Egyptian deity associated with the god Ptah. A living Apis bull was kept at the ancient Egyptian capital, Memphis; and Apis bulls were buried in the underground chambers in the Serapeum at Saqqara. The Serapeum was

14. Recumbent Ram

Mizpeh Yamim; excavations on behalf of
Haifa University by Rafael Frankel
Persian period, c. 586–332 B.C.E.
Bronze
H: 4.6 cm.; L: 6.1 cm.
Israel Antiquities Authority 87-1442

The pose of this recumbent ram, facing sideways with its legs folded under its body, is commonly portrayed on art objects throughout the ancient Near East and probably originated in Mesopotamia.

This feline is shown crouching on its haunches as if about to pounce. The face is deeply incised, its ears large and protuding. There is no molded mane, but the incisions on the neck and shoulders could represent the mane of a young animal. The body is not carefully molded, nor are the haunches distinguished. The long tail that terminates in a large tuft curves upward, and the anus is marked but the sexual parts hidden. The figurine probably represents a male.

The general proportions are those of a young animal. A hole through the back indicates that this piece was originally attached to another object, perhaps the rim of a crater.

This figurine does not conform to any of the various conventional ways of depicting lions known from the ancient world. Perhaps it was the work of a local artist who took a live lion cub as a model, for lions were still found in the region at this time.—*RF*

REFERENCES

Frankel, Rafael. "Har Mizpe Yamim, 1988/1989." *Excavations and Surveys in Israel* 9 (1989–90): 100–102.

Iliffe, J. H. "A Hoard of Bronzes from Askalon." *Quarterly of the Department of Antiquities in Palestine* 5 (1936): 61–68, pls. 29–34.

Lichteim, Miriam. "Situla No. 11395 and Some Remarks on Egyptian Situlae." *Journal of Near Eastern Studies* 6 (1947): 169–79.

Stern, Ephraim. *The Material Culture of the Land of the Bible in the Persian Period, 538–332 BCE.* Jerusalem, 1973: 214 (in Hebrew).

Winter, Erich. *Der Apiskult im alten Ägypten.* Main, 1978.

16. Jar Fragment with Inscription in Hebrew

Sepphoris; Joint Sepphoris Project
Hellenistic period, c. 2d century B.C.E.
Ceramic
L: 15 cm.; W: 8 cm.
Israel Antiquities Authority 95-3886

On this jar fragment, beneath the handle, are seven ink-written Jewish (square Hebrew) letters, typical of the second century B.C.E., that read as follows: *'pmlsĺš . . . [ ].*

Although there is no clear division between words, and the inscription is incomplete, it seems likely that the first five letters, *'pmls*, form a Greek word reminiscent of *epimeletes*, meaning "manager, overseer, one who is in charge." This word occurs in a Palmyrene inscription and in rabbinic literature (Tosefta, *Baba' Batra'* 10:5; Babylonia Talmud, *Baba' Batra'* 144b, *Menaḥot* 85b). The term is associated with *gabbay*, or "treasurer, manager."

In this jar inscription there is no letter *ṭet* to form the word *epimeletes*; thus *'pmls lš*[ ] may perhaps mean "caring for . . .,"

"to pay attention to . . .," or the like. If this inscription of a Greek word written in Hebrew letters does refer to an officeholder—a manager or overseer—it is a particularly noteworthy find. It would provide valuable archaeological evidence of a developed Jewish community in the city at a relatively early date, otherwise attested to primarily in literature.—*JN*

Roman-period Sculpture

17. Figurine of Pan (?) or a Satyr

Sepphoris; Joint Sepphoris Project
Roman period, c. 2d-3d centuries C.E.
Bronze
H: 6 cm.
Israel Antiquities Authority 95-3887

This small figure of a seated musician is identified as a satyr due to the presence of the pipes that he plays, his pointed ears just visible in the treatment of the hair, and the bunch of grapes held in his right hand (Meyers et al., 1986: 4; 1992: 24). Unlike earlier figures of Pan, this figure does not have the lower limbs of a goat. The presence of the grapes underscores the figure's associations with the cult of Bacchus/Dionysos and supports a banqueting context in a private home at Sepphoris.

In spite of the weathered surface and the loss of certain details (in particular the right foot), the satyr, depicted as seated on a rocky outcrop and seemingly absorbed in his music, is remarkably expressive. The treatment of the head and the softness implied by the limbs give the figure a childlike quality, in contrast to the often grotesque or even sinister representations of the rustic deity Pan.

Bronze statuettes depicting divinities or mythological figures were common items of domestic material culture throughout the Roman Empire. They represent either cultic objects from a household shrine or decorative attachments, often from furniture and thus devoid of explicit religious significance. Figurines of Pan became particularly popular during the Hellenistic period, when the bucolic god with goat's legs, human torso, horns, and lusty bearing represented pastoral life and, by extension, a nostalgia for simpler times. By the Roman period, the individual deity "Pan" had become conflated with the satyrs constituting the retinue of the wine-god Bacchus (the Greek Dionysos). Satyr figures therefore symbolized conviviality and often were featured in banqueting contexts, as attachments to banqueting vessels or furniture.

This satyr from Sepphoris displays an open stance and rounded limbs, like the figure of Prometheus found with it (see cat. no. 18); these features and other similarities—for example, the surface treatment—bolster the suggestion that they were created in the same workshop. In the absence of a direct monumental prototype, figurines of satyrs such as this are more

likely to represent Roman provincial reinterpretations of a Hellenistic type rather than a specific copy.—SHC

REFERENCES

Kozloff, Arielle P. and David Gordon Mitten. *The Gods Delight: The Human Figure in Classical Bronze*. Bloomington, 1988.

Meyers, Eric M., Ehud Netzer, and Carol L. Meyers. "Sepphoris, 'Ornament of All Galilee.'" *Biblical Archaeologist* 49 (1986): 4 19.

Meyers, Eric M., Ehud Netzer, and Carol L. Meyers. *Sepphoris*. Winona Lake, 1992.

18. Figurine of Prometheus

Sepphoris; Joint Sepphoris Project
Roman period, c. 2d–3d centuries C.E.
Bronze
H: 7.5 cm.
Israel Antiquities Authority 94-2592

Images of the mythical figure of Prometheus enduring punishment by being chained to a rock while an eagle consumes his liver are relatively rare on Roman objects. The image tended to appear on objects such as *terra sigillata* (stamped red ceramic ware), lamps, and gems. Although ancient authors mention the existence of statues of the bound Prometheus, this bronze statuette from Sepphoris constitutes the only extant example in-the-round from the Roman period (Meyers et al., 1986: 5; 1992: 24; *Lexicon Iconographicum Mythologiae Classicae*, 1994: 539, no. 50; 424, no. 50).

The statuette depicts Prometheus with his right foot raised, as if balanced on a rocky outcrop; his arms outspread, effecting a chained pose; his head to the side bent in pain. The pathos of the image is heightened by the figure's open mouth, evoking agony.

Given the small scale of the figurine, the modeling of the torso is remarkably subtle and expressive, especially in the curve of his spine and in his musculature. Accretions to the bronze have resulted in a blurred effect, which masks what must have been a highly polished surface treatment. In light of its small size, the Prometheus figurine was probably originally attached to a larger object by a tenon under his left foot.

That the Prometheus figurine was found in the same cistern as the figurine of "Pan" or a satyr (cat. no. 17) may imply that both were deliberately hidden there, possibly indicating their worth to their owner. The find spot indicates a domestic context in a residential area that probably was Jewish. However, their presence in a Jewish dwelling more likely reflects the influence of pagan decorative culture than the adoption of such religious beliefs or practices.—SHC

REFERENCES

Lexicon Iconographicum Mythologiae Classicae. Zurich and Munich, 1994: 7.1, 531–53; 7.2, 420–30.

Meyers, Eric M., Ehud Netzer, and Carol L. Meyers. "Sepphoris, 'Ornament of All Galilee.'" *Biblical Archaeologist* 49 (1986). 4-19

Meyers, Eric M., Ehud Netzer, and Carol L. Meyers. *Sepphoris*. Winona Lake, 1992.

19. Figurine of the Head and Forelegs of a Bull

Sepphoris; University of South Florida Expedition
Roman period, before mid-fourth century C.E.
Bronze
H: 7 cm.
Israel Antiquities Authority 87-900

20. Miniature Altar

Sepphoris; University of South Florida Expedition
Roman period, before the mid-4th century C.E.
Bronze: cast
H: 2.5 cm.; W: 1.9 cm.; L: 1.8 cm
Israel Antiquities Authority 87-902

This miniature cast bronze figurine was found in association with a small bronze altar (see cat. no. 20) and bronze bowl in a surface locus of Chamber 229. Its proximity to these other two bronze objects suggests that they were discarded as a group, and the altar may indicate that the group as a whole had cultic associations.

The high circular horns and, especially, the molded creases at the bull's neck indicate that this figurine belongs to the class of those representing Serapis, shaped as Apis, the bull god. The Ptolemaic (Ptolemy I, ruled 323–283 B.C.E.) cult of Serapis was associated with the sacred bull Apis into the Roman period. Apis was the bull worshipped at the temple in Memphis. His powers and his representation were taken over into Hellenistic and Roman worship of Serapis, both at his central shrine in Alexandria and throughout the Roman world (Cary et al., 1949: 68, 745, 793). Usually such depictions are life-sized, with Apis shown in a walking position, as in the Hadrianic-period (rule of Hadrian, 117–38 C.E.) example currently in the Graeco-Roman Museum in Alexandria (see Riad et al., n.d.; 67 and fig. 13). But miniature examples (c. 5 x 10 cm.) of the walking bull from the Roman period have been found in Yugoslavia (Poporic, 1969: 108, no. 157) and Savona, Italy (Comstock and Vermeule, 1971: 143, no. 169; note the hole between the horns for attaching a disc). However, a miniature bull or cow's head found at Rabat in Morocco indicates that figurines representing only the head also were cast; the neck served as a base so that the animal could gaze frontally at the viewer (Boube-Piccot, 1975: 322, no. 602 and pl. 262).

This find at Sepphoris is unusual in that the forelegs of the bull also appear, as well as the head and neck; and the hole at the base indicates that it ornamented something else, probably the head of a staff.— *DEG*

REFERENCES

Boube-Piccot, Christine. *Les bronzes antiques du Maroc.* II: Le Mobilier. Études et travaux d'archéologie marocaine, 5. Rabat, 1975.

Cary, M. et al., eds. *The Oxford Classical Dictionary.* Oxford, 1949.

Comstock, Mary and Cornelius Vermeule. *Greek, Etruscan, and Roman Bronzes in the Museum of Fine Arts, Boston.* Boston, 1971.

Poporic, Lj. B. *Anticka Bronza U Jugoslaviji.* Belgrade, 1969.

Riad, Henri, Youssef Hanna Shehata, and Youssef El-Gheriani. *Alexandria: An Archaeological Guide to the City and the Graeco-Roman Museum.* Alexandria, n.d.

This miniature altar was found in close association with two other bronze artifacts, a figurine of the head and forelegs of a bull (cat. no. 19) and a small bowl or laver. These artifacts lay on top of the fill in a cistern that was abandoned and sealed in the mid-fourth century. Although no precise parallels are known for this extremely small miniature altar, similar altars are not unknown (Pritchard, pls. 575, 579, 581). The function of this object remains uncertain, but the fact that several similar altars were used as incense burners, and the association of this object with the bull and laver, suggest that this is an artifact related to the practice of religious rites.

The altar stands on four short legs that form an arch at the bottom of each side. Above each arch is a round opening. The top is slightly larger than the base upon which it stands.—*TRWL*

REFERENCE

Pritchard, James B. *The Ancient Near East in Pictures Relating to the Old Testament.* 2d ed. with supp. Princeton, 1969.

21. Relief Plaque with Figural Scene

Sepphoris; Sepphoris Regional Project
Roman period, c. 1st century B.C.E.–
*   1st century C.E.*
Bronze
H: 4.9 cm.; W: 4.9 cm.
Israel Antiquities Authority 96-2222

This relief plaque appears to be broken along its upper edge; the remaining edges are intact. Within a U-shaped field, for which a horizontal groove serves as a groundline, a winged figure in right profile rides a horned and bearded goat (?). In front of them is what appears to be a table or altar, the side of which is ornamented with an "x" between a horizontal band above and below; there is a broad molding beneath. Resting on top of the table or altar is a tall conical object flanked by spherical ones.

Conical objects thought to be breads occasionally appear on offering tables or altars. The light-hearted character of this scene is frequently encountered in small-scale arts of the Hellenistic and Roman periods, particularly among terracotta reliefs with Dionysiac scenes.—*ER*

REFERENCES

Besques, Simon Mollard. *Catalogue raison-né des figurines et reliefs terre-cuite grecs étrusques et romains.* vol. 1. Paris, 1971: pl. 379 d, e, g.

Borbein, Adolf Heinrich. Campanareliefs: *Typologische und stilkritische Untersuchungen.* Mitteilungen des Deutschen Archaeologischen Instituts. Römische Abteilung. Ergänzungs-Heft 14. Heidelberg, 1968: pls. 2,21, 31.1.

22. Head of Dionysos

Not Illustrated
Purchased; reportedly found at Gadara,
*   Jordan*
Roman period, c. 2d century C.E.
Marble
H: 32 cm.
Israel Antiquities Authority 35-3254

This head is identified as the Greco-Roman god Dionysos by the band across his forehead and the wreath of ivy leaves, rosettes, and grape clusters encircling his head. The god's right hand is preserved; it rests atop his head, and clasps a left hand, either his own or that of a now-lost sub-sidiary figure. This gesture is related to that of a popular sculptural type of Apollo, known as the Apollo Lykeios (named after the Lykeion Gymnasium in Athens, where a statue of Apollo with his right hand atop his head stood).

This marble head, though not from Sepphoris, has been included in the exhibition as a complement to representations of the god in the Dionysos mosaic discovered at the site (see related article). Dionysos, the Greco-Roman god of wine and the theater, was widely worshiped in Palestine, where legend held that he was the founder of the city of Beth-Shean (Scythopolis). Also worshiped at such sites as Antioch and Baalbek in the wider region of the Levant (modern Lebanon, Syria, Israel, and Jordan), Dionysos was frequently honored by the display of marble sculptures; at least eight statues of the god have been found in the Levant.

To date, no such marble statuary has been recovered from the site of Sepphoris. One explanation is that marble sculptures may have been displayed at the site but not have survived in the archaeological record. In the Byzantine and Early Arab periods, marble artifacts frequently were burned to produce lime, a component of cement; indeed, a limekiln was discovered next to the theater. Alternately, marble sculptures may never have been displayed in the public buildings of Sepphoris because of the strong Jewish character of the city. The display of three-dimensional representations of pagan deities may have been foregone in accordance with the Second Commandment, which forbids the creation and worship of graven images. That no marble statuary has been recovered from Tiberias, the other major Jewish city of Galilee, supports this latter theory.

Because there is no native source of marble in the Levant, all marble artifacts discovered in this region were imported. This head of Dionysos probably originated in one of the famous sculptural workshops of Asia Minor because it has a thick, squared support at the nape of its neck, a technical feture unique to the sculptors of Turkey.—*EAF*

REFERENCES

Augé, Christian and Pascale Linant De Bellefonds. "Dionysos (In Peripheria Orientali)." In *Lexikon Iconographicum Mythologiae Classicae.* vol. 3. Zurich and Munich, 1986: 518, no. 36 (this sculpture).

Smith, Morton. "On the Wine God in Palestine." In *Salo Wittmuyer Baron Jubilee Volume II.* Jerusalem, 1974: 815–29.

Traditions and Rituals of Worship

23. Chancel Screen

Susita (Hippos); excavated by Moshe Dothan and Ruth Amiran for the Israel Antiquities Authority
Byzantine period, late 6th century C.E.
Marble
H: 87 cm.; L: 148 cm.
Israel Antiquities Authority 52-710

Both sides of this marble chancel screen are decorated with relief carvings set into rectangular panels. The front of the screen portrays a small architectural structure consisting of columns that support an arch adorned with a shell or with the radiating lines of a half dome. Hanging from the base of the shell or half dome is a round object, perhaps a lamp. The delicately rendered structure probably represents either the entrance to a monumental building (mostly likely a church) or the architectural decoration of the apse of the church.

The front of the screen also carries a Greek inscription flanked by two crosses. It reads: "In the time of Procopius the Presbyter." This presbyter is mentioned in another inscription in Greek discovered in the church where this chancel screen was found. The second inscription carries the date 591 C.E., enabling us to date the ecclesiastical activities of Procopius to the late sixth century C.E.

The back side of the screen is decorated with a large aquatic animal, probably a dolphin, a well-attested motif in Nabatean, Roman, Jewish, and Christian art (Goodenough, 1956: 11–13, 22–27). It has been slightly damaged, either by someone trying to efface or remove the representation or by chance.

This chancel screen was found in one of four churches that have been discovered at Susita (Hippos). The church in question, a triapsidal basilica, was richly decorated with marble columns and a marble floor in *opus sectile* technique. It was destroyed by an earthquake. It has been suggested that this church was Susita's cathedral, because of its large size (20 x 40 m.) and its opulent decoration.

Chancel screens were tremendously popular in the Late Roman and Byzantine periods (fourth to sixth centuries C.E.) throughout the Roman Empire, including Palestine. They were used in both churches and synagogues. Some chancel screens imitated lattice work; others consisted of a flat piece of stone decorated in relief, as does this example. Made of marble, and originating in marble workshops usually located in Asia Minor, these flat slabs of stone were used in churches as parapets that served to separate the apse and the area around the altar from the rest of the church. Chancel screens thus gave visible

expression to the existing liturgical division between clergy and laity. They stand at the basis of a development that in later Byzantine churches led to the construction of a more formal architectural division: the iconostasis or icon screen.—*LVR*

REFERENCES

Goodenough, Erwin R. *Jewish Symbols in the Greco-Roman Period.* vol. 5. New York, 1956.

Russo, Eugenio. "La scultura del VI secolo in Palestina." *Acta ad arch. et art. hist. pert.* 8, no. 6 (1987): 113–246.

Tzaferis, Vassilios. "Susita Awaits the Spade." *Biblical Archaeology Review* 16, no. 5 (1990): 50-58.

Ulbert, Thilo. *Studien zur dekorativen Reliefplastik des östlichen Mittelmeerraumes Shrankenplatten des 4.–10. Jahrhunderts.* Munich, 1969.

24. Model of the Basilical Synagogue from Gush Ḥalav

Not Illustrated
[The synagogue was constructed in the 3d century C.E., repaired and reconstructed in the 4th century, and destroyed by earthquake in the 6th century]
Wood
H: 100 cm.; L: 127 cm.
Prepared by the Israel Museum, Jerusalem

The model shows the ancient synagogue of Gush Ḥalav in Upper Galilee as it survived into the Byzantine period. It is a basilica featuring two rows of four columns on stylobates (continuous platforms) running north-south. The design of the main sanctuary with a central nave separated from two side aisles by rows of columns is typical of many ancient synagogues in the

Land of Israel. The southern wall, constructed of finished ashlar stones, faces Jerusalem and has a small raised *bema* or dais alongside the main entrance; the principle of sacred orientation to Jerusalem is thus maintained. An eagle is incised into the underside of the lintel of this doorway, likewise drawing attention to the southern end of the building.

Of special interest are the three interior areas to the west, east, and north. On the western side is a long corridor that apparently was used for the storage of construction materials for repairs or liturgical supplies; a coin hoard, preserved in a ceramic pot, was discovered here. To the north, another interior space or mezzanine perhaps provided extra seating. The space on the eastern side of the building may have been used for additional synagogue-related activities. The addition of these side rooms gives the building an overall shape that is nearly square (17.5 m. x 18 m.); but the hall itself (13.75 m. x 10.7 m.) has classic basilical proportions.

The model presents the roof as a shed construction. It is also possible that there was at one time a clerestory roof (having a row of windows along the uppermost part of the wall). The founding courses of the building are laid on the foundations of earlier structures, indicating a long period of occupation in this area.—*CLM AND EMM*

REFERENCE

Meyers, Eric M. and Carol L. Meyers. *Excavations at the Ancient Synagogue of Gush Ḥalav.* Winona Lake, 1990.

[handwritten margin note: Sentrums not E?]

25. Synagogue Mosaic with Dedicatory Inscription

Sepphoris; excavated by Prosper Viaud
Late Roman or Early Byzantine, 4th–5th
*   centuries C.E.*
D *(of medallion): 60 cm.*
Custody of the Holy Land

This ancient synagogue mosaic comes from one of the numerous Sepphoris synagogues mentioned in ancient rabbinic sources. The script and content of the Aramaic inscription suggest a Late Roman or Early Byzantine date. A large portion of the inscription on the right side of the medallion is missing, but some of its contents as well as the identity of Rabbi Yudan may be conjectured on the basis of a similar inscription at nearby Kafr Kana.

Aramaic text:
dkyr
[ltb] rby ywdn
[br tn] ḥwm wbr
dyhb ḥd

Translation:
Remembered
. . . for good, Rabbi Yudan,
. . . son of Tanḥum, son of . . .
. . . who gave one [dinar?].

Based on information in the Kafr Kana inscription, Rabbi Yudan can be identified as the son of Tanḥum and Butah. On the basis of a complete Aramaic inscription from Ḥammath-Gader in the Golan, the restoration of "dinar" for the amount of the donation may be suggested. The recent publication of the zodiac synagogue mosaic from Sepphoris has revealed a possible multigenerational connection in the Jewish community there. Several Aramaic donor inscriptions mention a certain Yose son of Yudan and Tanḥum son of Yudan, suggesting the possibility that Yose and Tanḥum could have been brothers. It is therefore quite possible that Rabbi Yudan of this inscription from beneath the church of Saint Anne was the father of Yose and Tanḥum who made donations to the recently discovered synagogue of Sepphoris. If such a suggestion is correct, the inscriptions provide a four-generation genealogy of a single Sepphorean family that lived in the late fourth and fifth centuries C.E.

Donor inscriptions in synagogues are very common in ancient Palestine and in the Diaspora. The colorful letters in this mosaic are very similar in form to ones found by the Joint Sepphoris Project in debris in the western summit excavations and to the script attested in the newly excavated Byzantine synagogue of Sepphoris. The well-known *archisynagōgos* inscription, also found on the property of the Church of Saint Anne, is probably Late Roman or early Byzantine as well.
—*EMM*

REFERENCES

Hüttenmeister, F. and G. Reeg. *Die antiken Synagogen in Israel.* Teil 1. Wiesbaden, 1977: 402–3.

Naveh, Joseph. *On Stone and Mosaic: The Aramaic and Hebrew Inscriptions from Ancient Synagogues.* Tel Aviv, 1978: 51–52, no. 29 (in Hebrew).

Netzer, Ehud and Zeev Weiss. *Zippori.* Jerusalem, 1994: 55–58.

Weiss, Zeev and Ehud Netzer. *Promise and Redemption: A Synagogue Mosaic from Sepphoris.* Jerusalem, 1996.

26. Mosaic Fragment with Greek Inscription

Ḥuldah; excavated by J. Ory for the Israel Department of Antiquities
Byzantine period, 5th century C.E.
Black border: 92 x 50 cm.
Israel Antiquities Authority 53–582

Located in Ḥuldah, some 8.5 km. southeast of Reḥovot, in the ancient territory of Lod-Diospolis, and near the important ancient Samaritan synagogue of She‘albim, the two-room building in which this mosaic was situated has not been identified with certainty. Although it was first thought to be a synagogue, now it seems more likely that it was a Jewish or Samaritan ritual bath complex. The closest parallel is the Samaritan site of Qedumim, which suggests that it could be associated with the olive oil industry.

Of special interest is the southern room with its mosaic floor of white tesserae and its plastered walls. The room has a round stepped pool (2.5 m. in diameter) with a sump in the center; the pool is connected by a lead pipe to a square basin that is shallower than the pool. The mosaic on display was set just south of the stepped pool; another Greek inscription in a medallion is located to its west. The organization of the Ḥuldah mosaic is as follows: a rectangular black border, 92 x 50 cm., encloses an assemblage of symbols, creating an oblong panel that consists of smaller and finer tesserae. The Greek inscription is situated slightly to the left of center.

The text of the mosaic is as follows:

eulogía   "Blessing
tō laō   to the People."

The use of Greek in Palestinian Jewish epigraphy is widely attested, especially in urban areas. Its use at Ḥuldah, in a presumably nonurban, Byzantine setting, is striking, as is the language, which is similar to that of Greek inscriptions from the Diaspora.

The symbols on the mosaic are part of the standard repertoire of late antique Jewish art; they are, left to right: *lulav* (palm branch) interwoven with two other species of branches; *etrog* (citron); incense shovel; *menorah* (lampstand); and *shofar* (ram's horn). The *menorah* has seven branches, each topped by a square receptacle and red wick. The *menorah* is the main symbol of Jewish iconography in antiquity and represents the Temple lampstand (see cat. nos. 32, 35, 41, 82–3, 117–18); the *lulav* and *etrog* are symbols associated with the feast of Succoth or Tabernacles; the incense shovel was used in the Temple service (but see cat. no. 27); the *shofar*, also associated with the Temple, where it was sounded to announce holidays and the New Year, is a symbol of redemption, reminiscent of the ram's horn in the story of Abraham and Isaac in Genesis 22 (see cat. no. 28). The fifth-century-C.E. synagogue mosaic excavated at Sepphoris by the Hebrew University features a *menorah* and other Jewish symbols, including the *shofar*, *lulav*, and incense shovel (see fig. 65).
—*EMM*

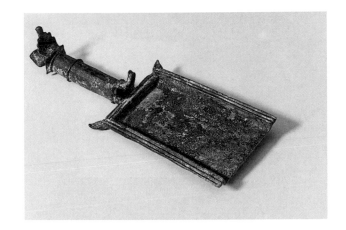

REFERENCES

Avi-Yonah, Michael. "Various Synagogal Remains: Ḥuldah." Louis M. Rabinowitz Fund for the Exploration of Ancient Synagogues *Bulletin* 3 (1960): 57–60.

"Notes and News." *Israel Exploration Journal* 3 (1953): 133–34.

27. Incense Shovel

Probably Eastern Mediterranean
Roman period, 1st–2d centuries C.E.
Bronze: cast
L: 29.21 cm.; W: 12.38 cm.
North Carolina Museum of Art G.78.15.1
Gift of Abram and Frances Kanof in Honor of Mrs. Fanny Heilig

The pan of this rectangular bronze shovel has an everted ledge rim decorated with parallel incised lines. The tubular handle terminates in a decorative leaf form. On two corners of the pan are small leaf-like projections, apparently intended to support flat cups for incense. Four bronze shovels found in the Bar Kokhba caves in the Judean desert feature similar brackets. The most complete of the four shovels retains incense cups, the short stems of which have been soldered to the brackets (Yadin, 1963: pl. 15, figs. 11 and 12). Similar shovels have been found at other sites in Israel, the Middle East, Italy, and France and have been connected by archaeologists with Greek and Roman and, later, Christian rituals. These shovels have been identified as fire-pans for burning incense: coals were placed in the pan, whereas the cups held incense to be sprinkled periodically over the coals.

Bronze shovels were among the implements of the Temple ritual, although their function has been a subject of debate among scholars. Some maintain that the shovels actually were used as incense burners, as suggested by Leviticus 16:12. Others argue, based on Leviticus 24:1–4, that they served as snuff dishes for cleaning up burned wicks from the *menorah* lamps or, as described in Exodus 27:3, for removing ashes from the altar.

Shovels were portrayed in synagogue mosaics in Israel from the fourth century on, appearing together with other symbols of the Temple, such as the *menorah*, the *shofar* (ram's horn), and the *lulav* (palm frond). See, for example, the mosaic from Ḥuldah (cat. no. 26) and the synagogue mosaic from Sepphoris (fig. 65). Erwin R. Goodenough suggested that the grouping of the shovel with symbols of great ritual significance in works of art may indicate that its use in the Temple had indeed been as a censer for cultic purposes rather than as a humble snuff dish (Goodenough, 1953: 197).—*RMN*

REFERENCES

Ackerman, Andrew S. and Susan L. Braunstein. *Israel in Antiquity from David to Herod.* Exhibition catalogue, the Jewish Museum. New York, 1982: 119, cat. no. 119.

From the Lands of the Bible: Art and Artifacts. Exhibition catalogue, America-Israel Culture House. New York, 1968: cat. no. 196, illus. p. 62 (this shovel).

Goodenough, Erwin R. *Jewish Symbols in the Greco-Roman Period.* vol. 4. New York, 1953: 195–208.

Hachlili, Rachel. *Ancient Jewish Art and Archaeology in the Land of Israel.* Leiden, 1988: 256–66.

Narkiss, M. "The Snuff-Shovel as a Jewish Symbol." *Journal of the Palestine Oriental Society* 15 (1935): 14–28.

Yadin, Yigael. *The Finds of the Bar Kokhba Period in the Cave of Letters.* Jerusalem, 1963: 48–58.

28. *Shofar*

German (?), 1751

Horn

L: 39.3 cm.

North Carolina Museum of Art G.75.16.3

Gift of Mr. and Mrs. Arnold Shertz

This *shofar*, or trumpet of ram's horn, is inscribed in Hebrew with the date 1751 and (on both sides) the words: "Happy is the people who know the joyful shout; [O Lord,] they walk in the light of your presence" (Ps. 89:15). Three bands of inscribed diamond fret patterns ornament the *shofar*, one near each end and one where the horn bends. Along the outside curve a series of scallops, some pierced with round holes, further enlivens the form.

The *shofar* has been used throughout Jewish history. In biblical times it was sounded for various reasons: to summon people in times of war, to warn them in times of danger, for the inauguration of kings, and to mark joyous occasions. The *shofar* was sounded in the Temple together with two trumpets to summon the faithful to repentance on Rosh Hashanah (New Year) and to mark the end of the fast on Yom Kippur (the Day of Atonement). After the destruction of the Temple in 70 C.E., the *shofar* was extensively used in the synagogues, where it was sounded to mark various distinctive occasions, such as the announcement of a new rabbinic decision,

at funerals, and during the High Holy days to remind the faithful to open their hearts to God's redemptive power. According to rabbinic teaching, the sound of the *shofar* also reminds God to move from the throne of judgment to the throne of mercy. The *shofar* as a symbol of compassion and redemption was closely associated with the story of Abraham and Isaac, in which a ram was substituted for Isaac as a sacrifice (Gen. 22:13); hence the *shofar* in art may generally be understood as a symbol of messianic hope.

The *shofar* may be made from the horn of an animal in the sheep or goat family, but by Greco-Roman times the curved horn of a ram was preferred. Beginning in the second and third centuries C.E., the *shofar* appears frequently in synagogue and funerary art, most often with other Jewish symbols, including the *menorah*, the incense shovel, and the *lulav* (a palm branch or bundle of branches), as on the mosaic from a synagogue complex in Ḥuldah in this exhibition (see cat. no. 26).—*RMN*

REFERENCES

Finesinger, Sol B. "The Shofar." In *Hebrew Union College Annual*. vol. 8–9. Cincinnati, 1931–32: 193–228.

Goodenough, Erwin R. *Jewish Symbols in the Greco-Roman Period*. vol. 4. New York, 1953: 167–94.

Hachlili, Rachel. *Ancient Jewish Art and Archaeology in the Land of Israel*. Leiden, 1988: 256–66.

29. Replica of *Menorah* from Hammath Tiberias

Not Illustrated
[*Original discovered by N. Slouschz in 1921
    on southwest shore of the Sea of Galilee*
*Late Roman or Early Byzantine, 3d–4th
    centuries C.E.*
Limestone
H: 46 cm.; W: 60 cm.; Thickness: 13 cm.
*Original: Israel Museum, Jerusalem 1729.66
    os]*
*Replica: Center for Restoration, Israel
    Museum, Jerusalem*

This cast of a seven-branched *menorah*, or lampstand, from Hammath Tiberias is a replica of the original found along the southwest shore of the Sea of Galilee by N. Slouschz in 1921. Cut out of a single block of white limestone, the *menorah* is decorated only on the front side and is carved in low relief. The exterior side and backside are unfinished, suggesting that the *menorah* was placed against or was attached to a wall or flat surface.

The lampstand consists of a central stem with three branches on either side. On top of all the branches is a horizontal crosspiece with seven hollow spaces, corresponding to the seven branches, in which glass or ceramic lamps could be inserted. The bottom portion and base of the lampstand are missing. Each of the branches is decorated with alternating pomegranates and flowers, no doubt echoing the arboreal origins of the *menorah* in the Tabernacle or Wilderness Shrine and the First Temple, which are reflected in the vision of Zechariah (chap. 4) for the Second Temple.

The Hammath Tiberias *menorah* is remarkable in that it clearly was intended to be used in the synagogue in which it

was found. Virtually all other examples have no functional use; rather they were incorporated as central items in the design or decoration of a special place in a synagogue, such as a lintel or mosaic. The date of this piece is probably Late Roman, though it could be Early Byzantine (4th-6th centuries C.E.). The *menorah* is the most distinguishing symbol of Jewish antiquity. Found most often in synagogues and tombs, it denotes either the Temple lampstand(s) or, more generally, Jewish identity, its lights signifying light and illumination. The *menorah* is especially common after 70 C.E., when the Temple was destroyed by the Romans.—*EMM*

REFERENCES

Israeli, Yael. "Menorah." In *Highlights of Archaeology: The Israel Museum*. Jerusalem, 1984: 102–3.

Sukenik, Eleazar L. *Ancient Synagogues in Palestine and Greece*. London, 1934: 55.

30. Replica of a Limestone Ark Fragment

[*Original Ark Fragment from Nabratein;
    Meiron Excavation Project*
Roman period, 3d century C.E.
Limestone
H: .58 m.; L: 1.30 m.; W: .50 m.
Original: Israel Antiquities Authority 81-507]
*Replica: Center for Restoration, Israel
    Museum, Jerusalem*

This finely carved limestone block is the pediment, or Syrian gable, from the Torah Shrine (Holy Ark) of the ancient synagogue of Nabratein in Upper Galilee. (A Syrian gable is one whose base is arched in the center.) At the beginning of the Late Roman period, this repository for sacred scrolls stood on one of the twin *bema*s, or prayer platforms, of a small basilical synagogue (11.6 m. x 13.75 m., external dimensions). This architectural fragment was damaged in the 306-C.E. earthquake that toppled the building, but enough of the key elements of its design have survived so that a precise reconstruction is possible.

A raised border, or raking cornice, 1.35 m. across the bottom and .62 m. high at its peak, defines the pediment. A frieze of egg-and-dart molding is interrupted by three rosettes inside the three angles. The twelve-petaled rosette at the peak is somewhat larger (10 cm. in diameter) than are the six-petaled rosettes (6.5 cm. in diameter) at the side angles.

The deeply sculpted arch within the Syrian gable is .36 m. high. The radiating lines within it may represent a scallop shell; or, given the structural nature of the block as the pediment of an aedicula, it may signify the half-dome ceiling of this portal to a shrine. In any case, the hole drilled through the top of the arch cornice apparently facilitated the hanging of a chain to

REFERENCES

Hachlili, Rachel. "The Niche and Ark in Ancient Synagogues." *Bulletin of the American Schools of Oriental Research* 223 (1976): 43–53.

Meyers, Carol L. and Eric M. Meyers. "The Ark in Art: A Ceramic Rendering of the Torah Shrine from Nabratein." *Eretz Israel* 16 (1982): 176–85.

Meyers, Eric M., James F. Strange, and Carol L. Meyers. "The Ark of Nabratein—A First Glance." *Biblical Archeologist* 44 (1981): 237–43.

Meyers, Eric M., James F. Strange, and Carol L. Meyers. "Second Preliminary Report on the 1981 Excavations at En-Nabratein, Israel." *Bulletin of the American Schools of Oriental Research* 246 (1982): 35–53.

(sanctuary) lamp

hold the lamp, or eternal light, that has been suspended in front of the Torah Shrine in synagogues from antiquity to the present.

The solidity of the gable is enhanced by the two rampant lions, nearly .70 m. from mane to paw, stretched above the raking cornices. The realistic modeling of these wild carnivores—with their taut bodies, open mouths, and erect penises—connotes strength and energy.

Architectural fragments with similar motifs, mosaic floors depicting Torah Shrines, and even an incised rendering of a Holy Ark on a ceramic bowl from Nabratein are well known from Palestinian antiquity, but the Nabratein gable is the first fragment that can be identified unequivocally as a functioning Torah Shrine. As such, this third-century pediment links the Torah Shrine, the architectural focus of synagogues as known from the medieval period to the present, with its biblical antecedent, the Ark of the Covenant.—*CLM*

31. Silver Relief Plaque with David Dancing before the Ark of the Covenant

German; Circle of Anton Eisenhoit (?)
c. 1550–1600 C.E.
Silver cast; silver gilt
H: 15.2 cm.; W: 16.5 cm.
North Carolina Museum of Art 83.4
Gift of Abram and Frances Pascher Kanof

This small, sixteenth-century German silver relief sculpture shows King David playing the harp and dancing before the Ark of the Covenant as another musician blows a long trumpet and four men carry the Ark by its staves. According to biblical tradition, the Ark served as a container for the tablets handed down by God to Moses at Sinai and represented the covenant between God and the Israelites. The cover was flanked on the ends by sculpted cherubim, who spread their wings to protect the Ark and to provide support for the invisible throne of God, which symbolized the divine presence in the Tabernacle (Exod. 25:1–22). The artist of the relief plaque has been fairly faithful to the biblical description of the Ark.

The Ark of the Covenant is the symbolic prototype for the Torah Shrine, or Holy Ark, a container for the Torah scrolls in the synagogue (see cat. no. 30). Despite these associations, this relief plaque has no apparent connection with Jewish ceremonial observance. Apparently it served as a decorative attachment; perhaps, given the religious subject, it adorned a type of domestic shrine ("Hausaltar") popular in Germany in the late sixteenth century (Kreisel, 1968: figs. 242 and 243).

In 1912 Otto von Falke attributed this relief to Westphalian goldsmith and engraver Anton Eisenhoit (von Falke, 1912: 48, pl. 40). In an unpublished letter to the North Carolina Museum of Art in 1983, Anna Maria Kesting suggested a more tentative attribution to Eisenhoit, reserving the possibility that the piece could have been made by a North German or North Dutch master working in close association with Eisenhoit. A goldsmith's mark (in the extreme upper left corner of the rectangle representing the ground) has yet to be identified.—*RMN*

REFERENCES

von Falke, Otto. *Die Kunstsammlung Eugen Gutmann*. Berlin, 1912.

Kesting, Anna Maria. *Anton Eisenhoit: Ein Westfalischer Kupferstecher und Goldschmied*. Münster, 1964.

Kreisel, Heinrich. *Die Kunst des deutschen Möbels*. vol. 1. Munich, 1968.

Burial Customs

BURIAL INSCRIPTIONS

Inscriptions in Aramaic or Greek that mention the names of the deceased are found in many tombs throughout Galilee, mostly at Beth-She'arim but also at Sepphoris, as exhibited here. Inscriptions were carved, incised, or painted on the tomb's entrance, its walls, or alongside the actual burial place. In most cases, an inscription was made directly on the tomb's wall or on the tombstone, though some inscriptions were on special plaques attached close to the resting place of the deceased (as in the case of HU 2409). Burial inscriptions were mounted on sarcophagi and small burial chests as well. Each inscription includes the deceased's name, to which additional information is added, such as the name of the father of the deceased, his or her age at the time of death, place of birth, occupation, and so on. Blessings for the deceased and curses on anyone who defiles the grave are found in some cases.

Because Sepphoris was one of the most important cities in Galilee, its cemetery was perhaps no less rich and elaborate than that of Beth-She'arim. Unfortunately, the various tombs around Sepphoris cannot be excavated because current antiquities law forbids the excavation of Jewish burials throughout the country. Perhaps future excavations on the necropolis of Sepphoris will be allowed; if so, they no doubt will produce important information regarding not only the burial customs of the ancient Jewish society at Sepphoris but also the actual burial places of some of the many rabbis who resided there during the Roman and early Byzantine periods.
—ZW

32. Tombstone with *Menorah* and Inscription

Sepphoris; chance find followed by excavations by Eleazar L. Sukenik for the Hebrew University of Jerusalem
Roman period (?)
Gray marble
H: 10.8 cm.; W: 10.8 cm.; Thickness: 2.3 cm.
Institute of Archaeology, Hebrew University of Jerusalem 2409

This tombstone is said to have been found in one of the many burial caves of ancient Sepphoris but not *in situ*. The square plaque is decorated with an incised, seven-branched *menorah*. An Aramaic inscription naming the person who was buried in the cave is incised along both sides of the *menorah*'s shaft. The inscription reads: "R. Yosa Hirorah." The title Rabbi might indicate that the deceased belonged to the rabbinic class. The meaning of the second name, "Hirorah," is unclear; it could refer to his family name or a nickname. The word "Hirorah," derived from the Aramaic word for "white," may indicate that he suffered from an illness, possibly an eye or skin disease. The use of a nickname appears in talmudic literature, for example, in the case of Rabbi Abba Semukah, who was a redhead (Palestinian Talmud *Berakhot* 9:1, 12a).—ZW

185

33. Tomb Inscription in Aramaic and Greek

Sepphoris; excavated by Adam Druks for the Israel Antiquities Authority
Byzantine period
Marble
H: 23 cm.; L: 27 cm.
Israel Antiquities Authority 80-886

Inscription: "This grave is of Nachum and Ya‿akov, sons of Rabbi Hosochi, may his soul rest in peace."—ZW

34. Tomb Inscription in Aramaic

Sepphoris; excavated by Adam Druks for the Israel Antiquities Authority
Byzantine period
Marble
H: 18.5 cm.; L: 39 cm.
Israel Antiquities Authority 80-887

Inscription: "Hoshea, son of Tanhum from Tiberias."—ZW

REFERENCES

Druks, Adam. "Zippori." *Excavations and Surveys in Israel* (1984): 18–19 (in Hebrew).

Naveh, Joseph. *On Sherd and Papyrus.* Jerusalem, 1992: 190–207 (in Hebrew).

Schwabe, Moshe and Baruch Lifshitz. *Beth She‿arim.* vol. 2. Jerusalem, 1974.

Sukenik, Eleazar L. "Two Jewish Tombstones from Sepphoris." *Bulletin of the Jewish Palestine Exploration Society* 12 (1946): 62–64 (in Hebrew).

Weiss, Zeev. "Social Aspects of Burial in Beth She‿arim: Archaeological Finds and Talmudic Sources." In *The Galilee in Late Antiquity,* ed. Lee I. Levine. New York and Jerusalem, 1992: 357–71.

35. Stone with Jewish Symbols from a Cemetery in Tiberias

Tiberias; excavated by Emmanuel Damati for the Israel Antiquities Authority
Byzantine period, 4th–6th centuries C.E.
Basalt
H: 40 cm.; L: 53 cm.
Israel Antiquities Authority 94-3336

This piece of unpolished basalt, probably part of a lintel from the entrance to a tomb in Tiberias, is decorated in low relief with Jewish symbols arranged within a circular band. The band is tied at the bottom in a large knot, from which one strand curves up on the right to terminate in a pomegranate design. The symbols are a seven-branched lampstand (*menorah*) with tripod base, a citron fruit (*etrog*) and a palm branch (*lulav*) to the right of the lampstand, and a ram's horn (*shofar*) to its left. A very similar stone reported to have been brought to Tiberias from Gadara, a few miles southeast of the Sea of Galilee, features the *menorah, lulav,* and *shofar* encircled by a wreath tied with a knot (Goodenough, 1953: vol. 1, p. 219; vol. 3, pl. 574).

The representation of ritual objects is characteristic of late antique Jewish art, in which they symbolize the Temple (the *menorah*) and the Jewish holidays of Succoth (the *etrog* and *lulav*) and Rosh Hashanah (the *shofar*). These are commonly found symbols in synagogues and in Jewish funerary art (Hachlili, 1988: 234–62). The pomegranate, though less frequently portrayed in Jewish art, epitomizes a decorative vegetative theme for which there are parallels (see, for example, Goodenough, 1953: vol. 3, pl. 563).

36. Decorated Ossuary from Mount Scopus with Inscription

Jerusalem, from a tomb on Mount Scopus;
excavated by Varda Sussman for the Israel
Antiquities Authority
Roman period, 1st century C.E.
Limestone
H: 45 cm.; L: 85 cm.; W: 39.5 cm.
Israel Antiquities Authority 89-2827

An ossuary is a container used in Roman-period Jewish practice for the reburial of the bones of the deceased. Despite biblical prohibitions against contamination through contact with the dead or the dessicated remains of the dead, both collective secondary burial (*ossilegium*) and reburial into individual ossuaries occurred over many centuries in antiquity, from the Iron Age into the Byzantine period, though individual receptacles were used for a more limited time. The custom of reburying the bones of the deceased is particularly well represented in western Galilee at the burial mound of Beth-She'arim, where the majority of interments are reburials. Even sarcophagi were used for multiple reburials, though some large rooms were used as common reburial places for bones.

Ossuaries were made of stone, clay, or wood; stone examples were fashioned after wooden prototypes. Some were lavishly decorated, as is this example from a tomb on the west slope of Mount Scopus; others were not decorated at all; and some, only modestly. The custom of individual reburial into decorated ossuaries is especially well documented in Jerusalem; in Galilee, the custom of reburial seems to have ended

This piece was found in one of the cemeteries of Tiberias. In antiquity Tiberias was known for having been built on a cemetery. In recent years archaeologists have discovered several of the ancient cemeteries of the city, but the majority of these excavations have yet to be published. Consequently, we are still ill informed about Jewish funerary customs in Tiberias during the period when it became one of the great centers of rabbinic Judaism.

The use of basalt, a stone of volcanic origin, is characteristic of the area surrounding the Sea of Galilee, as well as of the Golan. —*LVR*

REFERENCES

Goodenough, Erwin R. *Jewish Symbols in the Greco-Roman Period.* vols. 1–3. New York, 1953.

Hachlili, Rachel. *Ancient Jewish Art and Archaeology in the Land of Israel.* Leiden, 1988.

Hirschfeld, Yizhar. *A Guide to Antiquity Sites in Tiberias.* Jerusalem, 1992.

Levine, Lee I. "R. Simeon b. Yohai and the Purification of Tiberias: History and Tradition." *Hebrew Union College Annual* 49 (1978): 143–85.

at the end of the Roman period. This example dates to the first century C.E.

The decorations on ossuaries may have had significance, but there is no scholarly consensus on the matter. In general, the ritual of secondary burial was intended to reassure the living family members that the deceased had been judged by God, cleansed of sin, and entitled to resurrection.

Gabled lid: The front of the lid features a shallow relief of five vine leaves with two additional leaves extending left and right carrying grape clusters. Toward the ends of the lid the tendrils resolve into stylized lilies. A six-petaled rosette is inscribed on the right side of the lid; the left side is bare.

Ossuary front side: The center of the panel profiles an acanthus leaf cluster with its fruits. This cluster is flanked on either side by two plump grape clusters, with smaller clusters or rosettes hanging down from them. Both grape clusters are suspended from a bar that is attached to and extends across the top of the rectangular frame over the entire scene.

Inscription: Above central scene, from right to left, is inscribed, in Hebrew:

yhwsf br ḥnnyh hsfr

"Joseph, son of Ḥananya, the scribe"

Ossuary left side: A sunken panel is adorned with leafs and berries tied by a ribbon.

Ossuary right side: A sunken panel is decorated with a six-petaled rosette inside an egg-and-dart circle.—*EMM*

REFERENCES

Rahmani, Levi Y. *A Catalogue of Jewish Ossuaries.* Jerusalem, 1994: cat. no. 893.

Sussman, Varda. "A Burial Cave on Mount Scopus." *ʿAtiqot* 21 (1992): 89–96, ossuary no. 1.

37. Ossuary with Inscription

Qiryat Tivʿon; excavated by Fanny Vito for the Israel Antiquities Authority
Roman period, late 1st or 2d century C.E.
Limestone
H: 34 cm.; L: 59 cm.; W: 26 cm.
Israel Antiquities Authority 71-404

This roughly cut ossuary was discovered in a five-chambered, rock-cut tomb in western Galilee very close to the Jewish necropolis of Beth-Sheʿarim. It is one of five stone ossuaries, or bone receptacles, found there, along with fragments of three others, including a clay one. The material recovered with them clearly dates the ossuaries to the end of the early Roman period, circa 100 C.E. Attestation of secondary burial (reburial of the bones of the deceased) is widespread outside of Jerusalem, but more frequently than not, without the reinterment into an individual receptacle such as this. Two-thirds of the burials uncovered at the large burial mound of the sages at nearby Beth-Sheʿarim were secondary burials, mostly without individual receptacles for the dead. Most importantly, extreme care was lavished on the remains of the dead after initial interment, a concern that surely relates to a belief in an afterlife.

Inscription (not visible in photo):

"of Maia / [daughter] of Saul"

(*Maias,* genitive of the attested female name *Maia; Saoulos,* genitive of the common male name Saul.)—*EMM*

REFERENCES

Rahmani, Levi Y. *A Catalogue of Jewish Ossuaries in the Collection of the State of Israel.* Jerusalem, 1994: 172.

Vitto, F. "Notes and News." *Israel Exploration Journal* 24 (1974): 274.

38. Lead Coffin from Beit Ṣafafa

Beit Ṣafafa; excavated by Jacob H. Landau for the Israel Antiquities Authority
Byzantine period, late 5th century C.E.
Lead
H: 17 cm.; L: 89 cm.; W: 25 cm.
Israel Antiquities Authority 52-801

This Christian lead sarcophagus was found near the village of Beit Ṣafafa on the southern edge of Jerusalem when work on drainage led to the discovery of an underground burial structure that had been constructed of well-hewn ashlar stones and contained eight tombs. Six tombs contained lead coffins; two were empty. A simple white mosaic covered the floor of the structure, and each tomb had a stone covering slab. A funerary chapel was excavated north of the tomb structure.

All of the lead coffins were manufactured identically. The long sides and base were cast in a single mold, as were the two short sides, which were soldered to the base and two long sides; reinforcements were added at the corners. Each lid is slightly vaulted and is fastened with tongues that attach at the apex of the short side. All but one of the coffins were decorated in similar ways; they feature Latin crosses and cable-patterned circles or wreaths.

The long and lid sides of this example are divided by diagonal cables that form rhombuses. Each of the long sides contains three crosses; a large upright Latin cross is featured in the central rhombus. Similar but smaller crosses appear on each of the short sides. The side lid also is partitioned by diagonal cables and has large crosses in the two rhombuses; a third cross appears in an outer triangle. A circle appears in each of the flanking triangles, with one smaller circlet running down the fold on the narrow side.

The short length of the coffin suggests that it was used for a child—the larger coffins range from 1.69 m. to 1.82 m. in length. One other coffin in this group (IAA 53.1270), 93 cm. in length, also was intended for a child or infant. The coffins were locally made but are similar to ones found in Lebanon, in particular, Tyre. Lead coffins were also used at Beth-She'arim (about 16 km. from Sepphoris) in the burial mound of many of the Jewish sages. Although the use of lead coffins was not rare, it is nonetheless indicative of social standing if not wealth. The use of the Latin cross is surely a sign of the deceased's religion and an expression of faith.—*EMM*

REFERENCES

Landau, J. H. "Excavation of a Family Tomb in the Vicinity of Beit Ṣafafa." *Bulletin of the Department of Antiquities of the State of Israel* 5/6 (1957): 40–42 (in Hebrew).

Rahmani, Levi Y. "More Lead Coffins from Israel." *Israel Exploration Journal* 37 (1987): 139–46, pl. 17:c.

Yeivin, Shmuel. "Archaeology in Israel (1951-53)." *American Journal of Archaeology* 59 (1955): 166, figs. 24–25.

Amulets and
Mirror Plaques

AMULETS

Amulets are portable implements made from solid materials, such as earthenware or metal, or from soft materials, such as papyrus or cloth, incised with incantations and magical symbols. In antiquity, amulets made of soft materials usually were rolled, put in a case, and worn around the neck or hung in a room.

Both the literature of late antiquity and the archaeological record bear witness to the widespread popularity of amulets. Jews and Christians employed them as protection from disease, to promote fertility, to coerce someone into a love affair, or to bring ill fortune on an enemy or a competitor—powers derived from the incantations and magical symbols incised or written on the amulets. The incantations utilized names and formulas from across the spectrum of ancient Near Eastern and Mediterranean religions, although names and words drawn from the Jewish tradition were especially popular. Biblical (e.g., I-Am-Who-I-Am) and nonbiblical (e.g., Nereg) names for God, the names of angels (e.g., Gabriel), and biblical verses (e.g., Num. 12:13) were employed to capture power and to direct it toward the desired end. Magical symbols in the form of zodiac signs, letter permutations, or geometric designs likewise were used to ensure that the amulet became infused with the protective or coercive power drawn to it.—CTM AND BG-M

39. Aramaic Amulet against Fever

Sepphoris; University of South Florida
*   Expedition*
Byzantine period, 5th century C.E.
Bronze
8.2 cm. x 3.2 cm.
Israel Antiquities Authority 93-509

This bronze amulet was discovered in soil 55 cm. below the surface and 43 cm. above a mosaic carpet that covered the floor of the northwestern corner of the large basilical building situated on the eastern flank of Sepphoris (McCollough and Glazier-McDonald, 1996). The amulet likely was carried in a case and worn around the neck. When found, it was tightly rolled but not in a case or outer wrapping; nevertheless, it was remarkably well preserved. Unlike most amulets that have been recovered, the original edges of this one are intact. The difficult task of unrolling the amulet was performed by Joseph "Dodo" Shenhav of the Israel Museum in Jerusalem. The amulet was drawn by Ada Yardeni of Jerusalem.

The amulet is partially broken at the bottom, but it is unlikely that the incantation continued beyond the final row of letters. The language of the incantation is Palestinian Aramaic. Amulets for protection from disease apparently were the most common, and the incantation on this one, incised with a bronze stylus, is for the purpose of warding off a fever. Typical magical devices, including magical signs or symbols, series of magical letters, and names for God, are incorporated on this amulet. The letters and symbols are meant to draw to it the power necessary to heal a severe fever.

Because there is no personal reference, the amulet likely was produced by a dealer in amulets who, using manuals with prescribed magical formulae, could produce such devices cheaply and quickly. Literary evidence and the growing archaeological

record indicate that the desire for such protective magical devices was great in the Late Roman and Byzantine periods and that this desire cut across religious and social boundaries.

Translation of Text on Aramaic Amulet

1. An Amulet Against Fever

2. Protracted that Burns

3. And Does Not Cease.

4. (Three Magic Signs)

5. (One Magic Sign) Nun Nun (Final) Nun Waw He Yodh He Aleph Waw

6. Aleph Aleph Aleph Sin Sin Sin

7. An Amulet Against Fever

8. Protracted That Burns

9. And Does Not Cease (Magic Sign)

10. (Three Magic Signs)

11. Nun Nun (Final) Nun Waw He Yodh He

12. Aleph Waw Aleph Aleph Aleph

13. Sin Sin [Sin]

—*CTM AND BG-M*

REFERENCES

Bonner, C. *Studies in Magical Amulets: Chiefly Graeco-Roman.* Ann Arbor, 1950.

Gager, J. *Curse Tablets and Binding Spells from the Ancient World.* New York, 1992.

McCollough, C. Thomas and Beth Glazier-McDonald. "An Aramaic Bronze Amulet from Sepphoris." *'Atiqot* (English Series) 28 (1996): 161–65.

Naveh, Joseph and Shaul Shaked. *Amulets and Magic Bowls.* Jerusalem, 1987.

Naveh, Joseph and Shaul Shaked. *Magic Spells and Formulae: Aramaic Incantations from Late Antiquity.* Jerusalem, 1992.

Schrire, T. Hebrew Amulets: *Their Decipherment and Interpretation.* London, 1966.

ALSO IN THE EXHIBITION

40. Rolled Amulet

Palestine; exact provenance unknown
Byzantine period
Bronze
L: 2.5 cm.
Israel Antiquities Authority 57-5738

41. Mirror Plaque with *Menorah* and Birds

Palestine; exact provenance unknown
Byzantine period, c. 5th century C.E.
Limestone with traces of pigment
H: 34 cm.; W: 48 cm.
Institute of Archaeology, Hebrew University of Jerusalem 2474

The low relief decoration of this limestone plaque includes three architectural shrines flanked by columns. Each shrine has a circular depression for a mirror; traces of glass remain in the lower two shrines and in the eye of the bird on the left. The lower two shrines also have triangular gables within which are arched openings. Above them, the third shrine is topped by a pair of short columns, but other portions of its decoration are broken off. The center axis of the design is marked by a *menorah* (seven-branched lampstand), its shaft and branches defined by bead-like diamonds and circles. The profiles of two large birds, perhaps peacocks or doves, frame the entire composition. (A portion of the tail feathers of the bird on the left is broken off.) Rows of chevrons delineating their feathers enliven the surface of the plaque. It could have hung from the wall of a house or a tomb by means of various openings in the composition or small holes cut through the plaque between the leg and tail of each bird.

Other mirror plaques with a variety of Jewish, Christian, and Greco-Roman symbols have been found in Israel, mostly in tombs (see, for example, cat. no. 42). The portrayal of architectural shrines is common to the art of all three of these traditions, as is the depiction of birds, which often are associated with the soul and life after death. In this example, the *menorah*, a symbol specifically of the Temple in Jerusalem and more generally of the Jewish people, identifies the original owner of the plaque as Jewish (Hachlili, 1988: 236–56; 335–37).

Erwin R. Goodenough suggests that, on Jewish plaques, the combination of the *menorah* with light-reflecting mirrors symbolized divine light (Goodenough, 1953: vol. 1, pp. 174–77; vol. 3, figs. 140–42). Taking into account the use of mirrors on plaques with Christian or Greco-Roman symbols as well as such plaques with Jewish symbols, Levi Y. Rahmani has proposed that mirror plaques served their owners as talismans against evil spirits,

first in their houses and later in their tombs (Rahmani, 1964: 59–60). According to this interpretation, the mirrors were thought to deflect evil back upon itself and away from the owners of the plaques.

—*RMN*

REFERENCES

Avida, Uri. "Plaque against the Evil Eye." In *Treasures of the Holy Land: Ancient Art from the Israel Museum*. New York, 1986: 238–40.

Cohen-Mushlin, Aliza. "Plaque against the 'evil eye.'" In *Age of Spirituality: Late Antique and Early Christian Art, Third to Seventh Century*, ed. Kurt Weitzmann. New York, 1979: 388–89.

Goodenough, Erwin R. *Jewish Symbols in the Greco-Roman Period*. vols. 1-2. New York, 1953.

Hachlili, Rachel. *Ancient Jewish Art and Archaeology in the Land of Israel*. Leiden, 1988.

Mayer, L. A. and A. Reifenberg. "Three Ancient Jewish Reliefs." *Palestine Exploration Quarterly* 70 (1937): 136–39; pl. 7.1.

Rahmani, Levi Y. "Mirror Plaques from a Fifth-Century A.D. Tomb." *Israel Exploration Journal* 14 (1964): 50–60.

42. Mirror Plaque in the Shape of a Fish

From a tomb at Khirbet Dikhrin; chance find followed by excavations of the Israel Antiquities Authority
Byzantine period, 5th–6th centuries C.E.
Ceramic
L: 16 cm.; W: 8 cm.
Israel Antiquities Authority 62-286

This flat, fish-shaped plaque has been decorated in relief with raised outlines and small circles, each with a dot in its center. The large, empty circle on the fish's belly probably once held a mirror. The small hole near the fish's eye would have served to attach the object to the wall of a house or tomb. Although mirror plaques in the shapes of other animals are known, there are no parallels to this fish-shaped example (Rahmani, 1964: 54). Mirror plaques of various designs with Jewish, Christian, and pagan symbols have been found in graves in Syro-Palestine (see cat. no. 41). Levi Y. Rahmani and others have suggested that they were apotropaic, serving as protection against evil spirits (Rahmani, 1964: 59).

Talismans and amulets to protect their wearers against disease and mishaps were popular among virtually all peoples in the ancient world. Egyptians, Greeks, and Romans are known to have used them; their use was widespread also among Jews and Christians. According to a passage in the apocryphal Book of Maccabees (2 Macc. 12:40), the use of amulets among Jews was considered a sign of heathenism. Nevertheless, Jews continued to use amulets throughout antiquity.

The fish shape of this plaque reflects the fact that certain types of fish were considered sacred in various religious communities. For Christians the fish assumed a special meaning because the Greek word for fish, *ichthus*, was interpreted as an abbreviation for the name of *Jesus: Iesous Christos Theou (H)uios Soter*, "Jesus Christ, Son of God, Saviour." Because they frequently are represented as food, fish may also have a eucharistic meaning. According to other interpretations, which are based on the reading of such passages as Clement, *Paedagogus* 3.59.2, fish symbolize not Jesus but rather the believer in his or her capacity as having been caught (that is, saved) by the fisherman Jesus.

Among Jews, too, the symbol of the fish had strong symbolic associations. It was sometimes thought of as a good luck sign and in other contexts could have had eschatological connotations. Leviathan, a monstrous fish first described in the Bible, appears in some rabbinic legends concerning the messianic era, when he will serve, among other things, to feed the righteous.—*LVR*

REFERENCES

Bar-Ilan, M. "Magic Seals on the Body among Jews in the First Centuries C.E." *Tarbiz* 56 (1986): 37–50 (in Hebrew).

Dolger, Franz Joseph. *Ichthus: Das Fischsymbol in frühchristlicher Zeit.* 5 vols. Rome, 1910–43.

Engemann, Joseph. "Zur Verbereitung magischer Übelabwehr in der nichtchristlichen und christlichen Spätantike." *Jahrbuch für Antike und Christentum* 18 (1975): 22f.

Goodenough, Erwin R. *Jewish Symbols in the Greco-Roman Period.* vol. 5. New York, 1956.

Naveh, Joseph and Shaul Shaked. *Amulets and Magic Bowls: Aramaic Incantations of Late Antiquity.* Leiden, 1985.

Rahmani, L. Y. "Mirror Plaques from a Fifth-Century A.D. Tomb." *Israel Exploration Journal* 14 (1964): 50–60.

Robert, Louis. "Amulettes grecques." *Journal des Savants* (1981): 3–44.

Coins and Lead Weight

COINS OF SEPPHORIS

43. Coin

Minted at Sepphoris, 68 C.E.
Bronze
Obverse: Inscription in five lines surrounded
by circle and wreath:
LΔI / NEPΩNO / KΛAYΔIOY / KAICAPO / C
Reverse: Double cornucopiae crossed, caduceus
between horns and inscription: EΠI
OYECΠACIANOY EIPHNOΠOΛI
NEPΩNIA CEΠΦΩ *(Under Vespasian, in*
Neronias~ Sepphoris~Eirenopolis)
Israel Museum 2965

44. Coin

Minted at Sepphoris, 68 C.E.
Bronze
Obverse: Inscription in five lines surrounded
by circle and wreath: same as above
Reverse: In center, two Latin letters: S C
In field and around inscription: same as
above
Israel Museum 2966

Sepphoris first began to mint coins in 68 C.E., during the First Jewish Revolt against Rome (Meshorer, 1979). It was in this period that the city began to have its first dealings with Rome, and the history of that relationship can be traced on coins minted at Sepphoris.

The date of these coins refers to the fourteenth year of Nero's reign, which also corresponds to 68 C.E. The coins are identified as having been struck in Sepphoris, further identified as Eirenopolis, "the City of Peace," likely because of its pacifistic response to the revolt then taking place in Palestine. In his detailed account, the *Jewish War*, first-century Jewish historian Flavius Josephus reported that the residents of Sepphoris, being realistic people who would rather join the Romans than fight them, were desirous of peace. In contrast to the residents of most of the other Jewish cities in the Land of Israel, the Sepphoreans had welcomed Vespasian and his army in 67 C.E. and, according to Josephus, were the only Galileans who did not participate in the revolt. Josephus described the Sepphoreans as "people who 'think peace,'" and the word "peace" is used here as an additional name for the city. (For a more complete discussion of the history of the period, see Stuart S. Miller's article on Hellenistic and Roman Sepphoris in this catalogue.)

Sepphoris is referred to by another name as well, Neronias, in honor of the Roman emperor. Traditionally, when a city took on the name of an emperor—for its own prestige as well as to enhance that of the emperor—that name usually was retained after his death, sometimes for a lengthy period. The name Neronias, however, ceased to be inscribed on coins minted at Sepphoris immediately after

Nero's death, no doubt because the emperor's memory deserved condemnation.

They do not bear the image of the Roman emperor or any other pagan element that might have offended the religious sensibilities of the city's Jewish population. Also, considering that the double cornucopiae with the caduceus was a well-known motif in Jewish numismatics (it is on the coins of Herod the Great and his son Herod Archelaus, the coins of the Roman procurators of Judea, and the coins that Agrippa II struck in Panias), it seems certain that these coins were struck by Jewish authorities (Meshorer, 1978). (The double cornucopiae without the caduceus was an even more popular Jewish symbol; see Meshorer, 1976.) The two Latin letters, S C, also seem to represent the submission of the Sepphoreans to Roman rule during the revolt. They are especially interesting because they are characteristic of bronze coins struck in Rome by the Roman Senate, or, in Latin, the S[enatus] C[onsulto].—YM

46. Coin

Minted at Sepphoris, c. 98–117 C.E.
Bronze
Obverse: Portrait of the Emperor Trajan and
*   inscription: same as above*
Reverse: Palm tree with inscription below:
*   same as above*
Israel Museum 2968

_____

47. Coin

Minted at Sepphoris, c. 98–117 C.E.
Bronze
Obverse: Portrait of the Emperor Trajan and
*   inscription: same as above*
Reverse: Caduceus and inscription around
*   edge of coin: same as above*
Israel Museum 2969

_____

45. Coin

Minted at Sepphoris, c. 98–117 C.E.
Bronze
Obverse: Portrait of the Emperor Trajan and
*   inscription:* ΤΡΑΙΑΝΟΣ ΑΥΤΟΚΡΑΤΩΡ
*   ΕΔΩΚΕΝ*
Reverse: Laurel wreath with inscription
*   inside:* ΣΕΠΦΩΡΗΝΩΝ *("of the People of*
*   Sepphoris")*
Israel Museum 371

_____

48. Coin

Minted at Sepphoris, c. 98–117 C.E.
Bronze
Obverse: Portrait of the Emperor Trajan and
inscription: same as above
Reverse: Two ears of barleycorn and inscrip-
tion around edge of coin: same as above
Israel Museum 3531

These coins struck by local authorities at Sepphoris during the reign of Trajan (98–117 C.E.), though in the name of the emperor, were undoubtedly of Jewish origin. Indeed, the coins can be thought of as "Jewish-Roman" in that, whereas one side is dedicated to Trajan, the other depicts Jewish symbols. The coins are representative of four denominations, showing, from largest to smallest, a laurel wreath, a palm tree, the caduceus, and two ears of barleycorn. The reverse of each bears the same inscription: ΣΕΠΦΩΡΗΝΩΝ, meaning "of the People of Sepphoris."

The Jewish symbols on these coins distinguish them from coins minted elsewhere in the Land of Israel in this period. In addition, they also bear the highly unusual inscription ΕΔΩΚΕΝ around the head of Trajan. Meaning "gave" or "permitted," this expression is not found on other ancient coins. Customarily, only the name of the emperor and his title were inscribed around his image, without comment. This exceptional addition has particular significance and apparently reflects the special relationship between the council of Sepphoris (the *boulē*) and the Roman authorities, a relationship through which the Sepphoreans were permitted to mint coins that were distinctively Jewish.—*YM*

49. Coin

Minted at Sepphoris, c. 138–61 C.E.
Bronze
Obverse: Portrait of Antoninus Pius and
inscription: ΑΥΤ ΚΑΙ ΑΝΤΩΝΙΝΩ ϹΕΒ
Reverse: The city goddess Tyche in a temple
and inscription: ΔΙΟΚΑΙϹΑΡΙΑ ΙΕΡΑ
ΑϹΥΛΟϹ ΚΑΙ ΑΥ ΤΟΝΟΜΟϹ *(of Dio-*
caesarea, Holy City of Shelter,
Autonomous)
Israel Museum 2971

Toward the end of Trajan's reign Jewish communities in North Africa, Egypt, Cyprus, and Mesopotamia again revolted against Rome, and this insurrection was not suppressed until 117 to 118 C.E., the early years of Hadrian's reign. Whether or not the Sepphorcans were sympathetic to this revolt is not known, but at this time the city ceased to mint coins, and the right to do so was not renewed until the end of Hadrian's reign, 138 C.E. Both Tiberias and Caesarea, however, continued to mint coins under Hadrian. Perhaps because Sepphoris was regarded as a Jewish city, it was singled out for special punishment, as reflected by the cessation of minting there. Some scholars attribute Hadrian's punishment to the Second Jewish Revolt led by Bar Kokhba (132–35 C.E.), but that connection is less likely. Some fifteen years passed between Trajan's death in 117 C.E. and the Bar Kochba war, and during that time not a single coin was minted for Hadrian at Sepphoris. A different cause, one closely associated with the early years of Hadrian's reign is indicated, which, most likely, points to the Jewish revolt that began in the time of Trajan.

The minting of coins at Sepphoris recommenced in 138 C.E., under Antoninus Pius, who ruled until 161 C.E. Circumstances were much different, however. The name of the city had been changed to Diocaesarea (dedicated to Zeus), and the coins minted there no longer displayed Jewish motifs. Presumably as the city's ultimate punishment for betraying its 68 C.E. peace treaty with the Romans, its Jewish name, "Sepphoris," meaning "birdlike" (after the Hebrew word *zippor*), was changed to a pagan one, and all of the designs on coins were now pagan.

This coin depicts Tyche, the city goddess, in a temple; the accompanying inscription can be translated as "of Diocaesarea, Holy City of Shelter, Autonomous." After 161 C.E., no coins of Sepphoris-Diocaesarea are known until the reign of Caracalla (211–17 C.E.), during which coins were minted in the name of his mother, Julia Domna, the Syrian wife of and adviser to his father and predecessor, Septimius Severus.—*YM*

50. Coin

Minted at Sepphoris, c. 211–17 C.E.
Bronze
Weight: 25.65 gm.; Diameter: 35 mm.
Obverse: Portrait bust of Caracalla (laureate),
*   facing right; around, inscription:* AYT KAI
    M AYP ANT⍵NINOC CEB
Reverse: Inscription in five lines surrounded
*   by wreath:* ΔΙΟΚΑΙCΑΡ / ΙΕΡ ΑC ΑΥΤ /
    ΠΙC ΦΙΛ CYM / MAX · Ρ⍵ / MAI
*   (Diocaesarea the Holy, City of Shelter,*
*   Autonomous, Loyal [a treaty of] Friend-*
*   ship and Alliance with the Romans)*
Israel Museum 2964

Through the second century C.E. the Jewish assembly, or Sanhedrin, moved from place to place. (The history of the geographical changes of the Sanhedrin is described in the Talmud: *Rosh Ha-Shana* 31a,b.) Sometime around 200 C.E., during the last stage of his leadership, Rabbi Judah Ha-Nasi (the Patriarch) moved with the Sanhedrin to Sepphoris, which subsequently became a large Jewish center. Many talmudic legends refer to the special relationship between Rabbi Judah and his contemporary Roman emperor, called Antoninus (or Antonilus) in Jewish sources. The identity of this emperor is now generally accepted as Caracalla, described in the stories as a good friend and admirer of the Rabbi (Safrai, 1973).

It was during Caracalla's reign (211–17 C.E.) that this impressive medallion was struck at Sepphoris. The abbreviated inscription on the reverse of the coin can be translated as: "Diocaesarea the Holy, City of Shelter, Autonomous, Loyal [a treaty of] Friendship and Alliance with the Romans."

The treaty of friendship referred to here—and on other coins minted at Sepphoris during this period—was made between the two official establishments overseeing life at Sepphoris, the Roman Senate and the local council. It may well be that, during the time of Rabbi Judah, the Council of Sepphoris was actually the Sanhedrin, as during the period of Caracalla the Sanhedrin was seated at Sepphoris. Thus the coins struck at Sepphoris-Diocaesarea during the time of Caracalla suggest that the legendary relationship between Rabbi Judah and the Roman emperor was based on fact, and their inscriptions referring to a treaty between the people of Sepphoris and the people of Rome thus complement the imprecise literary sources.—*YM*

REFERENCES

Meshorer, Ya°akov. "The Double Cornucopiae as a Jewish Symbol." *Judaica Post* 4, no. 2 (1976): 282–85.

Meshorer, Ya°akov. "Jewish Symbols on Roman Coins Struck in Eretz Israel." *Israel Museum News* 14 (1978): 60–63.

Meshorer, Ya°akov. "Sepphoris and Rome." In *Greek Numismatics and Archaeology: Essays in Honor of Margaret Thompson.* Wetteren, 1979: 159–71.

Safrai, Samuel. "On the Chronology of the Patriarchs in the Second and Third Centuries." *Proceedings of the Sixth World Congress of Jewish Studies*, 2. Jerusalem, 1973: 51–57 (in Hebrew).

Also in the Exhibition

51. Cooking Pot of the Type Used for Coin Hoards

Not Illustrated
Sepphoris; Sepphoris Regional Project
Byzantine period
Pottery
H: 25 cm.
Israel Antiquities Authority 96-880

Bronze Coins from the Hellenistic and Roman Periods Excavated at Meiron in Galilee

Not Illustrated
Collection of the Department of Religion, Duke University

52. Coin from the Reign of Alexander Jannaeus (103–76 B.C.E.)

Minted in Jerusalem
Obverse: Anchor with circle of dots around Greek inscription
Reverse: Star with eight rays within diadem; Hebrew inscription between spokes
MI.3.41/R74247/3028

---

53. Coin from the Reign of Alexander Jannaeus (103–76 B.C.E.)

Minted in Jerusalem
Obverse: Hebrew inscription surrounded by wreath
Reverse: Double cornucopia with pomegranate between horns, struck off center
MV.4.17/L4001/R75069

---

54. Coin from the Reign of Agrippa I (37–44 C.E.)

Minted in Jerusalem in 42 C.E.
Obverse: Canopy with Greek inscription
Reverse: Three ears of barleycorn protruding from two leaves; date
M.VI.1.25/L1013/R75310

---

55. Coin from the Reign of Procurator Antonius Felix (52–60 C.E.)

Minted in Jerusalem
Obverse: Two shields and two spears crossed; Greek inscription around
Reverse: Palm tree with fruit; to either side Greek inscription
M.VI.1.25/L1013/R75312

---

56. Coin Commemorating the Jewish War against Rome

Minted in Jerusalem in 67 C.E.
Obverse: Amphora with Hebrew inscription around
Reverse: Vine leaf and branch and tendril with Hebrew inscription around
M.VI.1.7/L1001/R75092

---

57. Coin from Sidon

Minted in Sidon, 218–22 C.E.
Obverse: Laureate bust of Elagabalus, right; worn inscription
Reverse: Car of Astarte on two wheels; inside inverted crescent above sphere; two horns, figures at side; Latin inscription
M.VI.1.24/L1011/R75305

---

58. Coin from Antioch

Minted in Antioch, 244–49 C.E.
Obverse: Bust of Philip, right, laureate, wearing paludamentum and cuirass; Greek inscription
Reverse: Female bust (Tyche of Antioch), right, draped, veiled and turreted; above, ram running right, looking back, in field ΔE and SC; star beneath bust; Greek inscription
R77263

---

59. Coin from Tyre

Minted in Tyre, 253–60 C.E.
Obverse: Radiate, draped bust of Valerian, right; Latin inscription
Reverse: Two ambrosial rocks with olive tree between; below, palm branch, altar and murex shell; Latin inscription
M.I.8.07/L8001/R75221

---

60. Coin from the Reign of Maximianus Herculius (286–305 C.E.)

Minted in Cyzicus, 292–95 C.E.
Obverse: Radiate, draped, cuirassed bust, right; Latin inscription
Reverse: Emperor standing right, holding parazonium, receiving Victory on globe from Jupiter, standing left, holding scepter; Latin inscription
M.II.5.44/L5031/R771297

---

61. Coin from the Reign of Maximianus Herculius (286–305 c.e.)

Minted in Antioch, 305–6 C.E.
Obverse: Radiate, draped, cuirassed bust, right; Latin inscription
Reverse: Prince standing right, in military dress, receiving small Victory on globe from Jupiter, standing left, leaning on scepter; Latin inscription
M.I.3.49/L3029.1/R74405

62. Coin from the Reign of Licinius II (308–24 c.e.)

Minted in Arles in 318 C.E.
Obverse: Laureate, draped, cuirassed bust, right; Latin inscription
Reverse: Jupiter standing left holding thunderbolt, leaning on scepter, chlamys across left shoulder; Latin inscription
M.III.3/L3001/R2211

63. Urbs Roma (City of Rome) Coin

Minted in Siscia, 333–36 C.E.
Obverse: Helmeted bust left, wearing imperial cloak; Latin inscription
Reverse: She-wolf, standing left, suckling twins, two stars above; Latin inscription
M.II.5.39/L5025/R771195

64. Coin from the Reign of Constantine II (337–40 c.e.)

Minted in Antioch, 337–41 C.E.
Obverse: Veiled head, right; Latin inscription
Reverse: Quadriga ascending to right, in which Constantine stands, above hand of God; Latin inscription
M.II.5.23/L5012/R771040

65. Coin from the Reign of Constantius II (337–61 c.e.)

Minted in Antioch, 341–46 C.E.
Obverse: Pearl-diademed head, right, with one end rosette in the diadem; Latin inscription
Reverse: Within wreath, Latin inscription
M.II.4.79/L4024/R771162

66. Coin from the Reign of Constantius II (337–61 c.e.)

Minted in Cyzicus, 351–54 C.E.
Obverse: Pearl-diademed, draped bust, right; Latin inscription
Reverse: Virtue to right, with shield on left arm, spearing horseman falling from horse and raising arm behind him; Latin inscription
M.VII.1.20/L1010/R77052

67. Market Weight

Sepphoris; Joint Sepphoris Project
Roman period
Lead
9.7 x 8.8 x 1.3 cm.
Israel Antiquities Authority 95-3889

Inscribed on both sides in Greek, this artifact is of particular interest for its identification of two market inspectors. Although some of the letters are damaged or missing, the five lines of inscription on the reverse side can be translated to read: "Under the market inspection [of the two inspectors] Simon son of Aianos and Justus son of . . ." (This reading changes that published previously; see Meshorer, 1986.) The names of many *agoranomoi*, or market inspectors, are known, but this inscription is the first from Roman Palestine to identify men in this office who, to judge from the name of Simon (Shimon) son of Aianos, clearly were Jewish.

The front of the weight features three lines or registers. The top and bottom registers apparently depict rows of columns, perhaps in reference to the marketplace of ancient Sepphoris. The colonnade resembles one portrayed on the famous mosaic map from Madaba in Jordan, where columns line either side of the *cardo* (commercial street) of Jerusalem (Piccirillo, 1993: 94, fig. 63). The central line specifies the amount of the weight, which is 1,018 grams (36 ounces). This is the equivalent of three *libras*, the common unit of weight in the Roman world. The Roman *libra* (Greek *litra*) equaled approximately 340 grams (12 ounces) and often was used in multiples to weigh heavier items. The inscribed expression "half *litra*" on the Sepphoris weight refers to half of a six-*libra* unit.—YM

REFERENCES

Meshorer, Ya°akov. "The Lead Weight: Preliminary Report." *Biblical Archaeologist* 49 (1986): 16–17.

Piccirillo, Michele. *The Mosaics of Jordan.* Amman, 1993.

Ceramic Vessels and Objects

68. Inkwell

Palestine; probably from the Judean
wilderness, possibly from Qumran
Roman period
Ceramic
H: 5 cm.; greatest D: 3.8 cm.
Private collection, Durham, N.C.

This ceramic inkwell is typical of those used by Roman-period scribes in Galilee and Judea. Because most ancient peoples were either illiterate or barely literate, writing was often a professional function. Similar inkwells have been found in Jerusalem (Avigad, 1984: 127) and at Khirbet Qumran, the Essene settlement near the caves in which the Dead Sea Scrolls were discovered (Goranson, 1991, 1992, 1994; Olnik, 1983–84: 61, fig. 14.4). Although inkwells have not yet been found at Sepphoris, items such as this one likely were used there in business and legal transactions. A similar inkwell was uncovered in a grave in Meiron, Upper Galilee (Meyers et al., 1981: 109 and 118–19). That burial illustrates a rabbinic exception allowed to scribes: though Jewish burials are characterized by simplicity, usually avoiding the common ancient practice of interring "grave goods," it was considered acceptable for a scribe to be buried with the tools of his trade.

This ceramic inkwell was made on a pottery wheel, as can be seen by the circular tool marks around the body. Then the handle was added. (Many ancient inkwells lack the handle.) Particular care was directed to the sleeve or lip, which in this case descends 1.3 cm.; this lip helped prevent spills, it served for dripping back of ink when the stylus was touched to it, and in some cases it served to fit a stopper. Although no certain traces of ink are obvious in this case, typically, ink of the times was made of carbon black (lamp soot) fixed in a vegetable gum base binder diluted in water.—*SG*

REFERENCES

Avigad, Nahman. *Discovering Jerusalem.* Oxford, 1984.

Goranson, Stephen. "Further Qumran Archaeology Publications in Progress." *Biblical Archaeologist* 54 (1991): 110–11.

Goranson, Stephen. "An Inkwell from Qumran." *Michmanim* 6 (1992): 37*–40*.

Goranson, Stephen. "Qumran: A Hub of Scribal Activity?" *Biblical Archaeology Review* 20 (Sept.–Oct. 1994): 36–39.

Khairy, Nabil I. "Inkwells of the Roman Period from Jordan." *Levant* 12 (1980): 155–62 and pl. 25.

Meyers, Eric M., James F. Strange, and Carol L. Meyers. *Excavations at Ancient Meiron, Upper Galilee, Israel.* Cambridge, Mass., 1981.

Olnik, Yael. "Roman Period Ceramic Inkwells in the Land of Israel." *Israel: People and Land* 1 (1983–84): 55–66 (in Hebrew).

COMMONWARE VESSELS MANUFACTURED AT KEFAR ḤANANYAH

69. "Galilean Bowl"

*Sepphoris; Sepphoris Regional Project
Roman period, 2d–3d centuries C.E.
Pottery
H: 7.25 cm.; D: 27.3 cm.
Israel Antiquities Authority 95-3900*

70. Cooking Pot

*Sepphoris; Sepphoris Regional Project
Roman period, 1st–early 2d century C.E.
Pottery
H: 16.5 cm.; Maximum D: 23.5 cm.
Israel Antiquities Authority 95-3898*

71. Cooking Pot

*Sepphoris; Sepphoris Regional Project
Roman period, 1st–early 2d century C.E.
Pottery
H: 16.25 cm.; Maximum D: 19.75 cm.
Israel Antiquities Authority 95-3902*

72. Cooking Jug

*Sepphoris; Sepphoris Regional Project
Roman period, early 2d–3d century C.E.
Pottery
H: 20.25 cm.; Maximum D: 19 cm.
Israel Antiquities Authority 96-879*

These vessels recovered in the residential area on the western summit at Sepphoris are examples of the common kitchen wares used in Galilee during the Roman period. They are characterized by their well-fired metallic red ware; and they seem to come from the same manufacturing center, Kefar Ḥananyah. Located in Upper Galilee, not far from Sepphoris, Kefar Ḥananyah was responsible for manufacturing and supplying most of the cooking wares used in northern Palestine throughout the Roman and early Byzantine periods.

Most of these vessels show signs of charring by fire on their bases, indicating that they were set in fires and used for warming and for limited cooking. The cooking pot with the inverted rim and high neck is an early Roman type of the first to early second centuries C.E. (IAA 95-

3898). Although the cooking pot with the small, flattened, grooved rim and globular body is a common type used throughout the entire Roman period, this example is an early version dating to the end of the first or the beginning of the second century C.E.(IAA 95-3902). The open bowl with the flat base, a type often called a "Galilean bowl," was most likely used as a frying pan, although it does not have a long handle (IAA 95-3900). "Galilean bowls" were produced during the second and third centuries C.E. The cooking jug with globular body, spout, and strainer is the most complete piece of its type known (IAA 96-879). It dates to the early second or third century C.E.—*MB*

REFERENCE

Adan-Bayewitz, David. *Common Pottery in Roman Galilee: A Study of Local Trade.* Ramat Gan, 1993.

COMMONWARE VESSELS MANUFACTURED AT SHIKHIN

73. Storage Jar

Sepphoris; Sepphoris Regional Project
Roman period, 1st–3d centuries C.E.
Pottery
H: 39.25 cm.
Israel Antiquities Authority 95-3899

74. Jug

Sepphoris; Sepphoris Regional Project
Roman period, 1st–3d centuries C.E.
Pottery
H: 24 cm.
Israel Antiquities Authority 95-3901

75. Krater ("Sepphoris Bowl")

Sepphoris; Joint Sepphoris Project
Roman period, 2d–3d centuries C.E.
Pottery
H: 10.5 cm.; D: 17 cm.
Israel Antiquities Authority 94-2618

76. Juglet

See fig. 23
Sepphoris; Joint Sepphoris Project
Roman period, 1st–3d centuries C.E.
Pottery
H: 12 cm.
Israel Antiquities Authority 96-1549

These vessels were recovered from the residential quarter on the western summit at Sepphoris and came from the same context as the cooking vessels manufactured at Kefar Ḥananyah (cat. nos. 69–72). However, this group apparently comes from a different pottery manufacturing center, Shikhin, located 2 km. from Sepphoris. The Shikhin workshop, not yet excavated, probably specialized in the manufacture of storage jars, jugs, juglets, craters, and jar lids. Most of its products apparently went to the market of Sepphoris, where they are a common find. Some of the products were sold in nearby villages.

This storage jar (IAA 95-3899) is an early variation of the common Palestinian bag-shaped jar that was used for storing various materials such as water, oil, wine, or dry foodstuffs. The type is characterized by a cylindrical body and rounded shoulders, an everted rim, a ridge at the base of the neck, and two handles on the shoulders. This jug (IAA 95-3901) is a type common in Galilee. It has a globular body, rounded rim, and a flaring, ridged neck. The handle extends from ridge to shoulder. These two vessels, which were found together in a water cistern, are part of a large assemblage of vessels, many of which probably were used to draw water from the cistern. Some of them were broken, but some are completely intact.

This krater (IAA 94-2618) standing on three handle-like legs has a rilled hanging rim with a carination below; its rim is constructed to receive a lid. This form provides a convenient way of holding the vessel. This type of krater appears in different sizes and generally dates to the second to fourth centuries C.E., with slight differences that appear on the rim over this period. This example is a small variant and dates to the second or third century C.E. It may have been used as a chamber pot. Its especially widespread distribution at Sepphoris has led to its designation as the "Sepphoris Bowl." —*MB*

REFERENCES

Adan-Bayewitz, David and M. Wieder, "Ceramics from Roman Galilee: A Comparison of Several Techniques for Fabric Characterization." *Journal of Field Archaeology* 19 (1992): fig. 5

Strange, James F., Dennis E. Groh, and Thomas R. W. Longstaff. "Excavations at Sepphoris: The Location and Identification of Shikhin. Part 1." *Israel Exploration Journal* 44 (1994): 216–27; and "Part 2." *Israel Exploration Journal* 45 (1995): 171–87.

77. Juglet

Not Illustrated
From a burial cave near Nazareth; excavated
*   by Nurit Feig for the Israel Antiquities*
*   Authority*
Roman period, c. 2d century C.E.
Pottery
H: 10.8 cm.; Maximum D: 8 cm.
Israel Antiquities Authority 80-892

This small intact juglet was recovered along with other similar juglets and several Early Roman oil lamps in a burial cave near Nazareth. The juglet is characterized by a globular body, a small ring base, a flaring thickened rim, and a ridged neck. The handle extends from ridge to shoulder. This type, which probably was used as a small cosmetic container, was common mainly in Galilee, both in tombs and domestic contexts. It apparently was manufactured in the vicinity, perhaps in the pottery manufacturing center of Shikhin (see cat. nos. 73–6).—*MB*

REFERENCE

Feig, Nurit. "Burial Caves in Nazareth." *'Atiqot* 10 (1990): fig. 9:2 (in Hebrew).

CERAMIC INCENSE SHOVELS

78. Rectangular Incense Shovel

Sepphoris; Joint Sepphoris Project
Roman period, 2d-3d centuries C.E.
Ceramic
L: 23 cm.; W: 12.5 cm.; Depth: 1.75 cm.
Israel Antiquities Authority 95-2364

79. Round Incense Shovel with Cover

Sepphoris; Joint Sepphoris Project
Roman period, 2d-3d centuries C.E.
Ceramic
L: 18.75 cm.; W: 12.5 cm.; Depth: 2.5 cm.
D (of cover): 10.5 cm.
Israel Antiquities Authority 95-3882 and
*   95-3883 (cover)*

These two ceramic incense shovels are among the most interesting finds yet discovered at Sepphoris. Excavated in the residential quarter, an extensive domestic area located on the western summit, they are part of a larger assemblage of similar objects, constituting a corpus of around fifteen (mostly fragments). They represent the first-known exemplars of incense shovels in ceramic from ancient Palestine.

All of the examples from Sepphoris are covered with brownish-red slip and have burn marks on the interior. A few examples of rectangular and round lids also were recovered; all of the lids had molded holes and burn marks on the interior. The evidence of burning indicates that both rectangular and round shovels contained "burnt" materials and probably were used for incense. The perforated lids have no known parallels in metal or in artistic depictions from ancient Palestine. Objects similar in function, however, are known from Egypt and the Aegean world.

Bronze examples similar to this rectangular shovel are known from France, Italy, and Syria; they generally are dated to the first and second centuries C.E., as are the examples that come from the Judean desert (see cat. no. 27).

These ceramic shovels from Sepphoris were found in a cistern that produced a large assemblage of locally made ceramic vessels and oil lamps, all dated to the second and third centuries C.E. In that domestic context the shovels were used probably to burn incense, thus introducing fragrant smoke to interior spaces that often were not well ventilated. Although the ritual use of incense has attracted much attention, fumigation in ordinary households was probably widespread. —*MB*

REFERENCES

Meyers, Carol L. "Censers." In *Anchor Bible Dictionary*. vol. 1. New York, 1992: 882.

Meyers, Carol L. "Incense Dish." In *Anchor Bible Dictionary*. vol. 3. New York, 1992: 410.

Meyers, Eric M., Ehud Netzer, and Carol L. Meyers. *Sepphoris*. Winona Lake, 1992: 25, 27.

Netzer, Ehud and Zeev Weiss, *Zippori*. Jerusalem, 1994: 11.

80. Fine-ware Plate with Impressed Design

Sepphoris; Joint Sepphoris Project
Probably imported
Late Roman–Early Byzantine, 4th–5th
    centuries C.E.
D: 27 cm.
Israel Antiquities Authority 94-2632

This beautiful fine-ware plate belongs to the category of imported pieces known as African Red Slip Ware. Widely used throughout the eastern Mediterranean from North Africa to Athens, this ware has impressed designs that vary greatly but most usually indicate contact with mainstream Late Roman decorative art. The design of concentric circles is common, but that of the radiating palm leaves is less so. The combination of the two motifs, as on this plate, is unusual and appears to be uniquely African. The circles may derive from bone and ivory carving, and the shape of the flat plate with its turned-up lip may derive from a metal prototype. The fine-grained lustrous red ware of the Sepphoris plate is attested in the third to eighth centuries C.E., although the context of this particular piece is fourth to fifth century C.E.—*EMM*

REFERENCE

Hayes, John W. *Late Roman Pottery*. London, 1972: 230–36.

81. Flat-bottomed Dish

Sepphoris; University of Michigan Expedition
Byzantine period, late 4th or 5th century C.E.
Ceramic
D: 25.4 cm.
Israel Antiquities Authority 31-158

This flat-bottomed dish with the remains of a potter's stamp in the center and with a ring base was found in cistern no. 8 during the Michigan excavations of 1931. Dated to the late fourth or the fifth century C.E., it is most probably an imported piece of Late Roman C ware, a type of ceramic ware found extensively in Palestine in the early Byzantine period, though it continues to be used into the sixth century. The main competitor to African wares, Late Roman C ware was probably manufactured in Asia Minor or in the Aegean region. This ware was extremely common throughout the Eastern Mediterranean in the Byzantine period and was regarded as a "fine ware," that is, the best pottery available, not for everyday use.—*EMM*

REFERENCES

Groh, Dennis E. "The Fine-wares from the Patrician and Lintel Houses." In Eric M. Meyers et al., *Excavations at Ancient Meiron, Upper Galilee, Israel*. Cambridge, Mass., 1981: 129 ff.

Hayes, John W. *Late Roman Pottery*. London, 1972: 323ff.

REFERENCES

Hachlili, Rachel. "The Menorah." In her *Ancient Jewish Art and Archaeology in the Land of Israel*. Leiden, 1988: 236–56.

Meyers, Carol L. "Lampstand." In *Anchor Bible Dictionary*. vol. 5. New York, 1992: 141–43.

Meyers, Carol L. "Lampstand (candelabrum, menorah): Jewish." In *Encyclopedia of Early Christian Art and Archaeology*. New York, forthcoming.

Yarden, L. *The Tree of Light: A Study of the Menorah*. Ithaca, 1971.

82. *Menorah* Incised on Storage Jar

Sepphoris; Joint Sepphoris Project
Early Byzantine period, 5th century C.E.
Pottery
W: 18 cm.
Israel Antiquities Authority 96-2301

This *menorah*, or seven-branched lampstand, appears on a sherd that is part of a large ceramic storage vessel. The *menorah* extends 17 cm. across its branches; the preserved height of its central shaft is 4.7 cm., but originally it may have been double that. The *menorah* was incised on the vessel before firing, with its placement under the handle and high on the reinforcing ridge making it very prominent. The process of incising the wet clay was done after the handle had been added and also after the ribbing on the shoulder of the vessel had been formed. This sequence is clear because of the way the top of the central shaft of the *menorah* reaches the bottom of the handle and because the incisions of its branches obscure the ribbing beneath. The vessel itself descends from the bag-shaped storage jars of the Late Roman period, when the handles were placed somewhat lower on the shoulder of the vessel than on this later, Byzantine example. The strong reinforcing ridge on the shoulder and neck suggests that the vessel was meant to hold considerable weight, probably a liquid such as olive oil.

Although the simple, stylized seven-branched form of this *menorah* is not exceptional, its presence on a ceramic vessel is unique. The *menorah* is the most common and widely found symbol in Jewish art from antiquity to the present. Its appearance in the repertoire of motifs in Jewish art is so frequent that it can be legitimately called the dominant symbol of the Jewish people. Originating as a lampstand used in Temple ritual of biblical times, it proliferated in representational Jewish art in the Roman and Byzantine periods, especially after the destruction of the Second Temple in 70 C.E. It appears in public architecture (notably on lintels, capitals, and mosaic floors of synagogues), in funerary contexts, and on various artifacts, such as oil lamps and glass vessels. However, this example and several others from Sepphoris are the only ones in which the *menorah* is found on ceramic vessels. Perhaps in the pluralistic Byzantine community of Sepphoris, the contents of jars were marked for Jewish owners in order to maintain purity in keeping with Jewish practices.—*CLM AND EMM*

ALSO IN THE EXHIBITION

83. *Menorah* Incised on Fragment of a Vessel

Not Illustrated
Sepphoris; Joint Sepphoris Project
Byzantine Period
Pottery
L: 30 cm.
Israel Antiquities Authority 96-2287

84. Redware Bowl with Stamped Cross

Palestine; exact provenance unknown
Byzantine period, 6th century C.E.
Terracotta
D: 32 cm.
Studium Biblicum Franciscanum Museum,
Jerusalem
Custody of the Holy Land

This light reddish-orange colored terra-cotta bowl is completely preserved. It has been decorated on the inside with a stamped Latin cross (one on which the vertical arm is longer than the horizontal arm). Fine redware pottery, especially plates and bowls, enjoyed widespread popularity in late antique Palestine. This pottery is best known as *terra sigillata* or "stamped ware," a name that bears witness to the fact that the decoration (and sometimes also the potter's name) was stamped onto it. This well-fired, high-quality pottery, also known as "redware," is found in colors ranging from light orange, through reds, to light and even dark brown.

Very little redware pottery was manu-factured locally in Palestine in the fourth to sixth centuries C.E.; rather it was mainly imported from North Africa, Egypt,

Turkey, or Cyprus. The exact provenance of individual pieces is difficult to establish, however, despite attempts to do so by analyzing chemical composition and petro-graphical makeup. The presence of this pottery at various sites in Israel is a func-tion of the intensification of trade in this part of the Mediterranean world beginning in the fourth century C.E. From the middle of the fifth century onward, different types of crosses appear with greater frequency on redware vessels, and their presence can be taken as evidence of Christianity. Stamped crosses become especially widespread in the sixth century C.E., notably at Capernaum.

North African workshops are known to have produced pottery with Jewish icono-graphical motifs as well, but no redware vessels imprinted with Jewish symbols seem to have reached Byzantine Palestine.—*LVR*

REFERENCES

Egloff, Michel. *Kellia: La poterie copte.* 2 vols. Geneva, 1977.

Gunneweg, Jan, Isadore Perlman, and Joseph Yellin. *The Provenience, Typology and Chronology of Eastern Terra Sigillata.* Qedem 17. Jerusalem, 1983.

Hayes, John W. *Late Roman Pottery.* London, 1972.

Hayes, John W. *A Supplement to Late Roman Pottery.* London, 1980.

Loffreda, Stanislao. *Cafarnao.* II: *La Ceramica.* Jerusalem, 1974.

Loffreda, Stanislao. "Stampi su terre sig-illate del IV-VI secolo in Palestina." In *Studia Hierosolymitana, in onore di P. Bellarmino Bagatti. I: Studi Archaeologici.* Studium Biblicum Franciscanum Collectio Maior, no. 22. Jerusalem 1976: 189, 13 (Tav. 3:11; 5:3).

85. Fragment of a Redware Vessel with Stamped Cross

See fig. 28
Sepphoris; Joint Sepphoris Project
Byzantine period, late 4th or 5th century C.E.
Terracotta
L: 12 cm.; W: 7 cm.
Israel Antiquities Authority 95-3885

Despite its small size, the cross stamped on the inside of this red pottery fragment is elegantly rendered. The cross belongs to a type encountered relatively frequently on redware pottery: it has slender arms of unequal length, which are flanked by curls in each quadrant. Although the original shape of the vessel from which the frag-ment comes is not known, parallels suggest that it probably was a plate, a small platter, or a shallow bowl.

Redware vessels do not appear as fre-quently at Sepphoris as at other Palestinian sites of late antiquity, such as Capernaum. The appearance of pottery decorated with crosses in the residential quarter of the upper city of Sepphoris seems to suggest a shift in the population in this part of the city, which in the Roman period was largely Jewish. This example from Sepphoris may be dated to the period after the great earthquake of 363 C.E., but paral-lels to the cross stamped onto this plate generally are dated to the fifth and early sixth centuries C.E. (Hayes, 1972: 366, stamp no. 73).—*LVR*

REFERENCES

Hayes, John W. *Late Roman Pottery.* London, 1972.

Meyers, Eric M., Ehud Netzer, and Carol L. Meyers. "Sepphoris, 'Ornament of All Galilee,'" *Biblical Archaeologist* 49 (1986): 18.

Pilgrim Ampullae

In the decades following the conversion of Roman emperor Constantine to Christianity in 312 C.E., Christian pilgrims traveled to Palestine in increasing numbers from Europe and other Christian regions. Their principal destination was Jerusalem, but once in Palestine they often sought out other locations associated with biblical events and particularly with the life of Jesus. Around 570 C.E. an anonymous pilgrim from Piacenza, Italy, visited sites all over Palestine, including Sepphoris, where he reported seeing a flagon and a breadbasket that had belonged to the Virgin Mary.

Pilgrims were diligent in seeking a *eulogia*, or blessing, which could be obtained by visiting holy places and particularly by touching earth, water, or objects hallowed by association with some sacred event. Whenever possible, pilgrims liked to take home a blessing in material form, such as water from the Jordan River or earth from a sacred shrine. Oil might also be rendered holy by bringing it into contact with a sacred place or objects, such as the bones of a saint. Small ampullae or flasks of ceramic, metal, or glass served as containers for the holy oil, earth, or water.

The majority of pilgrim ampullae were very plain and were produced in large numbers to meet the demand from thousands of pilgrims. Some ampullae were decorated with Christian symbols; some even featured narrative scenes associated with a particular shrine.—*RMN*

86. Pilgrim Ampulla

Reported to be from a rock-cut tomb at
Einabus, Samaria
Byzantine period
Ceramic
H: 13.5 cm.; W: 10 cm.
Israel Antiquities Authority 42-95

This ampulla of light, buff-colored ware was formed in a double mold into a flattened shape with a handle attached to the neck from each shoulder. Relief decorations in three registers on either side of the body of the vessel include a cross with two doves, three amphorae, and two palmettes with what appear to be columns.—*RMN*

REFERENCES

Israeli, Yael. "Christian ampulla." In *Highlights of Archaeology: The Israel Museum*. Jerusalem, 1984: 112–13.

Vikan, Gary. *Byzantine Pilgrimage Art*. Dumbarton Oaks Byzantine Collection Publications, 5. Washington, 1982.

ALSO IN THE EXHIBITION

87. Pilgrim Ampulla

Not Illustrated
Purchase; provenance unknown; former
 collection of Father Godfrey Kloetzle
Byzantine period
Ceramic; light tan
D: 15 cm.
Studium Biblicum Franciscanum Museum,
 Jerusalem
Custody of the Holy Land

88. Pilgrim Ampulla

Not Illustrated
Purchase; provenance unknown; former
 collection of Father Godfrey Kloetzle
Byzantine period
Ceramic; black
D: 20 cm.
Studium Biblicum Franciscanum Museum,
 Jerusalem
Custody of the Holy Land

89. Arab-period Jug from Sepphoris

Sepphoris; Joint Sepphoris Project
Early Arab period, 8th-9th centuries C.E.
Ceramic
H: 32.5 cm.; Maximum D: 23 cm.
Israel Antiquities Authority 96-878

This jug is dated securely to the Early Arab period, probably to the eighth-ninth centuries C.E.; it is classified as a Khirbet Mefjar type vessel because of its distinctive ware. In the production of this pottery type, the clay is fired at a low temperature and remains soft. Its buff to white color often burns after firing to a green or pale buff. The fineness of the clay allows it to be thrown quite thin on the wheel and facilitates the application of the barbotine (items applied to the exterior surface) and the incised decoration so often found on these vessels.

This example is typical in shape, with its funnel-like neck with an everted rim, and in its decoration on the neck of repeating ovals arranged in horizontal bands and separated by hollow grooves. The application of two disc-like pellets above each of the wavy handles also is very common,

though the attachment of a ring to the left handle is less common. This jug has been extensively repaired but is nonetheless a very fine example of the enormous changes in technology and decoration that occurred in the Early Arab period.—*EMM*

REFERENCES

Delougaz , P. and R. C. Haines. *A Byzantine Church at Khirbet al-Karak*. Chicago, 1960: pls. 39:11, 41:7.

Loffreda, Stanislao. *Cafarnao*. II: *La Ceramica*. Jerusalem, 1974: fig. 15, nos. 11–13.

Meyers, Eric M., A. T. Kraabel, and James F. Strange. *Ancient Synagogue Excavations at Khirbet Shema, Upper Galilee, Israel*. Durham, 1976: pl. 7:22:28.

Tzaferis, Vassilios et al. *Excavation at Capernaum*. vol. 1. Winona Lake, 1989: fig. 61.5, nos. 3, 4.

Glass Vessels

Three Glass Bowls from Tombs in Galilee; see nos. 91, 92, and 90.

Large quantities of glass artifacts have been excavated throughout Galilee. Most date to the Roman period. The technology, which over time became immensely popular, probably was invented somewhere along the Syro-Palestinian coast. Before the invention of glassblowing, glass was shaped or carved much like stone, a process that was very time consuming and thus made glass a luxury item. The advent of glassblowing made it possible to create objects in a fraction of the time previously required, quickly making glass objects inexpensive and in turn ubiquitous. The earliest excavated glassblowing workshop in the Eastern Mediterranean, dating to 50 B.C.E., is in Jerusalem (Avigad, 1983).

The number of important glassmaking and -blowing sites in Galilee make it probable that the objects in this exhibition were made there. The sites of Beth-She'arim (Brill and Wosinski, 1965) and Ḥadera (Gorin-Rosen, 1993) appear to have been glassmaking centers during the Byzantine period, as large slabs of "raw" glass as well as the remains of furnaces have been found at both sites. It is important to note that these were glassmaking as opposed to glassblowing, sites. During this period it was typical for the "raw" glass to be made at one site and then sold to a glassblower elsewhere who would fashion it into objects. Glassblowing workshops were in operation at Sepphoris during the third to fifth centuries C.E., and it is possible that glassblowing took place there in other periods as well. The best-known glass factory in Israel, at the Late Roman site of Jalame near the Mediterranean coast, is sufficiently near Galilee to have influenced glassmakers and blowers there and perhaps to have supplied some of the glass objects (Weinberg, 1988).

After the advent of glassblowing, glass vessels often were used as containers, a function for which glass is uniquely suited. Because glass is relatively impermeable, a glass container, unlike one of pottery, will not absorb oils stored within it and therefore can hold different substances if cleaned between uses. Also, the general transparency of glass makes it possible to determine the condition and amount of the contents of a glass container without having to open it.—*AF*

THREE GLASS BOWLS FROM TOMBS IN GALILEE

90. Bowl

*Ha-Goshrim (Daphne); excavated by Gideon
    Foerster for the Israel Antiquities
    Authority*
Roman period, 1st–4th centuries C.E.
Glass
H: 7.5 cm., D: 29.2 cm.
Israel Antiquities Authority 55-67

91. Bowl

*Even Menahem; excavated by Emmanuel
    Eisenberg for the Israel Antiquities
    Authority*
Roman period, 1st–4th centuries C.E.
Glass
H: 18.5 cm., D: 11.5 cm.
Israel Antiquities Authority 75-1178

92. Bowl

*Ha-Goshrim (Daphne); excavated by Gideon
    Foerster for the Israel Antiquities
    Authority*
Roman period, 1st–4th centuries C.E.
Glass
H: 7.4 cm., D: 27.5 cm.
Israel Antiquities Authority 65-1265

Glass bowls of the types shown here were manufactured in Galilee for centuries, which makes dating them problematic. Such bowls were used primarily to hold food for consumption. Perhaps they, along with other objects, such as the glass cups in this exhibition, were meant to be part of glass "place settings." It should be noted that these particular vessels are grave goods and therefore were not intended for actual use; however, fragments of these same bowl types have been found in domestic contexts at Sepphoris. (See Edgar, 1974: pl. 1.)—*AF*

TWO CUPS WITH PUSHED-IN BASES FROM TOMBS IN GALILEE

nos. 93 and 94.

antiquity. Glass objects like those found in tombs were also in daily use within domestic areas, as indicated by the many broken vessel shards in household contexts. Because tombs are enclosed areas that are not disturbed by later occupations, glass objects placed within them are less likely to be broken and thus are far more likely to survive to the present. The only type of vessel typically found complete outside of tomb contexts is the smaller "miniature" vessel (see cat. nos. 99–101). Occasionally a larger vessel is discovered intact, but this is very rare. (See Weinberg, 1988: 62; Crowfoot, 1957: 408; Edgar, 1974: pl. 3.)—*AF*

93. Cup

Even Menaḥem; excavated by Adam Druks
   for the Israel Antiquities Authority
Late Roman-Early Byzantine, 4th-5th
   centuries C.E.
Glass; blue-green
H: 9.5 cm.
Israel Antiquities Authority 60-735

94. Cup

Even Menaḥem; excavated by Adam Druks
   for the Israel Antiquities Authority
Late Roman-Early Byzantine, 4th-5th
   centuries C.E.
Glass; amber
H: 8.5 cm.
Israel Antiquities Authority 60-738

The name for these cups derives from their method of manufacture. During the blowing process, a portion of the vessel base is folded in on the vessel in order to create a separate base feature without adding a second piece of glass. Another distinctive feature of these examples is the single thread that decorates the center of each vessel. These cups, which were very common throughout the Mediterranean, seem to have been everyday drinking glasses. It is possible that they were used in conjunction with glass bowls similar to those found in this exhibition.

Like many of the glass objects in this exhibition, these cups were found in a sepulchral context. The majority of whole glass vessels in existence today come from tombs, but this is not reflective of the original distribution of glass objects in

nos. 96, 98, 97, and 95.

JARS FROM TOMBS IN GALILEE

95. Jar

Lohame ha-Getaot; excavated by Gideon
Foerster for the Israel Antiquities
Authority
Late Roman–Early Byzantine, 3d–5th
centuries C.E.
Glass
H: 9.2 cm.
Israel Antiquities Authority 71-317

96. Jar

Tomb cave in Kabul (or Chabulon); exca-
vated by Vassilios Tzaferis for the Israel
Antiquities Authority
Late Roman–Early Byzantine, 3d–5th
centuries C.E.
Glass
H: 8.5 cm.
Israel Antiquities Authority 72-19

97. Jar

Beth-Shean; excavated by Nehemiah Tsori
for the Israel Antiquities Authority
Late Roman–Early Byzantine, 3d–5th
centuries C.E.
Glass
H: 7.5 cm.
Israel Antiquities Authority 57-1159

98. Jar

Beth-Shean; excavated by Nehemiah Tsori
for the Israel Antiquities Authority
Late Roman–Early Byzantine, 3d–5th
centuries C.E.
Glass
H: 10 cm.
Israel Antiquities Authority 57-1155

These glass jars, all found in tomb contexts, are examples of a typical Roman
Palestine vessel type. The vessel with green
zigzags is a type commonly found in the
tombs of the fourth to fifth centuries C.E.
The use of colored glass handles and appli-
cations was not uncommon in earlier periods, but at Sepphoris it is unusual to find a
vessel made entirely of colored glass from
before the third century C.E. The move
away from partial to full use of colored
glass may reflect an aesthetic shift, or it
may indicate that the raw materials for col-
oring class had become more accessible.
Glass is naturally a clear blue-green color,
and metal oxides must be added to change
the color. In order to make purple glass,
manganese must be added; blue glass is
achieved by the addition of cobalt; green,
by adding copper or iron. The green color
exhibited here is especially common in
Galilee, suggesting perhaps a nearby source
of the necessary oxide. (See Kuckmerman,
1988: 77–92; Tait, 1991: 21; Neuberg, 1962:
pl. 59.)—AF

nos. 101, 99, and 100.

99. 100. 101. Three "Miniature" Vessels

Sepphoris; Joint Sepphoris Project
Roman period
Glass
H: 2.5 cm.; 3.9 cm.; 2.3 cm.
Israel Antiquities Authority 95-3891, 95-3892,
* 95-3893*

Although these "miniature" vessels were found in an occupational context at Sepphoris, this type of object often is found in tombs. It is precisely because of their small size that these vessels survived intact. Larger vessels often are found broken and in many fragments.

Calling these vessels "miniature" presupposes that the glassblower was working from a full-size template, but it is often difficult to determine the type of vessel these were meant to imitate, as the tools the glassblower used were scaled to larger pieces, and that made it difficult to shape small glass vessels properly.

Miniature vessels like these were used throughout the Roman world, but their exact purpose is unknown. Perhaps small vessels of this type were meant to be children's toys, but this does not seem likely. Gladys Weinberg, who excavated a vessel similar to the tallest one shown here at the Late Roman site of Jalame, does not identify it as a miniature vessel but suggests

instead that it was originally the wick stand for an oil lamp (Weinberg, 1988: 85–86). Another possibility for this vessel is that it was meant as a "miniature" unguentarium, imitating the shape of the candlestick unguentarium in this exhibition. (See Auth, 1976: 154; Barag, 1970: 217–18; Winter, 1996: 98.)—*AF*

Three Unguentaria

102. Unguentarium

Tomb cave in Kabul (or Chabulon);
* excavated by Vassilios Tzaferis for the*
* Israel Antiquities Authority*
Roman period, 1st–4th centuries C.E.
Glass
H: 8.3 cm.
Israel Antiquities Authority 72-18

---

103. Unguentarium

Palestine; excavated by Eilat Mazar for the
* Israel Antiquities Authority*
Roman period, 1st–4th centuries C.E.
Glass
H: 15.5 cm.
Israel Antiquities Authority 91-410

---

104. Unguentarium

Beth-Shean; excavated by Nehemiah Tsori
* for the Israel Antiquities Authority*
Roman period, 1st–4th centuries C.E.
Glass
H: 11.5 cm.
Israel Antiquities Authority 57-1163

nos. 103, 102, and 104.

Unguentaria are thought to have been used to contain personal toilet items and cosmetics, such as perfumed oils or kohl (used as eye makeup), and often are found in grave contexts. Indented sides on the smallest of these three unguentaria give it an unusual shape and make it somewhat uncommon. The tallest one is of the typical candlestick type, which has been found in tombs all over the Eastern Mediterranean. The quadruple unguentarium was probably meant to hold cosmetics, with the four chambers making it possible to house four different substances. Because of their presence in tombs, unguentaria are sometimes incorrectly called "tear bottles," relating to the romantic notion that they were meant to catch the tears of those visiting the deceased. (See Barag, 1985: pl. 17; Crowfoot, 1957: 408; Neuberg, 1962: pl. 57; Winter, 1996: 97.)—*AF*

REFERENCES

Auth, Susan H. *Ancient Glass at the Newark Museum.* Newark, 1976.

Avigad, Nahman. "Jerusalem Flourishing: A Craft Center for Stone, Pottery and Glass." *Biblical Archaeology Review* 9 (Nov-Dec 1983): 63.

Barag, Dan. "Glass Vessels of the Roman and Byzantine Periods in Palestine." Ph.D. diss. Hebrew University, Jerusalem, 1970 (in Hebrew).

Barag, Dan. *Catalogue of Western Asiatic Glass in the British Museum.* vol. 1. London, 1985.

Brill, Robert and J. Wosinski. "A Huge Slab of Glass in the Ancient Necropolis Beth-She͏ᶜarim." *Annales du 7e Congres de l'Association Internationale pour l'Histoire du Verre.* Liege, 1965.

Crowfoot, G. M. "Glass." In *The Objects from Samaria,* ed. J. W. Crowfoot, G. M. Crowfoot, and Kathleen M. Kenyon. London, 1957.

Edgar, M. C. C. *Catalogue du Musée du Caire-Graeco-Egyptian Glass,* repr. ed. Osnabruck, 1974.

Gorin-Rosen, Yael. "Ḥadera, Bet Eliezer." *Excavations and Surveys in Israel* 13 (1993): 42–43.

Kuckerman, Onder. *Glass Beads: Anatolian Glass Bead Making.* Istanbul, 1988.

Neuberg, Frederic. *Ancient Glass.* London, 1962.

Tait, Hugh, ed. *Glass: 5,000 Years.* New York, 1991.

Weinberg, Gladys, ed. *Excavations at Jalame: Site of a Glass Factory in Late Roman Palestine.* Columbia, 1988.

Winter, Tamar. "The Glass Vessels." In *The Akeldama Tombs: Three Burials in the Kidron Valley, Jerusalem,* ed. Gideon Avni and Zvi Greenhut. Jerusalem, 1996.

105. Pilgrim Flask

Kafr el Makr; excavated by Pirhiya Beck for the Israel Antiquities Authority
Late Roman-Byzantine period, c. 4th–7th centuries C.E.
Glass; translucent blue-green
H: 18.3 cm.; W: 14.2 cm.
Israel Antiquities Authority 58-200

Glass pilgrim flasks derive their name from their similarity to ceramic canteen-like flasks once carried by pilgrims. The ceramic vessels, however, often are larger; it is assumed that they were meant to carry drinking water for travelers. Their flattened shape would make the vessels easier to pack or to hang from a saddle.

The limited volume of this translucent blue-green vessel, which at its thickest is only 2.2 cm., suggests that it was not meant to carry water for drinking but instead to carry some precious liquid, such as oil. The lack of handles suggests that the flask was placed within another container, possibly of woven straw or textile, so that it could be carried easily.

The vessel was made by flattening a large blown bubble of glass. Apparent near the base of the flask is the place where the two sides of the bubble met and were fused during this procedure. Also visible on the base is the round mark left where a metal rod (pontil) was attached to the vessel during manufacture, enabling the artisan to shape its rim.—*AF*

REFERENCE

Auth, Susan H. *Ancient Glass at the Newark Museum from the Eugene Schaefer Collection of Antiquities.* Newark, 1976: 135, no. 170 (for parallels)

Lamps

CLAY OIL LAMPS

The use of clay oil lamps was widespread in Roman Palestine during late antiquity, much more common than lamps made of glass, metal, or stone. Clay lamps were manufactured either on a potter's wheel or in a two-part mold carved in limestone, clay, or gypsum. Clay lamps have been recovered from a number of archaeological contexts, including pottery workshops, mines, houses, cisterns, catacombs, synagogues, churches, temples, and military installations. One lamp was even found in a first-century-C.E. fishing boat from the Sea of Galilee. Lamps of the Judean type (see cat. nos. 107–9) often feature decorative patterns from local folk art or motifs of daily life, such as baskets of fruit, bird cages, or jewelry. Other types, such as the discus lamp (see cat. nos. 111–17), bear more standardized motifs that are characteristic of lamps throughout the Roman Empire. These include Greco-Roman mythological characters, architectural features, floral patterns, and animal subjects. The Jewish *menorah* and Christian cross also appear, particularly on Late Roman- and Byzantine-period lamps. Although Palestinian lamps of the Roman period were significantly influenced in shape and often in decoration by Greek and Roman traditions, many types nonetheless reflect regional tastes. A small number even bear inscriptions with parallels in contemporary literary sources. In short, lamps like those excavated at Sepphoris and other sites in late antique Galilee and Palestine illuminate many aspects of daily life.—*ECL*

106. Knife-pared Wheel-made Lamp

Sepphoris; Joint Sepphoris Project
Early Roman period, late 1st century B.C.E.–
c. 70 C.E.
Baked clay
L: 8.8 cm.
Israel Antiquities Authority 95-3878

The knife-pared lamp is one of the most distinctive of Roman Palestinian lamps. Following Greco-Roman prototypes, the lampmaker fashioned a wide, angular (spatulate) nozzle and attached it to a wheel-thrown body with a large, round reservoir. Unique to Roman Palestinian lampmakers, however, was the technique of trimming excess clay from the body with a knife or scraper. Evidence for such lampmaker's tools made from broken Roman commonwares (and even shards of glass vessels) has been recovered in the hippodrome workshop at Gerasa (modern Jerash) (Kehrberg, 1995: fig. 18). Traces of the paring process are visible on the sides of the nozzle and body of this example. Although some lamps of this type feature simple geometric patterns, unadorned lamps such as this one are common. A wide ridge surrounds the large filling-hole. Traces of burning around the wick hole indicate use. The red clay fabric suggests a ferrous-rich clay type, whereas coarse sand-size grits suggest that ground limestone fragments were added by the lampmaker as temper.

Traditionally the knife-pared lamp has been called the "Herodian" type in reference to the Herodian dynasty (37 B.C.E.–c. 100 C.E.). This nomenclature is misleading, however, because this lamp type was not manufactured until the last years of the reign of Herod I, if not later, as archaeo-

logical evidence seems to suggest (Avigad, 1970; Kahane, 1961: 128–47). Further, the term implies that this lamp type was intimately linked to Herodian controlled lands, when in fact the lamp was also manufactured in neighboring Roman provinces under different rulership, such as Nabatea.
—*ECL*

107. Judean Molded ("Darom") Lamp

Sepphoris; Sepphoris Regional Project
Roman period, c. 70–135 C.E.
Baked clay
D: 8 cm.
Israel Antiquities Authority 95-3894

The Judean molded lamp closely resembles the contemporaneous knife-pared lamp in many respects, such as the splayed nozzle and round body and the use of double lines and concentric circles as decorative motifs. The shoulder of this example is decorated with three sets of double rings in molded relief, whereas the base is delineated by two sets of raised double rings. Unlike the knife-pared lamp, however, the Judean variety is mold-made and displays a far richer repertoire of decorative and iconographic elements. Also, the nozzle is wider and has pronounced flaring volutes. The round nozzle seen here is not as common as the spatulate variety, but parallels do exist (Sussman, 1982: 104, no. 190; 115, no. 222). The filling-hole is medium to large in size and is surrounded by a single or double ridge. The lamp handle is typically a small,

flattened vertical lug that is often pierced but is sometimes "pinched."

Lamps of this type have been found in significant numbers in Judea, hence the name. The type also has been referred to as "southern" (Hebrew *Darom*) or "Jewish" due to its frequent occurrence in the predominantly Jewish populated southern part of Palestine during the early Roman period. Scholars have recently shown, however, that "southern" is misleading because in antiquity the "south" referred to lands far more expansive than the distribution of this lamp type (Barag and Hershkovitz, 1994: 78). In addition, it has been shown that, although this lamp form probably was quite popular among the predominantly Jewish community inhabiting early Roman Judea, the large repertoire of motifs of daily life often portrayed on the lamps reflects the agricultural character of the region. The term "Judean," therefore, is more appropriate, as it accommodates the possibility that peoples other than Jews also may have manufactured, purchased, or used this lamp type. Although the most significant concentration of the Judean molded lamp type is Judea and the Shephelah, excavations at Sepphoris have unearthed fragments of several other Judean molded lamps. Along with this lamp, they represent the northernmost occurrence of this lamp type and indicate cultural contact between Galilee and southern parts of Roman Palestine where lamps of this type presumably were manufactured.—*ECL*

108. Judean Molded Lamp with Palm Trees and Basket of Fruit

Palestine; exact provenance unknown
Roman period, c. 70–135 C.E.
Baked clay
L: 9.1 cm.; W: 6.2 cm.
Israel Antiquities Authority 69-1270

The Judean molded lamp type has a vast repertoire of iconographic motifs associated with daily rural life and Judean folk art, motifs that usually appear on the upper surface of the nozzle and shoulder. Characteristic decorations include sheaves of grain, fruits, fluted chalices, amphorae, bird cages, combs, earrings, lamps, pitchforks, and architectural elements such as tomb facades. On this lamp (published by Sussman, 1982: 39, no.19), the nozzle is decorated with a basket of fruit, possibly dates. Two date palms adorn either side of the shoulder. Together these closely related motifs serve a didactic purpose. Not only is the kind of produce shown (dates) but also the source from which it was gathered (date palms). Although the palm tree—indigenous to the subtropical Jordan Valley—was used widely by artists in antiquity, it was commonly used to represent Judea and Judaism in Late Roman art (Fine, 1989: 105–18; Fine and Rugers, 1996: 1–23).

This lamp features a wide spatulate nozzle with pronounced volutes. The lug handle is pierced.—*ECL*

109. Judean Molded Lamp with Palm Tree and Sheaves of Wheat

Palestine; exact provenance unknown
Roman period, c. 70–135 C.E.
Baked clay
L: 10.5 cm.; W: 7.2 cm.
Israel Antiquities Authority 69-1231

On this Judean molded lamp, a palmette with seven leaves decorates the spatulate nozzle, which is narrow and plain with a large wickhole. A single ridge surrounds and encloses the shoulder, which is ornamented with two sheaves of wheat stemming from each side of the base of the pierced lug handle. The floral decorative scheme reflects the agrarian community from which the lamp originated. (See Sussman, 1982: 100, no. 179.)—*ECL*

110. Northern Stamped Lamp with Dolphins

From a tomb in Galilee, near Dishon; excavated by Nathaniel Tefilinski for the Israel Antiquities Authority
Roman period, 2d to 3d century C.E.
Baked clay
L: 9 cm.; W: 6.7 cm.
Israel Antiquities Authority 68-597

The Northern Stamped lamp is characterized by a pear-shaped or almond-shaped body. Among the most common handle types is the stout pointed lug sliding onto the discus (central medallion), as on this example, although some lamps of this group do not have handles. The central discus is typically depressed and oval in shape; here a plain round discus is surrounded by two prominent ridges, while a third ridge borders the central filling-hole. Two dolphins in molded relief decorate the slanting shoulders of the lamp. A trefoil motif, probably representing a stylized acanthus leaf or capital (Sussman, 1989: 25, no. 2a-b), ornaments the nozzle.

Lamps belonging to the northern stamped type were first discovered in significant numbers by Nahman Avigad in the 1950s during his excavations of the Jewish catacombs at Beth-She'arim in Lower Galilee; subsequently they were called Beth-She'arim lamps. Because examples of this type are found in the greatest numbers in the north, particularly at sites in Western and Upper Galilee, the term northern stamped, as as proposed by Varda Sussman, has been adopted in place of Beth-She'arim as being more descriptive and accurate (Sussman 1989: 23–24). The "stamped" portion of the nomenclature refers to the most characteristic feature of this lamp type, namely the often densely stamped decoration occurring on its body in variations on a basic repertoire of geometric and floral patterns.

Some examples of the northern stamped lamp have been discovered at sites in the coastal plain, Galilee,

Transjordan, and as far south as the Egyptian border. This wide distribution suggests cultural connections and even trade of this lamp type. The lamps predominate, however, in burials in the northern part of Israel, where unlike at burial caves elsewhere in Israel, they do not appear with many other types of lamps, including imports (Sussman, 1989: 24). The chronological range of this group is considerable, beginning in the second to third centuries and continuing until the seventh century C.E.—*ECL*

center of a corona. A single oil filling-hole is located below the head.

The motifs on Roman Palestinian discus lamps are considerably more standardized than are those that occur, for example, on local lamp types, such as the Judean molded variety. The discus motifs, commonly depicted on lamps manufactured throughout the Roman world, include mythological compositions, floral patterns, architectural features, and religious symbols. (Many examples, however, have plain discs, and some lack decoration entirely.) —*ECL*

113. Discus Lamp Medallion with Head of Medusa

Sepphoris; Joint Sepphoris Project
Roman period, late 1st to 3d century C.E.
Baked clay
D: 3 cm.
Israel Antiquities Authority 95-3888

The depiction of Medusa with characteristic wavy hair suggestive of slithering snakes adorns this discus lamp medallion. Because the filling-holes (usually two in number) on discus lamps are small, it was difficult to introduce oil into the reservoir. In order to facilitate filling, the user would often intentionally break out the discus center to create a larger filling-hole. The resulting medallion is often preserved in the archaeological record with the central motif still intact.—*ECL*

111. Discus Lamp with Male Head and Corona

From a tomb in Galilee; excavated by Dan
Barag for the Israel Antiquities Authority
Roman period, late 1st to 3d century C.E.
Baked clay
L: 9.5 cm.; W: 10.8 cm.
Israel Antiquities Authority 64-539

The Roman Palestinian discus lamp is characterized by a round body with a small nozzle. The lamp is made up of two halves, upper and lower, that are produced in separate molds and later joined together. Darts, acanthus leaves, or impressed ovals, as on this example, commonly ornament the shoulders. The central discus provided the lampmaker greater space for artistic expression. Here the central discus, surrounded by a double ridge, features a depiction of a male head positioned in the

112. Fragment of Discus Lamp with Floral Motif

Sepphoris; Joint Sepphoris Project
Roman, late 1st to 3d century C.E.
Baked Clay
D: 7 cm.
Israel Antiquities Authority 95-3879

A fluted *kanthoras* (vase) with two handles decorates the central discus of this lamp fragment. The vase holds a floral arrangement comprised of acanthus leaves, thistle, and a sheath of wheat. This type of decorative motif was widely used on lamps thgroughout the ancient Roman world. Impressed darts ornament the shoulder of the lamp fragment, on which traces of slip remain.—*ECL*

114. Discus Lamp with Erotic Scene

Sepphoris; Joint Sepphoris Project
Roman period, late 1st to 3d century C.E.
Baked clay
D: 8 cm.
Israel Antiquities Authority 95-3881

Recent excavations in Israel have shown that lamps depicting erotic scenes, primarily of heterosexuality and bestiality, were not uncommon in Roman Palestine. Significant numbers have been found at

Leader, King, Soldier" (Morgan, 1983: 71). Clay lamps bearing the image of Helios would also be expected from *mithrea*, as is the case at Caesarea Maritima, where members of the Mithras cult (particularly popular among Roman soldiers in the first century C.E.) gathered to worship the sun-god (Lapp, forthcoming).—ECL

Ashkelon, Dor, Jerusalem, and Sepphoris. A lamp fragment with an erotic scene was found also in the Jewish catacombs at Beth-She^{c}arim, near Sepphoris in Lower Galilee. Given the widespread expression of erotica in Roman art and the explicit references to sexual activity in rabbinic literature (Lachs, 1992), such an occurrence should not be viewed as extraordinary. The scene of the male and female lovers depicted here is typical; lamps depicting erotic scenes were popular throughout the provinces of the Roman East and elsewhere in the Empire.

Impressed ovals and two double-ax devices in molded relief decorate the shoulder, and two double volutes ornament the shoulder directly below the nozzle. The double-ax motif is characteristic of discus lamps from Roman Palestine and distinguishes them from other specimens found elsewhere in the Empire. A single prominent ridge surrounds the discus scene, and an oil filling-hole is located below it. No traces of slip are evident. (See Meyers, Netzer, and Meyers, 1987: pl. 35A; 1992: 23 and 26.)—*ECL*

115. Discus Lamp with Helios Motif

Nabratein; Meiron Excavation Project
Roman period, late 1st to 3d century C.E.
Baked clay
D: 8 cm.
Israel Antiquities Authority 95-3951

The central discus of this lamp depicts a motif of Helios, the Greco-Roman sun god, fashioned in molded relief. The worship of Helios was particularly popular among Syrians in the Roman period, and depictions of him appear throughout the archaeological record (as, for example, on a basalt lintel of the Chorazin synagogue). The symbolic rendition of Helios's chariot appears in the center of the zodiac wheel recently excavated at Sepphoris. (See the discussion on the synagogue mosaic by Zeev Weiss and Ehud Netzer in this catalogue.) This particular example of Helios is further paralleled on synagogue mosaics at Hammath Tiberias, Beth Alpha, Na^{c}aran, and Huseifa (Hachlili, 1988: 301–9). Acclaim for Helios as a leader is mentioned in a fourth–fifth-century-C.E. rabbinic text: "Holy Helios who rises in the east, good mariner, trustworthy leader of the sun's rays, reliable [witness], who of old didst establish the mighty wheel [of the Heavens], holy orderer, ruler of the axis [of the heaven], Lord, Brilliant,

116. Discus Lamp Fragment with Aedicula

Sepphoris; Joint Sepphoris Project
Late Roman period, 4th century C.E.
D: 8 cm.
Israel Antiquities Authority 95-3880

The aedicula, or shrine, depicted on the wide central discus of this lamp closely resembles images of the Torah Shrine found on other clay lamps, a gold glass bowl, catacomb wall carvings, and synagogue floor mosaics (Mann, 1989: 226, nos. 27 and 28; Lapp, 1991: Taf. 8a-d; Goodenough, 1953: no. 968; Mazar, 1974: 180, pl. 34; Hachlili, 1988: pls. 32 and 101–5).

The round demi-dome gable and columns with spiraling flutes are especially characteristic of, and are found on, for example, the Torah Shrine depictions from the synagogue at Hammath Tiberias and the Jewish catacombs at Beth-She'arim. Missing here, however, is any indication of paneled doors and steps leading to them, additional features commonly associated with Jewish or Samaritan Torah Shrines. Christian aediculae, too, possess similar features and on lamps are distinguished as Christian by the addition of one or more crosses, usually at the apex or at the ends of the pointed gable (Avigad, 1976: 173–75, pl. 63, no. 1 and pl. 65, no. 1; Mazar, 1974: 177, pl. 32, no. 3; Fine and Rutgers, 1996: 18–21, fig. 6). In the absence of doors, steps, or crosses, no explicit religious or ethnic affiliation can be associated with the aedicula rendered on this lamp.—ECL

prises rope-like branches and is supported by a curved tripod base. Jewish ritual objects such as the *lulav* (palm branch), *shofar* (ram's horn), and incense shovel often are depicted in association with the *menorah*; none, however, accompany this example. Two oil filling-holes pierce the discus on each side of the central shaft of the lampstand. An incised rope pattern surrounds the central discus and functions as a sort of decorative border and rim of the discus, whereas the shoulder of the lamp is plain. No slip covers the lamp. Two parallels were unearthed at Qaṣrawet in northern Sinai and at Jalame, northeast of Carmel (Oren, 1982: pl. 29, "B"; MacDonnell, 1988: 133, fig. 6-6, nos 83 and 84, pl. 6-3).—ECL

remains of a *lulav* (palm branch) flank the lampstand to the left. To the upper right a curved nodule could be the trace of a *shofar* (ram's horn). As ritual objects, both the *lulav* and *shofar* are commonly depicted in association with the *menorah* in ancient Jewish art. The representation of the *menorah* occurs as a widespread Jewish (and Samaritan) symbol on a number of artifacts and architectural features, including lead seals, clay lamps, gemstones, capitals, and synagogue mosaic pavements (MacDonnell, 1988: 133, fig. 6-6, no. 86, pl. 6-4).

The careless rendering of the *menorah* here is characteristic of the linear design that typically decorates the discs of this lamp type, known as the Caesarea round lamp, type 1 (Sussman, 1980: pls. 15-16). In 1960 the Negev excavations at Caesarea Maritima recovered limestone lamp molds from a deposit above the apse of a fourth-century building located south of the city wall. Two types of lamps were produced from these molds. The type 1 lamps are characterized by a large round body with a wide, short spatulate nozzle and a pyramidal, knob-like handle. Consecutive radial lines decorate the shoulder and create a ribbed appearance. The closed discus is quite broad and usually is decorated with a linear design fashioned in a haphazard manner by incising it freehand into the limestone mold (Sussman, 1980: 77). Various motifs are depicted on the discs, including geometric patterns, human and animal figures, floral designs, aediculae, and crosses. This example from Sepphoris is significant, for it represents the only known Caesarea round lamp the central discus of which is decorated with a *menorah*.—ECL

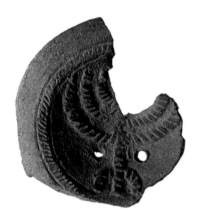

117. Discus Lamp Fragment with *Menorah*

Sepphoris; Sepphoris Regional Project
Late Roman period, 4th century C.E.
D: 6 cm.
Israel Antiquities Authority 95-3896

A seven-branched lampstand, or *menorah*, is depicted in molded relief on the discus of this lamp fragment. The *menorah* com-

118. Caesarea Round Lamp Fragment with *Menorah*

Sepphoris; Sepphoris Regional Project
Late Roman, 4th century C.E.
Baked clay
D: 7 cm.
Israel Antiquities Authority 95-3897

A *menorah* with multiple branches and a rectangular tripod base is depicted in molded relief on the central discus of this lamp fragment. Three branches stem from the central shaft of the *menorah* on the left; four (possibly five), on the right. The

119. Ovoid Lamp

Sepphoris; Sepphoris Regional Project
Late Byzantine to Early Islamic, late 6th to
*   first half of the 7th century C.E.*
Baked clay
D: 10 cm.
Israel Antiquities Authority 95-3895

Late Byzantine lamps served as prototypes for early Islamic lamps, which retain many of the same characteristic features: an ovoid body with pointed nozzle; a small, round sunken discus with sloping sides and a small central filling-hole; and a pyramidal knob "handle," too small to be usable. The decorative scheme employs simple patterns of floral, geometric, or zoomorphic motifs that cover the entire surface, exemplifying the aesthetic concept of *horror vacuii*, whereby no surface is left undecorated. Human representations are seldom found on lamps of this type or indeed on any lamps of the Islamic period (Rosenthal and Sivan, 1978: 130). On this example, the shoulders are ornamented with flower blossoms framed by spiraling vines; even the channel leading from the wickhole to the filling-hole is ornamented with a vine tendril. Radiating lines encircle the filling-hole.

Ovoid lamps are found in the northern part of Israel. Numerous examples have been recovered at Beth-She'arim. The lamps range in date from the late sixth to the first half of the seventh century C.E. —*ECL*

120. Ovoid Lamp

Nabratein; Meiron Excavation Project
Late Byzantine to Early Islamic, late 6th to
*   first half of the 7th century C.E.*
Baked clay
D: 10 cm.
Israel Antiquities Authority 95-3952

A single guilloche (ribbon twist) framed within an inner and outer ridge decorates the shoulder of this lamp, following the contour of the lamp body, central discus, and wick channel. A spiraling vine fills the channel space from the discus to the wick-hole. Raised round globules fill spaces inside and/or around these patterns. A small triangular handle merges into the discus. Traces of burning around the wick-hole indicate use.—*ECL*

REFERENCES

Avigad, Nahman. "Excavations in the Jewish Quarter of the Old City of Jerusalem, 1970: Second Preliminary Report." *Israel Exploration Journal* 20 (1970): 129–40.

Avigad, Nahman. *Beth She'arim. Report on the Excavations during 1953–1958. Catacombs 12–13.* vol. 3. New Brunswick, 1976.

Barag, Dan and Malka Hershkovitz. "Lamps." In *Masada IV: The Yigael Yadin Excavations 1963–1965 Final Reports*, ed. Joseph Aviram, Gideon Foerster, and Ehud Netzer. Jerusalem, 1994: 107–24.

Fine, Steven. "On the Development of the Visual Symbol: The Date Palm in Roman Palestine and the Jews." *Journal for the Study of Pseudepigrapha* 4 (1989): 105–18.

Fine, Steven and Leonard V. Rutgers. "New Light on Judaism in Asia Minor during Late Antiquity: Two Recently Identified Inscribed Menorahs." *Jewish Studies Quarterly* 3, no. 1 (1996): 1–23.

Goodenough, Erwin. R. *Jewish Symbols in the Greco-Roman Period*. vol. 3. New York, 1953.

Hachlili, Rachel. *Ancient Jewish Art and Archaeology in the Land of Israel*. Leiden, 1988.

Kahane, P. P. "Rock-Cut Tombs at Huqoq. Note on the Finds." *'Atiqot* (English Series) 3 (1961): 128–47.

Kehrberg, Ina. "Jerash/Gerasa, Hippodrome." In Patricia M. Bakai and Deborah Kooring. *American Journal of Archaeology* 99, no. 3 (1995): 528.

Lachs, S. T. "Sexual Imagery in Three Rabbinic Passages." *Journal for the Study of Judaism* 23, no. 2 (1992): 244–48.

Lapp, Eric C. "Zwei spätantike jüdische Tonlampen aus Kleinasien." *Jahrbuch für Antike und Christentum* 35 (1991): 156–58.

Lapp, Eric C. "The Cultural Significance of the Oil Lamp from Roman Palestine." Ph.D., diss. Duke Univ. Forthcoming.

MacDonnell, Anna M. "The Terracotta Lamps." In *Excavations at Jalame: Site of a Glass Factory in Late Roman Palestine*, ed. Gladys D. Weinberg. Columbia, 1988: 116–36.

Mann, Vivian, ed. *Gardens and Ghettos: The Art of Jewish Life in Italy.* Berkeley and Los Angeles, 1989.

Mazar, Benjamin. *Beth She'arim. Catacombs 1–4.* vol. 1. New Brunswick, 1974.

Meyers, Eric M., Ehud Netzer, and Carol L. Meyers. "Sepphoris (Sippori), 1986 (1)-Joint Sepphoris Project." *Israel Exploration Journal* 37, no. 4 (1987): 275–78.

Meyers, Eric M., Ehud Netzer, and Carol L. Meyers. *Sepphoris.* Winona Lake, 1992.

Morgan, M. A., trans. *Sepher Ha-Razim: The Book of Mysteries.* Pseudepigrapha Series, 11 (Chico, 1983).

Oren, Eliezer D. "Excavations at Qaṣrawet in North-Western Sinai: Preliminary Report." *Israel Exploration Journal* 32, no. 4 (1982): 209–10.

Rosenthal, Renate and Renee Sivan. *Ancient Lamps in the Schloessinger Collection.* Qedem 8. Jerusalem, 1978.

Sussman, Varda. "Moulds for Lamps and Figurines from a Caesarea Workshop." *'Atiqot* 14 (1980): 76–79.

Sussman, Varda. *Ornamented Jewish Oil-Lamps from the Destruction of the Second Temple through the Bar Kokhba Revolt.* Warminster, 1982.

Sussman, Varda. "Northern Stamped Oil Lamps and Their Typology." *Michmanim* 4 (July 1989): 22–58.

Yellin, Yosef. "Origin of the Lamps from Masada." In Dan Barag and Malka Hershkovitz. "Lamps." In *Masada IV: The Yigael Yadin Excavations 1963-1965 Final Reports*, ed. Joseph Aviram, Gideon Foerster, and Ehud Netzer. Jerusalem, 1994: 107–24.

121. Bronze Lamp

Sepphoris; Hebrew University of Jerusalem Expedition

Byzantine period, 4th-6th centuries C.E.

Bronze

H: 14 cm.; L: 17 cm.

Israel Antiquities Authority 94-2884

This oil lamp was found among the various bronze objects uncovered in the debris of the storehouse located to the south of the Crusader citadel. The lamp has a circular body with a projected round nozzle. The filling-hole at the top is covered with a round, hinged lid. It is decorated with various profiles and, at the top, a finial, which was used as a handle when opening to refill. The tall curved handle composed of two stems is decorated with a seated dove facing toward the body of the lamp. The disk base has a square hole to fit over the spike of a lampstand.

Decorated bronze lamps of this kind —a prototype for clay lamps—were popular in the region during the Byzantine period. Although the repertoire of bronze lamps in the area is limited, their decorative elements vary.—ZW

REFERENCES

Rosenthal, Renate and Renee Sivan. *Ancient Lamps in the Schloessinger Collection.* Qedem 8. Jerusalem, 1978: 160.

Tzori, Nehemiah. "Bronze Utensils from Byzantine Beth She'an." *Qadmoniot* 3 (1970): 68.

122. Polycandelon

Beth Shean; excavated by Nehemiah Tsori for the Israel Antiquities Authority
Byzantine period, 6th century C.E.
Bronze
D: 18 cm.
Israel Antiquities Authority 59-36

This hanging bronze polycandelon, or chandelier, held glass vessels containing oil and wicks in the six circular openings in the metal wheel or hoop. Lamps such as this were suspended from the ceiling of a home, from a pediment or other architectural element, thus providing illumination from above. They were used in addition to the more familiar portable clay lamps (see cat. nos. 106–20), which were placed at various points around the house or room.

The use of glass lamps became more common in the later Roman and Byzantine periods as blown glass became more available. Hence it was used for both domestic and nondomestic illumination. Because of its transparency, glass spread light more evenly. In order to prevent the heat from cracking the glass, water was inserted into the vessel before adding the oil, which rose to the top. The wick was soaked in oil before being inserted into the water. The glass vessels inserted into the circular receptacles cut into the wheel were nothing more than eating and drinking vessels adapted to a new use.

This example is very similar to one found in Upper Galilee, at the village of Kefar Makr, which may be related to the synagogue of Kefar Ḥananyah. An Aramaic inscription on that lamp uses the Semitic word for the bronze element of such a lamp, *kelilah*: "This kelilah was dedicated to the synagogue of Kefar Ḥananyah" (Naveh, 1978: 34–35, no. 16). Another close Byzantine parallel, dating to the sixth or the seventh century C.E., is the unpublished lamp, or polycandelon, found at the double church at Umm er-Rasas in Jordan and on view in the Madaba Museum in Jordan (on the church, see Piccirillo, 1993: 232–39). A hanging lamp of this kind or similar to it—possibly with a single glass vessel suspended—probably was hung from the pediment of the Nabratein Torah Shrine, a replica of which is presented in this exhibition (cat. no. 30) —*EMM*

REFERENCES

Meyers, Carol L. and Eric M. Meyers. "The Ark in Art: A Ceramic Rendering of the Torah Shrine from Nabratein." *Eretz Israel* 16 (1982): 176–85.

Naveh, Yose. *On Stone and Mosaic.* Jerusalem, 1978 (in Hebrew).

Piccirillo, Michele. *The Mosaics of Jordan.* Amman, 1993.

Zevulun, Uta and Yael Olenik, eds. *Function and Design in the Talmudic Period.* Tel Aviv, 1978.

123. Oil Lamp Filler

Sepphoris; Tel Aviv University Expedition
Early Arab period, c. 7th century C.E.
Bronze
L: 7.5 cm.; D: 5.3 cm.
Israel Antiquities Authority 96-425

This bronze vessel for filling oil lamps is in the shape of a hemispherical ladle with an open pouring spout extending from its lip (Tsuk et al., 1996: pl. 14:1). It could hold up to one-half ounce of oil. Its lip widens out on both sides of where it meets the spout, and a circle with a wide depression in its center is incised on each side. On the lip of the vessel, opposite these circles, are the remains of two or more such circles, as though the designer were trying to create a kind of decorative symmetry. There is also a strip around the inside of the ladle at the height of the spout.

Vessels for filling lamps from excavations at Kfar Saba (Roll and Ayalon, 1989: 169, fig. 108:4) and Ramat Gan (Brand, 1993: fig. 45) have been dated to the late Byzantine and early Arab periods (Rosenthal and Sivan, 1978: 168, nos. 695-97). A third vessel for filling lamps, exhibited in the Rockefeller Museum (Jerusalem), was found in the ancient synagogue at Naᶜaran; a fourth, in the cave of Araq e-Naasne in eastern Samaria, together with a large group of finds from the second century C.E. (Frumkin, 1981). Those finds were unstratified, however, so the lamp filler itself does not necessarily

date to the second century. The stamped decoration of two incised circles around central depressions on both sides of the spout decorate the Ramat Gan lamp filler; on the strength of that connection, the Sepphoris vessel can be dated to the early Arab period.—*TT*

Two Bronze Bells

124. Bell

Sepphoris; Tel Aviv University Expedition
Byzantine period, c. 4th–5th centuries C.E.
Bronze
H: 4.3 cm.; D: 3.0 cm.
Israel Antiquities Authority 96-426

This small, nicely designed bronze bell was cast in a typical mold (Tsuk et al., 1996: pl. 14:2). The iron bell clapper is missing. The well-shaped lip opens out and terminates in a thickened protuberance. Two groups of lines are incised on the outside of the bell, five on the lower part and four around the center. The top of the bell is designed with two round protuberances that apparently represent the points of connection between the bell and its perforated handle. Bells from the Early Roman period were more squat in shape, that is, not as tall but larger in diameter (Biran and Cohen, 1981: pl. 54:1). Shorter bells with larger diameters have been found in a tomb at Kibbutz Lohame ha-Getaot in Western Galilee (Peleg, 1991: 143, figs. 12:4, 13:19). Bells from Sajur (Braun and Hadas, 1994: fig. 5:5), el-Jish (Makhouly, 1938-39: pl. 31:14), and Tarshiha (Iliffe, 1934: pl. 8:13), all of which were found in tombs, bear a striking resemblance to this bell from Sepphoris. It may be that all four were created in the same foundry. These bells have been dated to the 4th-5th centuries C.E. They may have been placed in tombs to ward off evil spirits (Dellate, 1954; Russell, 1982).—*TT*

125. Bell

Sepphoris; Tel Aviv University Expedition
Byzantine period, c. 4th–early 7th century
C.E.
Bronze
H: 4.9 cm.; D: 3.4 cm.
Israel Antiquities Authority 96-427

This simple bell lacks any special design (Tsuk et al., 1996: pl. 14:3). The body of the bell and its handle represent a single cast unit. The iron clapper is missing. No parallels to this bell have been found, therefore, it has been dated in accordance with the archaeological context of the locus in which it was found.—*TT*

126. Ram-Shaped Pitcher

Sepphoris; Tel Aviv University Expedition
Byzantine period, c. 4th–early 7th century
C.E.
Ceramic
H: 9 cm.; L: 12.5 cm.
Israel Antiquities Authority 96-428

This zoomorphic "traveler's flask" was used for valuable liquids, probably wine (Tsuk et al., 1996: pl. 15:3, fig. 176).

Because of the shape of the head, the animal can be identified as a ram. The liquid was poured through a hole in the back of the beast above the tail, and it came out through another hole in the animal's mouth. A handle is located at the center of the back. The vessel is almost perfectly preserved except for three places: the right front leg is broken, the tail is broken, and there is a defect on the head. The eyes are formed by two incised circles with round depressions in their centers; this decorative motif is repeated above each leg and along the length of the neck. On the rest of the body deep lines are incised at an angle. The vessel's red slip is incomplete in most places. The clay is orange with a few white grits in it. No identical parallels have been discovered; the closest parallel is the Byzantine-period animal head unearthed in the excavations at Bab el-Hawa in the Golan Heights (Hartal, 1992: fig. 59).
—*TT*

127. Fragment of Vessel with Incised Cross Design

Sepphoris; Tel Aviv University Expedition
Byzantine period, c. 4th–early 7th century
* C.E.*
Ceramic
L: 13 cm.
Israel Antiquities Authority 96-429

Part of an inscription and a cross are incised on this sherd from a jug (Tsuk et al., 1996: pl. 14:7). The inscription was written on the upper part of the vessel near the neck, in an area where the ribbing has disappeared and the surface of the vessel is almost smooth. The clay is brown-orange. The incising was done before the vessel was fired.

In the inscription, the letters Δ Ρ Σ (delta, rho, sigma) are visible, though the letter that looks like a delta may be a cursive alpha. These three letters are at the end of a word—perhaps a name. There is also a fourth letter, which has barely survived and is totally illegible. The size of each letter is approximately 1 cm. Some 4 cm. to the right of the inscription is an incised cross, of which the upper half has survived. Its original size was 5 x 3.5 cm. Its rhomboid shape was achieved by connecting the end points of the transom and the upright by straight lines. The artist also used short straight lines to close the interior angles formed by the transom, the upright, and the connecting lines, thus forming decorative triangles at the points of connection (eight in the original).—*TT*

128. Cup-Shaped Vessel with Drain Hole

Sepphoris; Tel Aviv University Expedition
Byzantine period, 7th century C.E.
Ceramic
H: 13 cm.
Israel Antiquities Authority 96-430

This cup-shaped bowl has one handle (Tsuk et al., 1996: pl. 1:2, fig. 159). The rim is slightly closed, and its outer side is delineated by a groove that continues around the entire vessel a bit below the rim. The body of the vessel, which resembles a flower pot, has a pattern of shallow ribbing. The handle is crudely attached, particularly at the lower point of attachment. The flattened base is attached to the vessel in a clumsy manner and has a bulge in the center so that the vessel does not sit flat on its base.

The bottom of the vessel is pierced by a hole that apparently was drilled before firing. The hole seems to have been necessary to the function of the vessel, which may have been used for the filtration of water from the subterranean reservoir in which it was excavated.

The clay, a light brown, contains black grit and gravel and a few flakes of mica. —*TT*

129. Pouring Jug

Sepphoris; Tel Aviv University Expedition
Byzantine period, c. 7th century C.E.
Ceramic
H: 18 cm.
Israel Antiquities Authority 96-431

This vessel had a very specific use: drawing water and transferring it to a larger vessel (Tsuk et al., 1996: pl. 9:5, fig. 167). The vertical rim has a large opening and a triangular crosssection that tends slightly outward. The handle is crudely attached, particularly at the lower point of attachment. At this point, the wall of the vessel forms a sharp angle and also attains its maximum width. The body of the vessel is more or less cylindrical, with narrow, delicate ribbing. The base is crudely attached, but a recess in the center of the base ensures stability.

The clay is brown with white grits.

The vessel, found at the bottom of a sedimentation basin, belongs to the last stage in the use of the Sepphoris reservoir, apparently in the seventh century C.E.—*TT*

130. Jug with Black Painted Designs

Sepphoris; Tel Aviv University Expedition
Medieval period, 13th–17th centuries C.E.
Ceramic
H: 23.5 cm.
Israel Antiquities Authority 96-432

The spherical shape of this jug is typical of the Middle Ages (Tsuk et al., 1996: pl. 9:10, fig. 168). The lip turns down slightly toward the outside. The vessel features black geometric decorations, mainly triangles and stripes of varying thickness, over a white slip. The vessel was shaped by hand, rather than wheel-thrown. The ribbon-shaped handle is neatly attached to the vessel. The annular base is low. The clay is light brown with a gray core and contains straw and white grits. Similar vessels—handmade, slipped, and painted with geometric designs—have been found at Tel Yoqneᶜam (Ben-Tor et al., 1979: fig. 5:13). Vessels with similar geometric designs were also found at Taᶜanach (Ziadeh, 1995: fig. 7:4). —*TT*

REFERENCES

Ben-Tor, Amnon, Y. Portugali, and M. Avissar. "The Second Season of Excavations at Tel Yoqneᶜam, 1978: Preliminary Report." *Israel Exploration Journal* 29 (1979): 65–83.

Biran, A. and R. Cohen. "Aroer in the Negev." *Eretz Israel* 15 (1981): 250–73.

Brand, E. "Ramat-Gan." *Archaeological News* 100 (1993): 40–41.

Braun, E. Daupin and G. Hadas. "Tomb at Sajur." *ᶜAtiqot* 25 (1994): 103–15.

Dellate, A. "Une clochette magique." *Bulletin de la classe des lettres et des sciences morales et politiques, Académie royale de Belgique*, 5th series, 40 (1954): 254–76.

Frumkin, A. "Finds from Araq e-Naasne, Naᶜaran, and Wadi Murabbaᶜat." *Niqrot Zurim* (Journal of the Israel Cave Research Center) 4 (1981): 42f. (in Hebrew).

Hartal, M. In *Excavations and Surveys in Israel* 10 (1992): 64.

Iliffe, J. H. "A Rock-cut Tomb at Tarshiha." *Quarterly of the Department of Antiquities in Palestine* 3 (1934): 9–16.

Makhouly, N. "Rock-cut Tombs at el-Jish." *Quarterly of the Department of Antiquities in Palestine* 8 (1938–39): 45–50.

Peleg, M. "Persian, Hellenistic, and Roman Burials at Lohamei Ha-Geta'ot." *ᶜAtiqot* 20 (1991): 131–51.

Roll, Israel and Etan Ayalon. *Apollonia and Southern Sharon.* Tel Aviv, 1989 (in Hebrew with English summary).

Rosenthal, Renate and Renee Sivan. *Ancient Lamps in the Schloessinger Collection.* Qedem 8. Jerusalem, 1978.

Russell, J. "The Evil Eye in Early Byzantine Society." *Jahrbuch der Österreichischen Byzantinistik* 32 (1982): 539–48.

Tsuk, Tsvika, Arik Rosenberger, and Martin Peilstocker. *The Ancient Reservoir of Zippori, Excavations 1993–1994.* Tel Aviv, 1996 (in Hebrew with English summary).

Ziadeh, G. "Ottoman Ceramics from Tinnik, Palestine." *Levant* 27 (1995): 209–45.

Household Implements

131. & 132. Mortar with Lug Handles (illustrated) and Rubbing Stone (not illustrated)

Sepphoris; University of Michigan Expedition
Late Roman or Byzantine period
Basalt
H: 32 cm.; W: 29.3 cm. (mortar)
L: 6.5 cm; W: 4.6 cm. (rubbing stone)
Kelsey Museum of Archaeology 92997 (mortar)
    and 90107 (rubbing stone)

Mortars such as this one and rubbing stones were used to crush grain into flour for bread, among other domestic functions.—*RMN*

133. Spindle Whorl

Sepphoris; University of Michigan Expedition
Late Roman or Byzantine period
Stone; red
H: 0.9 cm.; W: 2.2 cm.
Kelsey Museum of Archaeology 90024

134. Spindle Whorl

Sepphoris; University of Michigan Expedition
Roman period
Terracotta
H: 1.0 cm.; W: 2.4 cm.
Kelsey Museum of Archaeology 90017

Spindle whorls were used in the making of thread. Fibers to be spun into thread were wound onto a spindle (a round stick with tapered ends). A whorl placed on the spindle increased its spinning momentum. —*RMN*

REFERENCE

Ackerman, Andrew S. and Susan L. Braunstein. *Israel in Antiquity from David to Herod*. Exhibition catalogue, the Jewish Museum, New York, 1982: 67, cat. no. 46; 120, cat. no. 120.

Jewelry and Other Small Personal Items

135. Crossbow Fibula

Palestine; exact provenance unknown
Roman period, c. 3d–5th centuries C.E.
Bronze: cast
L: 5 cm.
Israel Antiquities Authority 91-331

136. Crossbow Fibula

Palestine; exact provenance unknown
Roman period, c. 3d–5th centuries C.E.
Bronze: cast
L: 5 cm.
Israel Antiquities Authority 91-335

Bronze fibulae were used throughout the Roman Empire for fastening clothing. Those employed in the ancient Near East typically consisted of a bar bent outward into an arched bow shape, with a pin that moved on a hinge or a spring at one end and fitted into a catch at the other. The addition of a cylindrical or tubular cross-piece at the hinge end made the fibula resemble a crossbow; hence the name for the type represented here.

Crossbow fibulae, apparently brought to Palestine by Roman legionnaires, were among the most common of all Roman fibulae types during the third and fourth centuries. Because they exist in numerous decorative variations and degrees of quality in workmanship and materials, they probably originated from several production sites.—*RMN*

REFERENCES

Frisch, Teresa G. and N. P. Toll. "The Bronze Objects." In *The Excavations at Dura-Europas Conducted by Yale University and the French Academy of Inscriptions and Letters, Final Report IV,* ed. M. I. Rostovtzeff et al. New Haven, 1949: 51–61, pls. 11–15 (for parallels).

Needler, Winifred. *Palestine Ancient and Modern: A Handbook and Guide to the Palestinian Collection of the Royal Ontario Museum.* Toronto, 1949: 46, pl. 15.

GLASS BANGLE BRACELETS

137. Bracelet

Sepphoris; University of Michigan Expedition
Roman period, 2d–4th centuries C.E.
Glass; translucent blue-green
D: 7.5 cm.
Kelsey Museum of Archaeology 89820

138. Bracelet

From a tomb at Khirbet Gelilot (also known
as Gelil)
Roman period, 2d–4th centuries C.E.
Glass; opaque black
D: 6.2 cm.
Israel Antiquities Authority 52-983

139. Bracelet

From a tomb at Serakh Ilit; excavated by
Adam Druks for the Israel Antiquities
Authority
Roman period, 2d–4th centuries C.E.
Glass; translucent cobalt blue
D: 5 cm.
Israel Antiquities Authority 60-776

Glass bracelets seem to have been common throughout the Eastern Roman Empire, and many fragments of bracelets have been found by archaeologists at Sepphoris. Although it is unusual to find a complete bracelet, this well-preserved blue-green bracelet (Kelsey 89820) was discovered at Sepphoris by Leroy Waterman of the University of Michigan in 1931. The other two bracelets were recovered from tomb contexts. Because glass was inexpensive in the Roman period, such bracelets were accessible to everyone; however, they probably did not last long if worn often. They are found in large and small sizes, apparently intended for adults and children. Fragments of glass rings also have been found at Sepphoris.

The bracelets were manufactured by winding a trail of hot glass around a rod of the desired diameter made either of metal or wood. This process is apparent from the smooth interior of the bracelets and from the perfect circle formed by the interior circumference. The exterior surfaces of the bracelets are much less uniform. The opaque black bracelet (IAA 52-983) has a ribbed decoration. Due to the inconsistency of the spacing of the ribs, it seems likely that the ribbing was done manually, with each indentation created individually by the artisans.—AF

REFERENCES

Root, Margaret C. *Wondrous Glass: Reflections on the World of Rome, c. 50 B.C.–A.D. 650.* Ann Arbor, 1982: 35, no 27 (Kelsey 89820).

Spaer, M. "The Pre-Islamic Glass Bracelets of Palestine." *Journal of Glass Studies* 30 (1988): 51–61.

Winter, Tamar. "Jewelry and Miscellaneous Objects." In *The Akeldama Tombs: Three Burial Caves in the Kidron Valley, Jerusalem,* ed. Gideon Avni and Zvi Greenhut. Jerusalem, 1996: 111.

140. Gold Headpiece

*Sepphoris; University of South Florida
   Expedition*
Byzantine period, 6th century C.E.
Gold
L: 32 cm.
Israel Antiquities Authority 96-1094

This gold headpiece is composed of three strands of vine leaves connected to a central medallion. The fine leaves are decorated with gold granules. The medallion features a frontal view of a woman's face with turreted crown. She also wears earrings with two hanging decorations. To the right of the face is a cornucopia; to the left is the branch of a plant—both apparently symbols of fertility. Such portraits from the pre-Christian Greco-Roman world usually are understood to represent Tyche (Greek) or Fortuna (Latin), city goddesses of fortune and destiny. The medallion on this piece bears a Greek inscription—XAPIC—meaning "grace," which suggests that the medallion may be a Christian adaptation of an earlier art form. Symbols of women bearing gifts to the faithful are common in Byzantine Christian art.

The archaeological context of the headpiece was a shop of the sixth century C.E. located on the eastern slope of the hill of Sepphoris. The shop had been destroyed in a conflagration, and the gold was found in partially burned debris on the floor. Apparently it fell from a wooden shelf, which collapsed and snuffed out the fire from around the gold. Burned wooden beams lay within a few centimeters of the gold cache, which included, along with the headpiece, a gold disc, and a pair of gold earrings consisting of two chains (originally three) hanging from a loop, each chain ending in a seed pearl (see cat. no. 141). Another pair of earrings had all of its decorations, such as beads, pulled off so that only the central loops remained. About half of the gold headpiece also is missing, which suggests that the last owner was using it as a source of gold bullion.

In their original states, these elegant pieces of jewelry might have been worn to a public event, such as an athletic contest, a bishop's investiture, or some other occasion at which high-ranking officials gathered. How they got in a shop that burned can only be surmised.—*JFS*

REFERENCES

Gerscht, Rivka. "The Tyche of Caesarea Maritima." *Palestine Exploration Quarterly* 166 (1984): 110–14.

Ross, M. C. *Catalogue of the Byzantine and Early Medieval Antiquities in the Dumbarton Oaks Collection.* vol. 2. *Jewelry, Enamels, and Art of the Migration Period.* Washington, 1965: 31.

Weitzmann, Kurt, ed. *The Age of Spirituality.* New York, 1979: 33.

141. Loop and Chain Earring

*Sepphoris; University of South Florida
   Expedition*
Byzantine period, 6th century C.E.
Gold and seed pearls
D (of loop): 3 cm.
Israel Antiquities Authority 96-1095

This gold earring is part of a matched pair that was found in a burn layer in a shop dating to the sixth century C.E. Apparently these two gold earrings, a gold headpiece (see cat. no. 140), a gold disc, and two gold earrings from which the decorations had been removed constituted a gold cache that had been on a shelf in the shop. When the shelf collapsed it snuffed out the fire, which spared the earrings and the other gold pieces.

The loop that fits in each ear is a circle of 24-carat gold wire about 3 mm. thick and about 3 cm. in diameter. The ancient artisan soldered three small circlets of gold to the loops and attached a 3 cm. gold chain, formed of nine double links, to each small circlet so that three gold chains hung down from each large hoop; one chain has been lost. Each chain was finished with a seed pearl secured by gold wire that ran through the pearl and was attached to the end of the chain. The gold wire terminated in a gold-solder spherule, which prevented the pearl from dropping off. The seed pearls were damaged by the heat of the fire, but the gold of the earrings was not marred.

Pendant earrings appear in Byzantine art throughout the Mediterranean. Most commonly a matron is depicted wearing pendant earrings and a diadem or crown. Images of women wearing earrings and head coverings are well represented in Byzantine textiles, for example.

Interestingly enough, two years before this pair was uncovered, an identical earring with one chain missing and without seed pearls was found in a probe into an erosion layer some 75 m. to the southeast of the shop. That the latest materials in the erosion were all from the sixth century C.E. suggests a connection between them and local historical events. The burned shop was never rebuilt, nor was the gold cache rescued; and, at about the same time, buildings went out of use on the major east-west street southeast of the shop. The erosion that eventually resulted from disuse became the vehicle whereby the second earring was washed into the erosion layer next to the street.—*JFS*

REFERENCES

Ross, M. C. *Catalogue of the Byzantine and Early Medieval Antiquities in the Dumbarton Oaks Collection.* vol 2. *Jewelry, Enamels, and Art of the Migration Period.* Washington, 1965.

Ross, M. C. "Jewels of Byzantium." *Arts in Virginia* 9 (1968): 12–31.

ALSO IN THE EXHIBITION

142. Gold Earring with Pearl Pendants

Not Illustrated
Susita; excavated by Claire Epstein for the Israel Antiquities Authority
Roman period
Gold and pearls
D: 2.2 cm.
Israel Antiquities Authority 49-903

143. Gold Earring with Four Suspended Pearls

Hammath-Gader; excavated by Giora Solar and Yizhar Hirschfeld for the Hebrew University of Jerusalem
Byzantine period
Gold and pearls
D: 1.5 cm.
Israel Antiquities Authority 94-2113

144. Cross-shaped Pendant

Not Illustrated
Akko, El Machev; excavated by Jacob Ori for the Israel Antiquities Authority
Byzantine period
Bronze
L: 3 cm.
Israel Antiquities Authority 49-1106

145. Cross-shaped Pendant

Haifa, Tel Shikmona; excavated by Joseph Elgarish for the Haifa Museum of Ancient Art
Byzantine period
Bronze
L: 5 cm.
Israel Antiquities Authority 81-1235

146. Cross-shaped Pendant

Not Illustrated
Haifa, Tel Shikmona; excavated by Joseph Elgarish for the Haifa Museum of Ancient Art
Byzantine period
Bone
L: 3 cm.
Israel Antiquities Authority 81-1237

147. Kohl Applicator Stick

Not Illustrated
Caesarea
Roman period
Bronze
L: 9.5 cm.
Israel Antiquities Authority 51-688

148. Toggle Pin or Hair Pin

Nabratein; Meiron Excavation Project
Byzantine period
Bone
L: 10.5 cm.
Israel Antiquities Authority 80-457

149. Hair Pin

Sepphoris; University of Michigan
*   Expedition*
Roman period
Bone
L: 6.6 cm.
Kelsey Museum of Archaeology 90027

150. Hair Pin

Sepphoris; University of Michigan
*   Expedition*
Roman period
Bone
L: 7 cm.
Kelsey Museum of Archaeology 90066

151. Bodkin (Needle)

Sepphoris; University of Michigan
*   Expedition*
Roman period
Bone
L: 10 cm.
Kelsey Museum of Archaeology 89823

152. & 153. Two Dice Pieces

Sepphoris; University of Michigan
*   Expedition*
Roman period
Bone
1 cm. x 1 cm.; 1.2 cm. x 1.3 cm.
Kelsey Museum of Archaeology 89826 and
*   89991*

Ornamental Attachments

154. Statuette of a Female Lion
(Fragment of a Lampstand Base)

Sepphoris; Hebrew University Expedition
Byzantine period, 6th–7th centuries C.E.
Bronze: cast
H: 7 cm.
Israel Antiquities Authority 96-1643

This small bronze statuette of an animal was found among the various bronze objects uncovered in the debris of the storage building located to the south of the Crusader citadel. The statuette represents a leaping female lion. Her body is molded in profile, except for the head, which is turned to the right. The animal is rearing up on its hind legs, which stand on a small stepped base, as the forelegs thrust forward. Body parts, such as the eyes, ears, mouth, and long curly tail, are simply molded, as is the entire piece.

The forelegs of the lion are cut short, suggesting that the figure was once part of a larger object. Parallels to this piece indicate that the lion may be one of three legs, each shaped in the form of a rampant female lion, that composed the base of a lampstand.—ZW

REFERENCES

Lamb, Winifred. *Greek and Roman Bronzes*. Chicago, 1969: pls. 83–84.

Pettinau, Barbara. "L'illuminazione della domus: lucerne e candelabri." In *Il bronzo dei Romani*, ed. Lucia P. B. Stefanelli. Rome, 1990: 95–110.

ALSO IN THE EXHIBITION

155. Double Hook Decorated with Flowers

Sepphoris; Joint Sepphoris Project
Byzantine period
Bronze
L: 17.5 cm.
Israel Antiquities Authority 96-1550

156. Gold "Button" Ornament

Sepphoris; Joint Sepphoris Project
Late Roman or Byzantine period
Gold
D: 1.5 cm.
Israel Antiquities Authority 95-3890

157. Bone Carving of a Male Nude

Sepphoris; Sepphoris Regional Project
Byzantine period
Bone
L: 6.3 cm.
Israel Antiquities Authority 96-881/1,2

Also in the Exhibition

158. Section of Ornamental Molding from Theater

Sepphoris; Joint Sepphoris Project and
*   Hebrew University Expedition*
Roman period, early 2d century C.E.
Limestone
L: 65 cm.; W: 70 cm.
Israel Antiquities Authority 96–1642

159. Hunter Mosaic from the Nile Festival Building

See fig. 33
Sepphoris; Hebrew University Expedition
Byzantine period, c. 5th century C.E.
Stone tesserae
H: 3.21 m.; W: 1.52 m.
Israel Antiquities Authority 93–2887

160. Replica of the "Mona Lisa of Galilee" from the Dionysos Mosaic

The original is illustrated in fig. 45
[Original: Sepphoris; Joint Sepphoris Project
Roman period, early 3d century C.E.]
Stone tesserae
H: 62.23 cm.; W: 89.53 cm.
Replica: Center for Restoration, Israel
*   Museum, Jerusalem*

161. Replica of Scenes of Dionysos and Herakles from the Dionysos Mosaic

The originals are illustrated in figs. 48 & 49
[Original: Sepphoris; Joint Sepphoris Project
Roman period, early 3d century C.E.]
Stone tesserae
H: 45.08 cm.; W: 88.9 cm.
Replica: Center for Restoration, Israel
*   Museum, Jerusalem*

162. Two-part Model of Excavation Sites at Sepphoris

Not Illustrated
Fabricated by Lindsey Bute, A.I.A.

163. Model of the Dionysos Mosaic Building

Not Illustrated
Fabricated by Lindsey Bute, A.I.A.

164. Model of a Typical Roman-period House at Sepphoris

Not Illustrated
Fabricated by Lindsey Bute, A.I.A.

165. Model of the Crusader Church of Saint Anne at Sepphoris

Not Illustrated
Fabricated by Lindsey Bute, A.I.A.

166. Model of a Vertical, Two-Beam Loom Typical of the Late Roman Period Onward

Not Illustrated
Fabricated by Cynthia Baker

167. Replica of a Spindle with Spindle Whorl

Not Illustrated
Fabricated by Cynthia Baker

Books and Manuscripts

To be exhibited in Raleigh only, on a rotating schedule

Adrichem, Christiaan van (1533–85)

168. Theatrum Terra Sancta et biblicarum historiarum, cum tabulis geographicis aere expressis

Cologne: Idodocum H. Kramer, 1682
26.7 x 38.1 x 5 cm.
Special Collections Library, Duke University
EfA243

Pococke, Richard (1704–65)

169. & 170. A Description of the East and Some Other Countries, *vol. 2*, Palestine

London: W. Bowyer, 1743–45
26.6 x 42 x 6.4 cm.
Special Collections Library, Duke University
EfP741D v.2; and the Rare Book Collection, Wilson Library, University of North Carolina at Chapel Hill F915 p741d v.2

Josephus, Flavius (37–100[?] C.E.)

171. The Genuine Works of Flavius Josephus, the Jewish Historian, *2 vols.*

Translated and edited by William Whiston and Samuel Burder
Boston: S. Walker, 1825
28 x 23.5 x 5 cm.
Special Collections Library, Duke University
Eq#668 v.1

Josephus, Flavius (37–100[?] C.E.)

172. The Famous and Memorable Works of Josephus

Translated by Thomas Lodge
London: Humfrey Lownes, 1609
32.2 x 22.7 x 6.5 cm.
Burke Library, Union Theological Seminary
EG/EL8

Josephus, Flavius (37–100[?] C.E.)

173. The Works of Josephus

Translated by Thomas Lodge
London: Abel Roper, 1693
39 x 24.5 x 5.5 cm.
Library of the Jewish Theological Seminary of America RB1801:2

174. Yihus ha-tsadikim u-tefilot ᶜal kivrehem [*Casale Pilgrim Manuscript*]

Israel (?); 17ᵗʰ century
19 x 14 x 3.5 cm.
Library of the Jewish Theological Seminary of America MS3571.1

Uri ben Simeon of Biala (16th century)

175. Cippi Hebraici

Translated by Johann Heinrich Huttinger (1620–67)
Heidelberg: Samuel Broun, 1662 (2d ed.)
16.5 x 10.5 x 2 cm.
Library of the Jewish Theological Seminary of America DS106.U72 1662

176. Talmud Yerushalmi (*editio princeps*)

Venice: Daniel Bomberg, 1523
39.5 x 26 x 5.5 cm.
Library of the Jewish Theological Seminary of America SHF1727:6

177. Talmud Yerushalmi

Krotoschin: Dov Behr Mannes, 1866
39.5 x 28.5 x 4 cm.
Library of the Jewish Theological Seminary of America BM498 1866

Selected Bibliography on Sepphoris

Dessel, J. P. "'Ein-Zippori, Tel." In *The Oxford Encyclopedia of Archaeology in the Near East*, vol. 2, pp. 227–28. New York and Oxford, 1997.

Meyers, Carol L. and Eric M. Meyers. "Sepphoris." In *The Oxford Encyclopedia of Archaeology in the Near East*, vol. 4, pp. 527–36. New York and Oxford, 1997.

Meyers, Eric M., Ehud Netzer, and Carol L. Meyers. "Sepphoris, 'Ornament of All Galilee.'" *Biblical Archaeologist* 49 (1986): 4–19.

Meyers, Eric M., Ehud Netzer, and Carol L. Meyers. "Artistry in Stone: The Mosaics of Ancient Sepphoris." *Biblical Archaeologist* 50 (1987): 223–31.

Meyers, Eric M., Carol L. Meyers, and Ehud Netzer. *Sepphoris*. Winona Lake, Indiana, 1992.

Netzer, Ehud and Zeev Weiss. "New Evidence for Late-Roman and Byzantine Sepphoris." In *The Roman and Byzantine Near East*, ed. John H. Humphrey, pp. 164–176. Journal of Roman Archaeology, Supplementary Series, no. 14. New York, 1995.

Netzer, Ehud and Zeev Weiss. "New Mosaic Art from Sepphoris." *Biblical Archaeology Review* 18, no. 6 (1992): 36–43.

Netzer, Ehud and Zeev Weiss. *Zippori*. Jerusalem, 1994.

Strange, James F. "Sepphoris." In *The Anchor Bible Dictionary*, vol. 5, pp. 1090–93. New York, 1992.

Waterman, Leroy, et al. *Preliminary Report of the University of Michigan Excavations at Sepphoris, Palestine, in 1931*. Ann Arbor, Michigan, 1937.

Weiss, Zeev and Ehud Netzer. *Promise and Redemption: A Synagogue Mosaic from Sepphoris*. Jerusalem, 1996.

Weiss, Zeev. "Sepphoris." In *The New Encyclopedia of Archaeological Excavations in the Holy Land*, vol. 4, pp. 1324–28. Jerusalem and New York, 1993.